Executive Hobo

Riding the American Dream

By Bo Keeley

Free Man Publishing Co.

Published 2011 by Free Man Publishing Co.

Executive Hobo
Riding the American Dream

Printed in the United States of America

Disclaimer

Freight hopping is potentially dangerous and is illegal. The author and publisher do not condone that anyone engage in illegal activity. The usual penalty for getting collared by 'the bull' is being ordered off the premises or a petty trespassing charge. The author and publisher recommend that no one hobo without permission from the railroad. Historically, freight jumping is encouraged to transport seasonal laborers who run the same risks as executives on the rails.

Dedication

For Steam Train Maury Graham who told me to go to the rails and byways to see America first-hand, Hobo Herb who instructed me there in boxcars, and Todd 'Adman' Waters who shoved me off Amtrak and onto the educational 'iron elephants.' Like doomed ships on an iron road we pass in the night, remembering around the crackling fires in the hobo jungles...

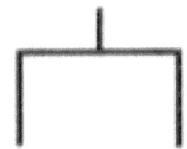

I don't ever remember anyone telling me a real fairy story...but the tales of the gandy dancers, and of the bundle stiffs, of their jobs in the wheatfields of Minnesota... the breathtaking yarns of mushing in Alaska, or getting pinched in San Francisco... were thrillers I remember to this day.

— Boxcar Bertha in The Autobiography of Boxcar Bertha

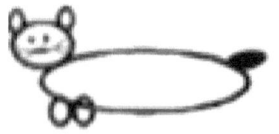

Bo Knows Hobos

I've always been fascinated with hobos. But unlike Bo Keeley, I'd pretty much viewed these vagabond rail riders from afar.

That obviously didn't satisfy Bo's curiosity. He decided to get to know and understand them up close and personal... by becoming one of them.

As you turn the pages ahead, you'll become a bit of a hobo yourself. Be prepared to think you're *there* with Bo, hearing the cackle as you ride the rails...feeling the wind whirling around the boxcar... bobbing and swaying as you roar through the lonely night... kept awake by the piercing whistle as you approach the backside of town after town.

For most of us, unlike Bo, this is as close as it gets to experiencing this kind of risky adventure. And you get to do it without fear of the "bulls" or the bruises accompanied with jumping on and off moving freights.

Oh, oh... hobo at the door

My personal fascination with hobos began in rural Iowa. The farmhouse in which I was born was only 200 yards from a railroad, and I often sat on the bridge over those tracks and waved at the conductors. Obligingly, they'd smile, wave, and sometimes even hoot their loud whistle at me.

But the scary part of living that close to the tracks back then was the hobos. Every couple of weeks during the summer months, one would show up, tap at our screen door and ask for food. They were usually darkly bearded men, and since no one else I knew had a beard, they appeared all the more scary.

I could tell by her tight voice and her actions that my mom was scared of them, too. After all, Dad and my older brothers were usually out on the north forty or somewhere, and it was just her and me—a little squirt then—in an unlocked farm home.

She never turned down a request for food. She'd cut thick slices of her homemade bread, cover it with butter and homemade jelly, and hand it to them with a cup of coffee.

I'd then watch through the screen as they sat on our front step, apparently in no hurry to enjoy the snack. Most were very polite and thanked her before leaving.

But one morning when there was a tap at that screen door, and a huge, bearded hobo stood there, Mom panicked a bit. She was out of bread.

She looked about, not knowing what to do, until she spotted a stack of pancakes that were left over from breakfast. So she spread jelly on a few of them, folded them and handed them out the door to the hobo.

That guy must have thanked my mother a dozen times, bowing each time he did. He'd apparently gotten so tired of all those homemade bread sandwiches wherever he stopped that those jellied pancakes were a real change-of-pace treat!

But the problem was, the more she fed the hobos, the more of them came.

Did they use 'symbols?'

My dad had heard that hobos used some type of 'codes' and left them as markers for those who followed, indicating where they could get free food or whatever. That made us curious, so my brothers and I studied the wood pilings of the bridge closely. But other than some scratches, we could never detect anything.

I could tell by her tight voice and her actions that my mom was scared of them, too.

About 40 years later, I learned those 'scratches' meant more than we thought. I was on the phone with a draft horse friend from Britt, Iowa. That was when I first learned that Britt hosted an annual hobo convention. When I expressed surprise, my friend informed me that, in fact, he had a hobo named Steamboat Charlie in his house at that very minute.

"Can I talk to him?" I asked, and in a minute Steamboat was on the phone. It was a very interesting conversation. But after about five minutes, when I mentioned how impressed I was with his eloquent vocabulary, he seemed to take it as a bit of an insult!

"Don't ever confuse a hobo with a tramp!" he reprimanded me. Then he explained his point of view that while 'tramps' were shiftless and couldn't be trusted, true hobos provided a real *service* in early years when most people weren't able to travel.

As he saw it, hobos enlightened these people with their stories and descriptions of far-away places they would never have heard from anyone else, and the food and shelter (most often the soft haymow of the family's barn) they were given in return was 'just payment.'

He also pointed out the names of many famous authors, including Ernest Hemingway, who were vagabonds for part of their lives, and during that time they gathered much of the material and experiences they shared later. It was an interesting point of view.

Did a deal with a hobo

Hesitatingly, I asked him whether it was true that hobos had their own code, and whether they left markings for their counterparts.

"Absolutely," he replied. "We did it to help each other and survive."

So I asked him if he would be willing to share those code markings with me if I sent him a $100 check in advance. I thought it would make an interesting story for the readers of *Country*, a magazine I was editing at the time.

He readily agreed to do so, and he sounded trustworthy, so I sent the check. Two weeks later, I got this written response with 10 simple markings, and the meaning of each.[1]

As I studied them then, I did note he hadn't included any special code marks for jellied pancakes.

So, there, that's my hobo story. But it's nothing like the hobo story you're about to read. After all, it's written by one of them.

Roy Reiman

> Roy Reiman is the founder of Reiman Publications, which is best known for country-oriented magazines and books that often convey a childhood penchant for hobos. Mr. Reiman built the country's largest, private subscription-based publishing company without selling a single ad. In 2003, one out of every eight American households subscribed to a Reiman magazine. — ed.

---

[1] Appendix G reprints these codes exactly as Steamboat drew them, plus others, except his writing is changed to type to be more legible.

CONTENTS

Hobo life began for me in 1949 at six months, whisked in a New York laundry basket on the back seat of a '40 Mercury to Santa Cruz, Ca.

The first freight I caught was on a locomotive cowcatcher in a VW van crash and carried 200 yards on for the first hobo ride.

It struck me over the years every time I saw a fellow in oversized coveralls with everything he owned in them poking a smile from a boxcar that one day I was going to be that guy.

The first experimental ride was from Salt Lake to the Ogden Golden Spike. I paused at the library to read in Daniel Leen's *Freighthopper's Manual* 'Piss out a boxcar once, you're hooked,' but was past it. And Doug Harper's *Good Company* braced me to stroll back into the Union Pacific yard in coveralls and a three-day beard like I owned it, and solicit a car knocker to help me get on Dirty Face to California.

Two good tramps in route instructed me on 'gooseberry picking' socks from a clothesline, catching pigeons to cook over a jungle fire with their wine fed stories for dessert, and more. Movin' on felt good, and I stayed a Boxcar Tourist for ten summers before forming an executive hobo service.[2]

The *caste* of characters along the ballast starts with the lowest-class *bum* who is too lazy to roam around and never works. Next up is the *tramp*, a traveling nonworker moving from town to town but never willing to work for the handouts or welfare he begs. My definition of a modern *hobo*, especially in depressed times, is one who reads the *Wall Street Journal* and stuffs it inside his clothes for insulation, riding freights from town to town seeking work.

However, I'm of the popularly ignored breed called a Boxcar Tourist. We hop freights across North America for pure joy and the education of seeing great nations over their backyard fences, industrial parks, skid rows, and panoramic countrysides... waving out at others to join. My credential in catching about 360 freights is hung early in the next frontpiece, Hat on Head Timeline.

---

[2] Executive Tour Services by Bo Keeley, Appendix I.

Attending five Britt, Iowa, National Hobo Conventions was a springboard for many stories in riding or getting helped on freights by celebrity hobos like Hobo Herb, Ad Man Waters, Iowa Blackie, Hobo Hafey, North Bank Fred, Fry Pan Jack, and in the cherry Cadillac of the King of the Hobos: Steam Train Maury Graham, bringing cheer to old folks.

These mentors bolstered courage in my grimy bibs one day to butt into the Dean of Sociology office at a Michigan college and ask to teach Hobo Life in America. That jammed class into which a Southern Pacific RR bull strode during final examination caused such a public uproar that after one term the college president sent me packing to the rails.

Since, I've held down boxcars with hoboettes who adore the rails and take colorful monikers like Boxcar Beetle, Dirty Face Dolly, Silver Sidekick, and ChooChoo Chelsea. The chauvinistic advantage is that tagging after the right lady opens doors in railroad yards, jungles, skid rows, and across the tracks in citizens' homes.

I've gone low tech nearly dying in snow-blown boxcars across the High Line, and with computer techs manned w/ scanners, infrared goggles, laptops, and cell phones across the Low Line.

And across Canada, through Mexico atop slow grumbling freights with Central Americans to the USA border. They must be illegal because they ride the length of Mexico to work in the Promised Land, where once I got caught knee deep in the Rio Grande by a US Border Patrolman with arched eyebrows.

There have been Kings of the Road, mighty anonymous men with a little bit of nothing nowhere, and business executives living their version of the American Dream. I took 'em as they came—a financier, commodities broker, shrink, attorney, medical device president, CFA, CEO, computer programmer, pilot, politician, gold trader, and an Albertson's chief grocery clerk—they got hooked and struck out solo.

I still steal executives to the rail and use freights as personal transportation because it's faster, educational, and cheaper than Greyhound, and more exciting and safer than Amtrak.

But I prefer it alone with a knapsack, bottle of water, L'Amour western, hammock, and jump rope, dressed like a crewman… to stroll into any RR yard in America, or thumb a ride in a Renzenberger crew limousine.

And by time we're dropped at the lead locomotive, hopefully, I've talked my way onto it.

Before I saw the hobo way, I was a respected and productive member of society. Now I ride the rails, and if you follow my stories you can hobo them, too.

Doc Bo Keeley
June 30, 2011
Phoenix, Arizona

My first hobo ride was in a laundry basket, the next on the cowcatcher of a freight train, and then the rail journeys roll in this hobo life overview.

Aug 22, 1900	<ul><li>The first Hobo Convention is held at Britt, Iowa, and to this day hobos and the curious gather with execs in the hobo jungle. There is a *Hobo* newspaper, a grapevine of symbols on RR water tanks, and the most successful hobo college in a Chicago hub of the expanding rail network.</li></ul>
1949	<ul><li>Steven 'Doc Bo' Keeley is born in Schenectady, NY</li><li>At six months whisked in a laundry basket on the back seat of a '40 Mercury to Santa Cruz, Ca.</li></ul>
1978	<ul><li>While driving a VW van, I'm hit by a freight train and carried 200 yards on the cowcatcher for the first hobo ride.</li></ul>
1981	<ul><li>Experimental ride with Freedom Frey from Salt Lake to the Ogden Golden Spike.</li><li>Ride the rails from Salt Lake City to LA and learn the hobo ropes from two masters.</li><li>Nabbed by Canadian immigration during an unplanned border crossing inside a grain car.</li><li>Havre, Mt., to Minneapolis by rail and caught by the first bull who issues a warning.</li><li>Robbed by Minneapolis tramps and ask police to sleep the night in an empty cell.</li></ul>
1982	<ul><li>Sell Michigan *Garage Nirvana* to tramp the country.</li><li>Cross-country hitchhike with twelve rides in four days from Michigan to San Diego.</li><li>Travel to southwestern missions with a Franciscan monk.</li><li>Pinned on an LA sidewalk by a demented man with a .45 pistol and a tin leg.</li><li>Join a Clydesdale wagon acting troupe along the California coast for a week.</li><li>Hobo throughout the West standing in food lines and staying in missions.</li><li>Invent boxcar handball.</li><li>Visit the Rajneesh ashram in Antelope, Oregon.</li><li>Climb Mt. Rainier.</li><li>Sacramento to the Britt, Iowa, National Hobo Convention, and back by freight.</li><li>First executive hobo trip Denver to Grand Junction with a Denver</li></ul>

businessman and Australian pilot.

- Second executive hobo trip Las Vegas to LA with two San Diego businessmen and a psychologist.
- Surrounded and punched by four hoods while rescuing a San Diego victim.
- Drunk redhead begs to show what's 'inside her pants' and pulls out a hunting knife.
- An epoch ends of spending one hour for about 3000 straight nights standing without a drink in bars across the country.

1983	<ul><li>Finance travel with annual writing storms to create backlogs for mother to submit to magazines.</li><li>Drive a Chevy van around the USA with an invisible fish-line attached to a 7' rabbit riding shotgun to wave down interesting people.</li><li>Sacramento to Salt Lake to Denver to Chicago to Minneapolis to Seattle to Sacramento by rail.</li><li>Near suffocation riding near the locomotives through the 6-mile Colorado Moffat Tunnel.</li><li>LA to Jacksonville to Newark by freight.</li><li>Freight from California to Dallas on the old Southern Pacific for a family Christmas.</li></ul>
1984	<ul><li>Sacramento to Britt with hoboette ChooChoo Chelsea for the National Hobo Convention.</li><li>Caught on a moving freight ladder over the Salt Lake Causeway.</li><li>Hitchhike to the Sturgis Motorcycle Rally, and freight the transcontinental rail to California.</li><li>LA to Dallas and back by boxcar for a family Christmas.</li></ul>
1985	<ul><li>Near-death from exposure trapped on a winter flatcar between Colorado Springs and Denver.</li><li>Say, "That's enough!" through spaghetti in frozen beard on the high rail between Spokane to Minneapolis.</li><li>Sleep in a coffin lined with electric blankets through the Michigan winter.</li><li>Teach a sociology course "Hobo Life in America" at Lansing Community College in Michigan.</li><li>Write Hobo Training Manual for the course.</li><li>Profiled in a documentary hobo film.</li><li>Volunteer stints at Lansing nursing homes, adolescent and geriatric psych wards, orphanages and schools for the blind in a one year study of the mind.</li><li>Speak to the NYC Junto on hoboing.</li></ul>
1986	<ul><li>"Hobo Life in America" is cancelled after one term by the college</li></ul>

president due to an uproar—"The bum is teaching our kids to be tramps."

- Wilderness survival class from Peter Carrington.
- Michigan to Indiana by rail with Locomotive Lotus for 'Hands Across America.'
- Minneapolis to Spokane to Sacramento to St. Louis to Chicago with celebrity hobo Iowa Blackie.
- Fall asleep covered with cockroaches on a Minneapolis kitchen floor when a lasso of Borax fails to repel them.
- Hitch to the Missouri national Rainbow Gathering.
- Sacramento to Britt with Hobo Queen candidate Silver Sidekick.
- North Platte to Denver by freight with celebrity Hobo Herb.
- First tattoo at a skid row parlor of a Road Mouse with a smile and teardrop.
- Address the Aspen Eris Society about Executive Hobos.
- Grand Junction to Sacramento by boxcar with financier Doug Casey.
- Spokane to Chicago to Toledo by rail with hoboette Boxcar Beetle.
- Chicago to LA and hook up with the National Hobo Association of movie star and yuppie riders.
- Contributor to the NHA *Hobo Times*

1987	
	- Hike three months on the California Pacific Crest Trail from Mexico to Lake Tahoe with a custom fanny pack.
	- Sacramento to Britt to the Eris with hoboette Mappy.
	- Ride in his cherry Cadillac and the rails with Hobo King Steam Train Maury Graham
	- Third executive hobo trip from Grand Junction, Co., to Roseville, Ca., with Doug Casey and LinuxCare CEO Art Tyde.
	- Nabbed by the Salt Lake bull and to court where the judge slams the gavel, 'dismissed with prejudice.'
	- Three days in the LA County Jail for jaywalking from a bank robbery in progress.
	- LA to North Carolina by rail for a family Christmas.
1988	- Freight the USA perimeter working odd jobs and frequenting the Willies, Sallies, and Goodies for collectibles.
	- Hardest day's work ever ketchin' 2500 chickens with four retarded youths in deep Georgia.
	- Bay Area's 'Best Sunday Magazine Feature' with a hobo ridealong reporter to Mt. Shasta.
	- Escort hoboettes Mappy, Silver Sidekick, and ChooChoo from Sacramento to the Britt convention and back.

- Caught skinny dipping with the three hoboettes by the North Platt RR bull.
- Recumbent bicycle with a wind sail the 500-mile Baja Cortez coast.

1989	- Sacramento to Grand Junction to Eris by freight with hoboette Silver Sidekick.

- Grand Junction to Portland by rail with Doug Casey to inspect gold mines.
- Save the life of an Oregon 'apple knocker' stuck on the latch of a rolling boxcar.
- Ride the RR 'low line' from Washington to Chicago to Pittsburgh visiting a string of associates.
- First and only life drunk on hopping down from a boxcar near Wilmington, De., to visit a girlfriend bartender.
- Start cheap living to save money for travel: French-fry hotels, basement, shed, garage, cellar, laundry room, trailer, motorcycle sidecar, and a boat.

1990-4
- Mother dies in my arms.
- Tour NYC subway and steam tunnels to ferret out HUDs (human underground dwellers).
- Hike and canoe the Okefenokee Swamp; swept to sea on a tidal bore.
- Travel under a backpack to 100 countries.

1995
- Return to Manhattan to compile a list of 'Low-Life Indicators' for commodities such as long cigarette butts in a bull market that catches print in the *New York Observer* and *Barrons*.
- Ride a boxcar from Jacksonville, Fl., to New York and borrow a suit to wear to a meal with George Soros at the Four Seasons restaurant.
- Explain hobo economics at global banking seminars.
- Cast a skeleton list of near-deaths in writing *Catman Keeley's Memoirs* during a one-year sequester in a Connecticut stairwell.

1996
- Artist Linda Mears paints *Hit by Train* as part of Adventure Art that become jigsaw puzzles.
- Return to alma mater MSU to lecture on hobo and world travel.

1997
- Hike the 500-mile Long Trail of Vermont.
- Hike the 600-mile Florida Trail alligator gauntlet from the Everglades to Georgia.
- Black Friday, October 27, 1997, Dow mini-crash and *The New Yorker* takes a swat at Keeley for it.

1998
- Walk the 130-mile length of Death Valley and stumble on the bleaching bones of a mysterious man.

	• Hike the 600-mile Baja coast from Cabo San Lucas until forced out by rattlers.
	• Hike the Colorado Trail 500 miles through the Rockies from Denver to Durango.
	• From *Education of a Speculator* (1998, Victor Niederhoffer)— "When all's said and done there's the Hobo (Bo)."
1999	• Retire to a desert burrow as a hermit near the California-Mexico border.
	• The turn of the millennium passes unnoticed in the desert with Sir the Sidewinder doorkeeper and laptop computer.
2000	• Second person to walk the 220-mile Mojave Road from Needles to Barstow.
	• Hike with a llama two weeks along the Sierra Nevada crest.
	• Freight from Reno to Colorado for Eris.
2001	• Fifth executive hobo trip from Sacramento to Denver and back with the LinuxCare CEO, a Canadian stock broker, NY speculator, and Bay Area head of emergency response. Trip ends on 9/11 terrorist attack, which clamps security on hoboing.
	• First person to walk 250 miles on the California Heritage Trail.
	• Begin a series The Desert News in scorching Sand Valley, Ca.
2002	• Hitchhike the perimeter of Baja Mexico.
	• Hike from Mexico to San Bernardino on the Pacific Crest Trail.
	• Walk 24 hours waterless and lost in a Sonora desert, near death.
2003	• *Liberty Magazine* article shames a Florida peace officer after '36 hours in the Broward County Jail.'
	• One hundred posts of hobo and travel yarns at Websites of *Daily Speculations*, *International Man*, *Swans Commentary*, and *North Bank Fred*
2004	• Resident consultant to *Rancho Costa Nada: The Dirt-Cheap Desert Homestead* (Phil Garlington).
	• Trapped by flash floods in Sand Valley for one summer as three die in the heat.
	• Spokesman for the Canadian Safety Pak for survival.
2005	• Rail across Canada with South African CPA Tom 'Diesel' Dyson.
	• Ride disguised as Mexicans with Diesel Dyson and Central American immigrants through Mexico to the USA border.
2006	• Executive Hobo trip with Baby Jack Black (Hollywood TV show) from Eugene to Seattle.
	• Grammy songwriter Shandi Sinnamon writes and performs 'Baby Black Jack and Bo Kerouac.'
2007	• Bo Keeley Executive Tour Services founded as a businessperson's

	'outward bound' on the rails.
2008	▪ Executive outing to the Baja Santa Maria Mission ruins.
2008	▪ Belen, NM, to Clovis, NM., and back with retired IBM Applehead.
2009	▪ "Lost on the Rails" from Colton yard San Bernardino with computer executive Rail Mariner.
2010	▪ Ride the Mexican rails with anthropologist Boxcar Dolly and Central Americans from Guaymas to Juarez.
	▪ Orange County district court switches DNA on a Conservancy trespass charge resulting in case dismissal.
	▪ Executive trip with Rev (Medical Devices president) from Colton RR yard to Tucson.
	▪ Peter Gorman's *Renaissance on the Rails* profile wins 1st place for the Association of Alternative Newsweeklies 'best feature of the year.'
	▪ Halloween trick or treat on the rails with Boxcar Dolly from Sacramento to Cheyenne to Portland.
2011	▪ Take to the rails on being fired trying to stop a 'playground war' at the Blythe, Ca., Middle School.
	▪ *Keeley's Kures: Alternative healings from the trails and trials of a world-champion hobo-adventurer* published.
	▪ *Executive Hobo: Riding the American Dream* published.
	▪ Become an itinerant expatriate writing from select global Shangri-Las including Iquitos, Peru, San Felipe, Mexico, and Lake Toba, Sumatra.

Hobos are America's historic backbone. Reams of books describe how townspeople, and even RR bulls during the Great Depression, helped them get to the fields and orchards to get the crops to market and feed the citizens.

The definition of a hobo is a train rider who rides from jobs to kind words and helping hands. He knocks apples in Washington and plucks oranges in California but no longer cuts ice from lakes in Wisconsin. The RR bull turns a blind eye during harvest seasons if the hobo doesn't spend his wages on alcohol and can speak polysyllables on the way to the boxcar.

A King of the Road by wit, guile, and grace doesn't lose a finger or end up in jail after decades on the rails. Pretenders seat him in the warmest spot near the campfire to prove himself with stories of the fast freight.

An Executive climbs in the business world by making the fastest decisions that are usually right. He comes packed with the hobo traits of intellect, humor, humility, alert drive, brinksmanship, and good cheer in a storm.

The meeting place of the King of the Road and the Executive is the American Dream. The King wishes dearly to pursue the financial American dream and the Exec asks himself, "Do I dare to live the American Dream of independent travel?"

One man's dream is another man's nightmare.

Their intelligence surpasses any in 150 years of hobo history. Arthur "The Wiz" Tyde shoots aerial photos of the catch-out yard from his Cherokee Piper, Omid "Big Apple" Malekan downloads train data from the Pacific to the Rockies, Byron "Pronto" Mulver personally reconnoiters the first jungle, and Lise "Clown" Bradley shapes the group as a professional humorist. They call me Doc Bo, a hobo college professor and alpha of this brainy pack of business executives. We're outward bound by freight train for 2500 miles that, strangely enough, will end with 9/11.

Part 1: The Pacific

Follow any hobo on a California railroad track far enough and you penetrate the sprawling Davis Yard in Roseville, Ca., sixteen miles northeast of Sacramento. This is the Pacific junction, the largest rail yard on the west coast, with coastal Canadian northbounds and Mexican southbounds, and daily hotshots east to all points on the USA track gridiron. The Davis Yard, once in the heart of the gold rush, historically smothers America with freight traffic, and hobos.

It is sunset on July 25, 2001 as four business executives creep waist-deep the golden grass where nineteenth century tramps ducked bulls to grab the same 'Dirty Face' freight on to better fortunes. We enter our exec hobos jungle, a spare opening in a Live Oaks copse littered with bottles, cardboard that train tramps call 'thousand-mile paper,' and a ring of seatless chairs. We sit on the frames and evoke the first fast freights, their rolling steel wheels called cookie-cutters, and the joys of escape into a gritty, strange world.

Soon, we walk 100-yards through a red dusk to the Davis perimeter fence and part the barb-wire strands for each other to insert. Beyond lays our iron road, the original 1865 Transcontinental RR. It still runs east up the Pacific lowland, over the coastal Sierra, a flash through the Great Basin, along a

3

steel ribbon above the Great Salt Lake, out the Rockies, and down beyond to the executives' Denver destination. This rail is also the executives-to-hobos birth canal.

Hobo numbers swell and fall with the financial times. The rails blackened with men and families during the Great Depression. They slackened in the 1950s with the loss of steam engines as the new diesels started faster and, with no need to take on water, there became fewer cross-country pauses. In 2001, I estimate there are 20,000 train tramps but only a few hundred out tonight on the rails and, certainly, we are the only executives.

Look at us, interchangeable with the overall tramps we'll face during the journey. Each thought to grow a week's beard in his respective workplace before the shove-off. Everyone's outer clothing is dark as the night, boots are steel-toed, and each sports a baseball cap with a tether string against the freight wind. The rest is in their noggins... or deep in their packs: we carry clip-on ties for eventual business meetings, tablecloths for storm tarps, sleeping bags, gallon water jugs, two-days food ration, short libraries, and individual kits of high-tech instruments.

I feel like a Mensa scout leader. Meet Arthur Tyde III (The Wiz), the founder and CEO of Linux-Care computer systems; Byron Mulver (Pronto), the Bay Area Chief of Disaster Response; Omid (Big Apple) Malekan, a New York computer programmer for high-roll investors; and Lise Bradley (Clown), a Toronto stockbroker and professional comedian who'll board in Colorado for the return to the Pacific.

"Men with packs are sneaking into the yard!" comes a muffled voice inside Wiz's pack. Another responds, "I'm on them!" The Wiz, grinning, pulls a police scanner from the pack and adjusts the volume. He has preprogrammed the device for every yard frequency from Davis to Denver. He reaches deeper and comes up with, "Brownie anyone? My wife makes double-chocolate so I'll come home faster after business trips." "Later! Let's exit the yard," orders the disaster expert, Pronto. Big Apple, silently calculating probabilities, motions me, and I lead the team out the barb wire just in time.

Car lights crack the night 400-yards away pursuing two other unlucky tramps. We're safe. The bulls (railroad police) are the hobo nemesis cruising the tracks in white Broncos with phallic CB antennas. Hobos use various evasion tactics: hide in the weeds next to the rail to board a freight 'on the fly,' secret inside a train car before it rolls, or use hobo interference as we do tonight. With the bulls busy in a snarl of headlights and shouting tramps, we boldly retrace a short distance to the mainline and continue deeper into the yard to ask yard workers for train info.

"Tonight's puzzle is peculiar to the Davis yard," I brief the squad inside the yard. I point at starlight running along the main south, swing a finger to dozens of darker parallel tracks coursing into the stockpile area, up the yardmaster tower rising like the dollar's eye a quarter-mile to the north, and finally rest it on a narrow bridge a quarter-mile beyond the tower. "The north mainline that we'll ride tonight branches just after the bridge to send a track north and another track east. We want the latter, but without foreknowledge or at least 'reading' a train before its departure, there's no way to tell if the next rolling freight will go straight after the bridge to Seattle or bend west to our Salt Lake, our wish."

Apple scuffs the grit and nods south without looking up, and says, "For example, that approaching dot could be the headlight of our ride, or not." Pronto murmurs, "We're exposed!" Wiz poohs, "What the hell, the bulls are busy." The bright dot enlarges, engines thunder, the ground trembles and the locomotives trudge ten feet from us and stop.

Before us sits a mixed freight that we read car-by-car, salivating. I urge the others, "Speed-read it in five minutes before the crew changes and it changes out." Pronto evaluates, "There are three locomotives pulling mostly empty lumber flatcars. I bet it's going north, not our way." "However," inserts Apple, "We can board now and connect east later, according to the maps I've memorized..." "Hey guys," injects Wiz, "let's just listen in." In seconds, "Highball!" screams the scanner as the truth-or-consequences freight pitches north. We miss it, and stand stupidly in the track watching the red taillight wink and disappear under the bridge.

I clarify at trackside to the execs that the train indeed changed crew on the fly, in minutes, which is standard in a lively yard. Ready as the wheels quit turning, the old crew—engineer, conductor, and maybe a brakeman—squeezed out the lead unit and the new crew in. They tested the brakes and bolted like a race car from the pit. That leaves us standing with a midnight lesson learned the hard way inside the Davis Yard.

"In smaller yards," I pacify, "it's less hectic." Trains are more leisurely 'called.' This term is vital anywhere. The call time is the moment a new crew is notified at their homes or motel an hour prior to the approximate arrival of a freight into the yard. The call time gives the crew an hour to clean up and drive or get picked up by a company van for the yard. The call time in a small yard is often premature so the train sits unmanned on a track for up to a couple hours, and the savvy tramp sashays the drag to pick the finest ride before it pulls out.

We look both ways along the Davis long mainline and seeing no action, just hundreds of dormant cars on the bowl of 50 tracks, head back to the Live Oak jungle. As we hike, I reconstruct the common techniques hobos use to board a freight in a yard. "We just tried the most popular method of waiting at rail-side until a freight materializes and then boarding as the crew changes. We have also tried to solicit information or a call time from yard workers who seem nonexistent at this hour. Shortly, we'll try the third method from the jungle of sending an advance team to scout the 'building yard.' Big RR spreads like Davis have a makeup yard at either end where car strings are connected to build trains to which units are added, and then the whole shebang pulls onto the main, the crew boards, and they sally day and night."

We know from the aerial photos that the Davis Union Pacific Yard sprawls for five-miles with 60-miles of inside track and a half-mile makeup yard bracing each end that lead to two arrival and departure mainlines. The north makeup yard is identified by a 'hump' and the snort and crash we hear every few minutes from the jungle of freight cars being pushed up a 30-foot hill and released at the top to glide by gravity onto assorted destination tracks.

Wiz volunteers to take Apple from the jungle into the north building yard to solicit information from a worker. In forty-five minutes, the pair returns through the tall grass with Wiz strutting up front like a superhero. Dressed in black from boot to cap with night-vision goggles, he exclaims, "The night goggles work well outside the yard but inside the yard the sodium lights flood them out." Apple then reports that a worker informs him there are no eastbounds being built tonight, however the sure bet is to secret along the mainline where there's frequent traffic.

Accordingly, we rap and nap under the oak overhangs for another hour until a through freight puffs to rest 100-yards from us on the main. I stalk out the jungle and up to the units throwing quakes in a 50-yard radius. The engineer in the head loco calls down a warning that's lost in the clamor. "I can't hear," I yell up. Instantly a lower voice sounds behind my back, "He says, 'Watch out for the bull.' Please don't move!" A black man with a silver star 'Special Detective' steps around into the train headlight and grins sphinx-like at me. I ask, "How does a tramp know if this freight goes north or east?" The bull snorts, "You don't, and I can't tell you. Exit the yard now or I'll arrest you." He is a polite but firm railroad policeman. "Thanks," I reply brightly and walk away. In a few seconds he yells after me, less harshly, "Wait safely under the bridge like everyone else."

I take an indirect path in case the bull follows back to the jungle where a debate sparks. Freight hopping is like chess; now the team faces three possible moves. I notify them, "The first option is to go wait a half-mile away under the bridge as the bull suggested." "I really don't think the new talent is equipped to board a moving freight," vetoes Pronto. The second choice is to keep to this jungle to monitor in-coming trains by sight and scanner. "That has a strong chance of getting the prevalent eastbound weighed against the slight chance of ending up north off-track," regards Apple. The third is for one or two of us to probe even deeper into the yard for info, but I tell them that I'm against the group splitting for such a long interlude. "There's a fourth option... that I'm not going to tell yet," brain-teases Wiz. "Just remember," I close tonight's game, "At sunrise we become sitting ducks for the bull."

Four men slumber in cold fits on thousand-mile paper in a century-old jungle near the mainline awaiting a train. On my advice, they catnap ready in boots with strapped packs. Stars prick the sky and move as the creator intended. I crack an eye sometime in the night and note that only Wiz refuses to sleep—wearing five layers of T-shirts for warmth and with one ear to the scanner. He sees me and mumbles, "I like to work nights."

Dawn first touches the control tower north of the jungle. This white obelisk is the yardmaster's crow's nest with an internal function like a central nervous system.

"I can't hear," I yell up. Instantly a lower voice sounds behind my back, "He said, 'Watch out for the bull.' Please don't move!"

Here the master oversees and controls arrivals and departures, yard workers, crews, and bulls. Hidden in our oak and willow jungle, we awaken with the early light and circle Wiz for the promised final option. He summarily grasps Apple by the elbow, wheezing oddly, "You are my ten-year old grandson." Then he plucks a cell phone from his pocket and dials: "Hallo," he gasps like a codger. "Is this the yardmaster?" Apple on cue anxiously blurts, "Grandpa! When is the big train coming?" Pronto squeals like a background infant, so the whole family is on line. The yardmaster happily divulges our train time, track number, and destination to us under the branches two-hundred yards away. After fond goodbyes, Wiz hangs up and rasps, "Our train leaves in fifteen minutes, folks."

We move speedily out of the jungle and through the barb wire. The forecast freight slides to our feet. Four behemoth units growl and shake the earth like dinosaurs. Some greenhorns' legs turn to Jello and others faint at this initial encounter; nonetheless the execs gawk but a second, pivot and crunch along the trailing string to spot rides. We shall pair in twos on separate cars and remain in radio contact.

This short, mixed freight offers empty flatcars, closed boxcars, shoebox gondolas, and—at the tail—a couplet of grain hoppers linked like fat sausages. We hike to these last two cars where I glimpse the front and back 'porches' for clean rides, and kick the sides to assure loads for smooth travel. "All aboard!" I sanction via the radio, and the team in pairs piles on. Instantly, an electric click sings along the brake line that keys the charge, the units rev, smoke blows high, and the train tugs heavily with the drumbeat of advancing couplers. Our final cars leap, and the freight reaches speed under the bridge.

"Yeahhh!" the execs scream like newborns toward sunrise.

Part 2: The Sierra

This executive hobo trip started a month ago amid a flurry of emails at two financial-intellectual interchanges: Daily Speculations and the Eris Society. Days later, the Cherokee Piper's right wing dipped in reconnaissance to expose the Davis Freight Yard from 800-ft. "That clump of trees is the jungle," Wiz hollered from the pilot's seat. "Right next to the mainline!" I cheered back.

Then yesterday, hours before the freight catchout from Davis, those aerial photos wallpapered a den at Pronto's nearby San Francisco home. His wife served the execs preparatory crackers and water. Hobo gear was strewn wall-to-wall, and with our tiny packs to fill like three Chinese puzzles: what to bring? What to leave behind? The Wiz, Apple, Pronto and I sifted carefully for four hours knowing this stage would structure the entire journey. Hobos are individualist packers: most modern tramps go 'streamline' with just a day-pack for single city leaps, while old-timers lug 70-lb. homes with tied-on fishing rods. I urged the execs to compromise and drove the point home with a reading of a prior email titled "Standard Hobo Issue."

The upcoming 2500-mile rail journey will take about two weeks and includes America's best scenery from the summer desert floor to the Rockies continental divide. Each member should bring a soft pack with items selected from the list below that totals less than 40 lb., and be able to carry it a mile at a time when hungry."

The men grumbled inside the den, until I handed out complimentary three-pound "survival kits." They eagerly pulled out RR maps, can openers, rope, garbage-bag ponchos, jungle condoms, and Gatorade powder. Then they stuffed these into their packs and circled for inspection around the bathroom scale.

Apple strained to lift his green rucksack to the scale—50 lb.—and sorrowfully left behind six hardcover books and blue pajamas. Wiz was overweight too and hastily chewed double-chocolate brownies. Pronto's newlywed requisitioned pink flip-flops (for mission showers) from his fireman's pack. No one in the den would meet my eye.

Apple then conceded, "I've never put on a pack before," so after quick instruction he drilled fifty times in front of the bathroom mirror. Then the three bright recruits lined the wall for final inspection. I clipped short the dangling pack cords and tied square-knots in their bootlaces that might tangle in moving freight parts. Ultimately I pronounced, "Ready for the rails!" The golden glow of electric light through the den window suggested a coming hobo trip with the better elements of technology and corporation heads.

America doesn't know where to put its geniuses, so many like these break personal business trails. Arthur "Wiz" Tyde III graduated in telecommunications from Michigan State University in 1985 and took my college hobo course his senior year. After dual diplomas, plus a visit to the National Hobo Convention in Britt, Iowa, he caught a solo westbound freight to the Pacific coast. There he founded Linux-Care and became the computer magazine cover boy of Silicon Valley. "I couldn't see myself sitting in a boxcar or an office cubicle for the rest of my life, so I became a private eye, learned some tricks, and, after, head-hunted the world's best computer programmers. I tailed two Italians in Rome for three days and made them an offer they couldn't refuse— shares of the fledgling Linux-Care." The company flourished to 140 employees with offices in San Francisco, Amsterdam, and Hong Kong. "I delegated responsibility to competent people and traveled with a checkbook to write bonus checks. With so much free time I bought an airplane, and started playing with the freight trains again. Isn't play the purpose of starting a business?"

Byron "Pronto" Mulver, the unemployed guy next door who played champion bagpipes at night, also monitored emergency radio frequencies through the late 80s from his San Francisco apartment. He picked up calls and chased down accidents, crime, and fire scenes. "I was looking for a suitable slot." He had been a cowboy, rodeo clown, firefighter, hotel dick, EMT, US Mint guard, and drumming champion. Finally, a year ago, he interviewed for Chief of Bay Area Disaster Response. He got the job by throwing a lighted match into a wastebasket before the startled hiring committee and asking who knew the location of the nearest fire extinguisher in the skyscraper. He has since wanted to hobo as a break from safeguarding millions of souls from chemical spills to tsunamis, and to investigate boxcars as a possible terrorist transportation. Pronto finds openings where others face barriers in life.

Omid "Big Apple" Malekan has one cerebral hemisphere in the Middle East and the other in the West, providing an edge for the team. He was born and raised in Tehran, Iran, and left at age 10, in 1990. "My family moved from a dying and corrupt society that had been ravaged by war and offered no opportunities. Father, an entrepreneur, still loves the country but sought the financial and family advantages of America." Omid enrolled in Columbia University and while still a student worked as the head of business development of a small online brokerage and market company. "I worked my way up through the minor to the Double-A leagues of trading until finally starting to manage my own as well as clients' money, a peculiar rags-to-riches dream come true."

They call me Doc Bo from a 1985 college course "Hobo Life in America." I'm no genius like the others, but I am well-traveled. I used to blindfold hobo undergrads for "Pin-the-Tale on the RR Map:" Where it stuck, I opened class with a personal hobo anecdote. I've been a veterinarian, professional athlete, publisher, world traveler, and, after all that, retired to an underground burrow near the Needles, California, railhead. Then this executive hobo trip popped up.

The executives don't stop screaming to the Sierra summit.

Our two grain cars at the train tail have a couple of built-in amenities. At either end, each car's 8-in. x 10-ft. steel platform (called a front and back porch), is tops for sightseeing. A 3-in. portal leads from the porch into a hobo 'hotel room' like a steel pup tent within the bulwark. Tramps cruise on the porch and hide in the room through yards or bad weather. Pronto and I occupy the front porch while Wiz and Apple hold down the rear porch. The pairs communicate with hand signals around the convex cars' sides and with two-way radios. Wiz listens with the scanner to the crew in the lead unit chitchat with approaching yards, and puts the speaker to the radio mike for the other execs to hear.

Suddenly, our freight slows to 5 mph in a yellow Sierra meadow where all mouths gape ahead at a fresh derail. Three overturned freight cars have gouged the rich, brown earth for a hundred yards along a sharp rail curve. The metal car sides are shredded and the wheels askew or upside down like dead bugs. Our cameras click. Our own 4-ft. wheels sing slowly and toss sparks along the bend that an earlier engineer had taken too fast. I radio the others not to worry; the freight derail is an exception and, "Nine-out-of-ten hobos prefer freight trains over Amtrak for safety." We slide past the meadow wreck and into a late-summer afternoon on the finest free mechanical ride in the world.

Once our freight crests the California Sierra, we settle for the long rail down to the Great Basin Desert. The diesel-electrics groan and brake like restrained dinosaurs down the extended eastern slope. Fifty couplers jam tight on curves along the half-mile train. We sit back and watch the passing pines and exodus of birds. The glory of the railroads is this 20-yard swath through nature, and our right-of-way is 150-years old and fairly untouched by roads. We glide through dozens of old tunnels and snow sheds, some etched "1935" on the concrete entries.

Suddenly, our freight slows to 5 mph in a yellow Sierra meadow where all mouths gape ahead at a fresh derail.

Because the mountain rail is single lane for stretches, our non-priority mixed-freight sides hourly for priority trains to pass in the same or opposite direction. When this happens we jump down and stroll ten minutes to stretch the legs along these mile-long sidetracks as the "hotshot" approaches, whizzes, and flees. Then the execs clap each other on the backs in the fresh mountain air and climb aboard the grain cars chewing portions of ten-pounds of Texas Beef Jerky donated by New York speculator Laurel Kenner.

Toward evening the radios crackle, "What is that blue pool way down there?" Pronto and I look around the fat cars to see Apple on the back porch leaning out and pointing. "Donner Lake!" exclaims Pronto. "I fought a fire near there once."

The sun sinks over our shoulders, cold air hits you hard in the face at this altitude, and the executives enter their respective hobo hotel rooms to bed inside the wobble and sway. There is no better sleep than a freight car like a cheap hotel vibrating mattress—despite a premonition of tomorrow's heat—as the rail twists down to the desert.

In the morning, abruptly, the Sierra edges away on a high overlook of the Great Basin desert. It lies like a white bowl under a larger blue one. We peek out the room portals. "Beautiful!" shouts Apple. "The ride of my life!" cheers Pronto. "Beats the office chair," delights Wiz. "It's the hobo way!" I join them on the radios.

Part 3: Great Basin

The serpentine rail grabs a stairway of valleys down to the desert floor. The tunnels cease on one step, the snow-sheds on the next, and the Juniper pines fade lower on. The last stage is a long bend of the rail where the couplers finally stretch and brakes silence. The freight slithers like a coughing snake out of the Sierra foothills, straightens and empties us into the Great Basin Desert.

The train breaks a thermal wall on the desert floor and cuts directly and flat to the eastern horizon. Air burns our elastic lungs and sweat drips from two-day grizzled chins to the sizzling platforms. The Great Basin Desert is the largest in the USA. It covers 200,000 square miles bounded by the Sierra Nevada on the west and the Rocky Mountains on the east. Over the miles and hours, we discover that the dry expanse is actually a honeycomb of smaller basins divided by north-south mountains—all falling between the grand ranges of the Sierra Nevada and Rockies.

The freight runs up a 1000-ft. divider mountain, swoops into a ten-mile wide shallow, followed by another range and basin. The repetition and midday glare are finally cut in the east by a civilization sprawling like a spider on a white trap. "Reno!" Pronto shouts standing next to me into the radio. The pair a car back hoorays. The freight slides at 5 mph through that gamblers' paradise and on into the Sparks Yard at the east city edge, and parks on the main before the control tower. The other two execs trudge forward from their rear grain car like desiccated cowboys after a long drive, and we join them sheltered from the tower eye between our train and a string on the adjacent track. In the next few minutes, before the crew changes and the freight rolls, we must decide the next move.

"Our options are to press on, or to rest a couple of hours here before the next through train. Let's put it to a vote," I suggest. "Stick with the sure ride," Wiz casts first. Apple likewise points to our freight. Pronto nods. "All right," I say, "conserve your water because it's at least eight hours and 100-degrees to the next division town."

Abruptly, the crunch of ballast on the far side of our train halts our chat. A brakie (brakeman) stops, stoops, and shouts, "Hallo!" under our grain car. I hunker down for a look back. Brakies and switchies (switchmen), in western RR yards, are regularly cheery to earnest tramps. "Gents," exhorts the man in a hardhat, "This tail gets shuffled before she pulls out. The last six cars get cut and a new dozen added. Be quick to find a ride because I hear the 'hog' (work engine) coming." He rises as we shoulder our packs, uncouples and cuts the brake line, and the huffing hog latches the string including our car and transfers it to an inner rail for storage. Soon the yard engine chugs back with the new string of black oil tankers, plus a solitary cement car hooked on the tail like a stinger. This silver curved-hopper takes on cement or dry chemicals through roof hatches, empties out the bottom, and has front and rear steel porches like the grain car for hobos. On quick examination, both end platforms are dusty and the interior rooms floorless and useless.

Pronto kicks the concave hopper to receive a hollow twang and grimaces, "Empty! But there's no other." So he and I scale the front porch ladder while Wiz and Apple mount the rear even as the grinning brakie adjoins the brake line and couples. "Helluvaride!" he groans, and crunches off shaking his hardhat. Soon the airbrakes hiss in filling, an electric click tests them from the lead a half-mile ahead to our last car, and the freight plunges forth into the desert.

Our carrier is Union Pacific, the largest American railroad. Its route map in our Rand McNally Railroad Atlas covers most of the western and central USA. The company runs about 100,000 cars on 30,000 miles of mainline track hauling consumer goods, coal, chemicals, lumber, aggregates, grain, and other commodities. Reno-Sparks is the principal division point and building yard on the western margin of the Great Basin. The execs' eastern goal is across Nevada and Utah to the Great Salt Lake, and beyond to the Rockies.

The big hurdle is not the heat but the empty cement car we occupy. It rests high on the springs and bounces crazily along the rail. This car at the tail end also whips side-to-side. It's the most teeth rattling ride at

50mph in hobo history. The freight sides hourly, to our great relief, and we jump eagerly to the hot grit to chew beef jerky and the fat.

Soon the airbrakes hiss in filling, an electric click tests them from the lead a half-mile ahead to our last car, and the freight plunges forth into the desert.

At one in the endless ligament of sidings, I distribute a short hobo library to the execs including *The Freighthopper's Manual for North America* (Daniel Leen), *Bound for Glory* (Woody Guthrie), *Riding the Rails* (Michael Mathers), *A Guide to Division Points* (Norton), and *Hobo Life in America*—my college class training manual. In every direction, silent and white, extends the desert.

The engineer in the lead unit must know of passengers since he kind-heartedly toots for us to board after each priority train passes. Then the couplers tighten, the cars lunge and the freight pulls east, now into the desert twilight. This cool blessing rocks the executives fast to sleep for the night.

Sunrise hits Pronto and me hard in the faces on the twitching front porch. We rig a shade from tablecloths and resolve to ride the day out. This track runs 600 miles between Reno and Salt Lake City but our pokey freight with frequent sidings and car drops could take 30 hours, as opposed to a third of that on a hotshot.

Pronto stands on the top rung of the moving ladder to find his land legs after the night's sleep. He sighs and jumps back onto the porch, a dusty cartoon in a black head bandana with bug yellow goggles against the desert glare. Now he slips them up to reveal raccoon eyes over cracked lips, smiles, and crackles, "If it's Nevada, it must be red."

I squint into our Security Chief's blue eyes questioning his mind. He plucks a freshly-pressed red bandana from his pack and replaces the blue one, wearing a dry smile beneath. "I researched the FTRA (Freight Train Riders of America) before we left and matched the regional gang colors with our route. One of us might as well blend in with any hot-headed gangs we encounter." The Freight Train Riders of America is an exaggerated mob of men who use the rails to move about the country. The FTRA allegedly color-codes their regional factions with bandanas seen in yards, boxcars, and jungles—hobohemia. The media and bulls inflate the FTRA, and I personally see more color-coded bandanas in an hour sub-teaching at the Blythe, California, high school.

The optimal party size to ride the rails is two people: one fetches info or supplies while the other guards the gear, plus there is companionship and mutual protection. Yet, seasoned hobos more often travel alone as 'lone wolves,' knowing that a single traveler evades the bull and blends into division point towns better than a pair. Enlarging the party, a tramp triad creates continuing inefficiencies including boarding and dismounting a car, and cramming into a hopper's interior room. A group of four is normally out of the question unless the team splits, as we have, and rides with radios and well-thought-out contingency plans.

At this fiery passage, we would almost welcome a tiny calamity to break the white monotony. Our freight goes "in the hole"—onto a desert sidetrack—every thirty minutes. These periodic mile-long sidings branch from the single main, run a parallel mile, and there our freight pauses with heated units to wait out a priority train to overtake or pass from the opposite way. On the priority scale, Amtrak is the highest, container cars and piggybacks (boxes and semi-truck vans) next, and miserable mixed-freights like ours fall last. The repeated few-minute breaks on the farm for passing trains allow the execs to vault to the grit, exercise the legs, and converse a bit until the priority train clears. Then our apathetic freight reenters the mainline to poke along.

On the second day, in such a dry hole of the Great Basin, Wiz radios us that his timetable predicts an Amtrak is about to barrel through. Astonishingly, it never appears. So we convene at the next siding where he turns his nose up from the page and asserts, "The timetable is always accurate for Amtrak. The only other reality is that we're lost." "Can a train on a track get lost?" asks Apple. "No," I answer, "but tramps can." "Maybe the track branched as we slept in the night," wonders Pronto. Wiz consults the RR Atlas and confirms a fork in the rail behind us near the Nevada-Utah border. We had expected to climb out of the Great Basin at Salt Lake City, but now our GPS receiver pinpoints us on a rail bent north and coursing to Ogden, fifty miles north of Salt Lake City.

There are four west-east major rails commensurate to the great auto Interstates of this country: two iron roads run the northern latitudes from the Pacific to Great Lakes, our historic first transcontinental rail carries us from Sacramento via Ogden to Omaha, and the former Southern

Pacific track I used to ride to Texas for Christmas goes Los Angeles to Dallas. As with auto super-highways, the RR mainlines are bolstered by a gridiron of lesser rails. Hobos traffic mostly west of the Mississippi River on the four main trunks.

The old-fashioned way to determine location *en travel* is to scrutinize the rail mileage markers and crossing names, highway signs, towns, or simply to walk forward during a siding to ask the engine crew. That's too far today with no feasible ride along the string if the freight jump starts. Instead, Wiz reaches again into his sackful of gadgets. He has preprogrammed the scanner using The Compendium of American RR Frequencies with every frequency along our projected odyssey. But, he implores us to keep our eyes peeled, "The scanner frequency guide is useless without a town name."

We ascend the ladders as the freight jerks east somewhere near the Nevada-Utah border to scan all horizons for geographic clues. The fantasy is soon to roll into a division point and decide the next move. A train runs for twelve hours maximum by law, and then a new crew must man the units. These crew changes occur along a string of dots—either small towns where you watch paint peel off the old stationhouses or inside metropolitan centers. Every veteran rider carries inside his skull a map of the division points along the American routes because at these junctures he shall disembark to rest, change trains, or continue.

We have held down this hot hopper at the whiptail end of the train since Reno. That's like four horseflies riding a donkey's ears jogging across Death Valley. Wiz is gaunt and spent, Apple is paste, I have heatstroke, and only Pronto is in glory at sidings medically tending us with water, jerky, and cool words. Years ago, he broke wild horses and seems to have an acquired immunity for the bucking car. But where, even he starts to wonder, is the next division town?

At the noon zenith, Pronto and I gratefully claim our day's first sliver of shade on the front porch. The rear porch duo must now begin to suffer the direct sun, or erect a tablecloth tarp. An hour later, our respite is cut short on a sidetrack when the rear pair climbs down with packs and staggers forward the ballast to our porch step. "We think we're getting the raw end of the deal," Wiz objects. "The platform bucks like it's trying to jump off," Apple protests. They aver that the sunned rear porch is like riding in a tumble-drier across the desert, and flatly refuse to return. Pronto and I glance at each other and, though we could cram four men and packs in the spare space among the shifting mechanical arms on the 8-ft. x 20-ft. platform, we acquiesce to test the tail of the train ourselves.

In the first minute on the whip, Pronto and I agree it's the wildest ride short of a rodeo, but we stick with it out of pride.

Hours later, the freight sides and the group rallies on the gravel in the thin north shade of the cement car. I take a deep breath of hot air on a whim, and start, "I want to speak to emergencies. Pronto, this is your specialty so interrupt me anytime. A crisis is when the expected doesn't occur and there's danger. The hobo probability from my experience is that one time on each cross-country voyage an emergency crops up. Our conduct then changes instantly. Sorry, but we go from democracy to my authority until you learn the ropes. If I'm out of commission then Pronto takes charge. If it gets real bad, it's every man for himself. Your successes off the rail will carry a cool head to the worst of times here on the road. That's all." They gape at me until Pronto intones, "Well said." Then our freight brakes release, we scale the ladders, the couplers tighten in a fore to aft drumbeat, and the wheels spin.

We have held down this hot hopper at the whiptail end of the train since Reno. That's like four horseflies riding a donkey's ears jogging across Death Valley.

At dusk many hours later, a golden glow rising above the eastern desert takes every exec's eye. The freight rumbles into an unnamed desert town that is igniting with streetlights. Hot, tired, and lost on the rails, the execs detrain and stare grimly at me on the ballast. Their drawn faces beg for a hint of change in this trying journey.

The executive trip wasn't to have been this blitzkrieg. Conventional tramps wind a leisurely path, jumping down to refresh in Goodies and Sallies at division points every day, sitting out full days in jungles next to brooks and over a cooking pot of beans like a water cooler. However, the execs have had to lay a fast, hot trail because Big Apple must catch a Denver flight to New York in four days on the same day Wiz is due to speak at the Aspen Eris Society.

"That's the skinny," I sum. "And, the freight may roll again as I speak." Wiz slips around the front platform to pace the line like a ghost. "There's no time to hike to the power or find a worker to inquire," I forbid them. "Our options are three: Stay on this mystery freight, get off here to rest and risk the deadlines, or split up in pairs and meet later."

"The team doesn't split," says Pronto off the bat. "That's right," agrees Apple. "You've all missed one option," comes a fading voice over the walkie-talkie.

"Wiz..." I wail, but he doesn't turn around. His voice breaks the airwave, "Mates, sorry to bail but I can hardly put one foot in front of the other. I've slept one hour in the last two days. I spotted the lights of a Holiday Inn rolling into town. I'll hook up with you again... somewhere down the line." He walks off dressed in black from boot to cap. "I feel like the hangman," he mutters and vanishes into the city.

The train jumps east with three execs.

Part 4: Milk and Honey Route

The executive hobos railed across the Great Basin as best can, suffered the rest, and lost one good man to the desert. The reward for the surviving three is a whooping ride across the Great Salt Lake Causeway.

The short history of the causeway is intriguing. The 1869 first transcontinental railroad traveled north around the thirty-mile wide brine lake. At the turn of the century, embankments from the west and east shores of the lake connected at the center with a 12-mile wooden trestle. Later, in the 1950s, the unsafe timbers were replaced by the present rock and gravel causeway. We execs watch seabirds roost, preen and flick off the timber tops and early telegraph poles a quarter-mile north of the present rail bed.

The train trudges off the eastern causeway and soon into Ogden, Utah. We jump down on a slow, 5-mph roll just outside the yard perimeter to steer clear of the reputed no-nonsense bulls. We hump the packs a mile around it for the same reason, and by luck stumble into a work train crawling the south rail toward Salt Lake City. We jump one-at-a-time as prerehearsed into the yawning "window"—open door—of a 2-mph boxcar, boosting each other safely in. Then the train paces from the historic Promontory Point where, in 1869, the Gold Spike was pounded to celebrate the completion of the first transcontinental railroad.

The local work train threads little burgs south next to I-15 for one hour and on into Salt Lake City. This is a high desert Mormon and hobo stronghold blockaded on the west by the Great Salt Lake and on the east by the Wasatch Range of the Rocky Mountains. Dirty Face trundles through the north city industrial parks and soon alongside the square-laid city streets and avenues that in early morn bustle with the 'busy bee' citizenry. "There's the gold-dome capitol atop the hill!" points Pronto.

The freight then slides past the giant Union Pacific red-and-blue badge above the old UP yard. Millions of hobos rolling through history similarly gaped at the towering marker but none were executives with gold crowns. The freight creeps through the downtown UP yard to the smaller Roper Yard in south city, and ceases.

We jump to the dirt behind two tramps pressed against a building wall peeing. Their indifference to our intrusion suggests a long road to disaffiliation. Furthermore, they see us as peers. I wave and they nod over their shoulders and turn again to face the flat wall. Salt Lake has the stains of hobohemia for a century as a rail junction and division post. It is still called the 'City of Manna' by tramps, and railroads ply the 'Milk and Honey Route' through Utah. Surely the burning issues— "Do American hobos crave to live aside society?" and "Is that where society wishes them?"—will be answered as we transition for a day here from the rail culture and into the city.

The brash urinaters zip and wheel to us. They wear blue-jeans and sweatshirts, baseball caps, and rail grime everywhere. I open, "Must have been a long night... beer?" They grin pleasantly. Their packs are hidden at a nearby stream bank where they drank last night, but soon they'll catch a westbound to the coast. "Why do you ride?" I ask. "Hell," one replies. "I don't have anything else to do." The other sniffs, "Should we work when we don't need to?" That statement hammers the divider between tramp and society: these riders and thousands like them take occasional jobs, recycle bottles and donate blood as businesses when they want flash money, and then hardly see the next day. In contrast, regular society delays gratification and squirrels their nuts.

We separate from the pair and I advise my comrades as we walk, "It's curious that we passed as tramps. Moreover, that they place themselves at a rung above the rest of society." "Food for thought, all right, but how about breakfast?" urges Pronto. "I gotta pee but I think it can wait until the Golden Arch," cracks Apple. We spot an Interstate viaduct a half-mile to the south and strike out for McDonald's on its near side.

The first thing a smart rider does on alighting on a new town turf is to wash up. This usually occurs at a stream, filling station bathroom or fast-food joint. Very dirty tramps pay four-bits at a self-car wash. A hobo wears a grime coat of grease, earth, and sweat that fills the pores and grows out only after two weeks. However, the outer layer lifts immediately with a good scrub of hot water and soap. We order a dozen Egg McMuffins—on sale for a buck each—and coffee, and take a corner table. The executives take turns washing the monkey out of the bathroom mirror until breakfast arrives. The food disappears fast, and we lean back to discuss the dichotomy of citizens and tramps: Them and Us.

I advise my comrades as we walk, "It's curious that we passed as tramps. Moreover, that they place themselves at a rung above the rest of society."

"Did you see the way people stared at us on the sidewalks? It was a strange look of awe and distrust," declares Apple. "The water jugs gave us away along with freight odors. And I think everyone has a romantic notion of hobos," inspires Pronto. "Though passersby looked oddly at us," continues Apple, "when I observed you guys I found myself gawking the same way. I'm confused." I jump in, "You guys are floating between Them and Us!"

After a pause, I resume. "The prejudice ranges from mild in Mormon towns to getting chased by rednecks in Texas... Weary Willies stick out like sore thumbs." Do train tramps get a doormat treatment everywhere you go?" asks Pronto. "Yes," I answer, "Unless you take these three easy measures to blend in after you get off the freight: Wash up, do laundry, hide the pack, and walk the sidewalks like an upright citizen."

"How prevalent and how deeply do the dual societies run?" asks Apple. "Everywhere freights run through towns," I retort. "It's tough to be girdled by good citizens who believe that a fitting member has a job, bank account, home, significant other, and takes vacations. Those are their requirements for an identity. Without them, you become Us."

Apple confesses, "I find myself during this journey identifying more with the hobo ways but condescending as an executive. It's not an identity crisis, but approaches it." I respond, "That rub stops when you remain on one or the other side of the tracks for a few days to rearrange your reactions to a single environment. We just immersed abruptly into the rail world and out this morning in Salt Lake, so for the remaining day we'll be in a transition shock. Take heart: the advantage, after bouncing from easy street to the gutter and back enough times, is to render compassion at each."

"Art Linkletter was another tramp turned millionaire," I inform. He writes fondly in his memoirs *Hobo on the Way to Heaven* of riding the rails penniless during the depression. However, he held two aces: a YMCA card and a skill to type 100 words per minute without error. The first ace let him check into a facility after getting off a freight in any city. The next day, showered and shaved, he played the second ace where typists were needed in the work force. He spent two years hoboing the country in this fashion."

"That's what all tramps need," insists Apple: "A place to clean up, a job, and a million dollars."

"For now," charges Pronto, "Let's find a motel near the tracks. Then we'll go to town." We push back from the table, rise, and Apple introspects out the door, "We bounce like dry leaves, and Them don't care where we land except Us do."

The following thing the hobo does on stepping down in a new town, after washing up, eating and gauging the citizenry, is to stash his pack. It can be stuck in the jungle weeds, or in a Greyhound or Amtrak station locker. The execs have ridden an extreme one-thousand rail miles from the Pacific without respite, so we select a classier option, the thin Siesta Motel on 3200 St. South next to a strip mall just a few blocks from the tracks. The hot shower is a luxury, but Apple refuses to shave his fledgling beard. Next the clothes are laundered at the motel machine, lifting the lid once for a longer soak cycle. The day sparkles outside, and after cleanup we can blend with the public.

The Salt Lake Light Rail trolley conveys us for $1.50, our first paid ride, to downtown where we saunter Trolley Square, an upscale marketplace inside four historic buildings. Shoppers nod warmly, and we buy snacks at every other food shop. "A tramp is always hungry," lips Pronto. "Let's go eat at the Sally," agrees Apple. A street person provides us directions to Pioneer Park where the homeless and hungry wait for a free meal across the street at the Salvation Army. The Park loungers recognize us as kin by the laundered albeit wrinkled shirts, quick feet in heavy boots, and grime wedged in the nose pores.

The Salvation Army is the new-tramp-in-town's best friend with thousands of outposts scattered about the United States and the world. We walk from the Park a block over to the food line stretching around the block with a hundred hungry men darkened by sun and dirt, with faces creased by hard lives. A dozen women and children take priority slots up front. Throughout the queue, one-in-twenty appears to be a freight rider with boot toes scuffed, evenly flattened soles, clean clothes but grease-spotted, and those familiar noses like shields on somber faces. Pronto, the outdoorsman knows how to walk the street walk and hobnobs easily with the rest, whereas Apple's intellect broadcasts far and wide as he listens aside to the strange conversations. I spend the time in line in a personal kick quantifying types of men and their traits.

This good company closes in on the mission door for the strict reason of hunger. Once entered, seated at the large tables in the dining area, and the main course served—a thick potato soup—talk is sparse. The Salvation Army is a boon to the homeless man intent on starting from the streets up and into a productive life. Here daily he can eat, shower, get clothes vouchers for the Willie (Goodwill), and find temp work. He also may be referred to a large nearby shelter for a maximum free three-month stay as the new, productive life gels.

We egress the Sally to investigate the nearby UP railroad yard. An old codger at the end of a busy rake in a freshly mowed yard catches our eyes on the way to the yard. "Why do you do this?" I ask in earnest. "It's just going to grow back." He eyes us up-and-down before replying, "I'm Mormon, and you know what that means?" We're unsure. "Hard work over time creates discipline, and the community looks well at that, as well as the yard. Now you've looked and heard, so I'll get back to work."

Further on, we get waylaid by a quaint event: the rodeo is in Salt Lake City... Downtown jumps! Banners stretch between telephone poles encircling the midtown Delta Convention Center screaming "Days of '47 Rodeo." Horses are parallel parked on the Main Street tethered to parking meters. Yips crack the air.

Former rodeo clown Pronto assumes a bowlegged swagger down the middle of the sidewalk and slants toward a youngster in a huge cowboy hat twirling a bigger lariat. Time and again, the loop drops like a frown to the street. "Can you teach me that?" Pronto asks the boy. "I reckon if you got the time and the talent, cuz ropin' ain't easy." "I got the time anyway," laughs Pronto. In the next minute the tyke runs through the steps of forming the loop, twirling it larger and larger until ultimately... it droops from gross weight. Now the adult grabs the course rope to try but seems all thumbs, and soon hands it back for more demonstrations. The kid finally shrugs in exasperation, "Sorry, mister, but I guess you ain't got what it takes tonight." Pronto smiles, takes the rope in his calloused hand and twirls an awesome loop that he jumps gracefully through. He hands the coil back to the wide-mouthed boy with, "You sure are a good teacher!"

We leave the main stem of click-heeled cowboys slaloming thousands of horse droppings for the Light Rail, and return to the Siesta Motel. Pronto phones his newly wed he actually lassoed on a San Francisco sidewalk to propose, and tonight tells his wife to go out for their anniversary dinner alone. None of us is a TV hound, so the room lights go down early in anticipation of a sunrise freight into the Rockies.

At 7 a.m., bagpipe music erupts in my ear, and I slide my head beneath a pillow. Pronto drums with pencils the pillowcase until I throw it off. "I practice drumming each morning accompanied by my mini-recorder," he says switching off the recorder. "You're just in time; I finished practice."

As the sun peeks over the Wasatch Range, we hike with coffee, bagels, and the morning edition of the *Salt Lake Tribune* to the Roper freight yard, and crawl under a small bridge in the center to strategize. Our timber nook is located under the eastbound main and a brook gurgles at our feet. The only missing link is a freight.

Pronto schemes to parade the yard to seek a worker for train info. Today's bandana, Utah sky blue, he slides down the forehead to around his

We leave the main stem of click-heeled cowboys slaloming thousands of horse droppings for the Light Rail, and return to the Siesta Motel.

neck and fluffs it. He states, "I researched the FTRA (Freight Train Riders of America) website before we left. The group says it stands for hanging together and making sure you don't get robbed or killed by assholes, helping each other out with places to crash, and with ways to pick up some cash." I then tell the duo what I know. A seed core of thirty riders banded loosely in Montana in the 80s and spread as new geographic sets adopted trademark colors. The railroad police overplay their numbers with incredulous comments like, "If there's railroad tracks running through your town, chances are you have FTRA members nearby." Pronto informs, "A website advised not to get on a car with a group wearing bandanas unless you have one the same color. Hence my crayon selection throughout the journey—safety in camouflage."

He stands tall to the bridge rafters. "Watch my pack. I'll explore the yard for workers and if I'm not back in an hour turn on the radios." We're confident he'll get the info—train number, time, destination, and track—because any bloke with coveralls and a neckerchief inside a rail yard will be mistaken not as an FTRA but as a RR employee.

In thirty minutes, he struts back like a prizefighter and exclaims, "I talked to some guys in a work truck who said the track west of Salt Lake City is blocked due to construction. It's an odd situation with trains bypassing this yard and being shuttled north through Ogden. There won't be a Denver Man until the line clears late this afternoon, but at that point they should run regularly."

Apple wonders aloud, "What took you so long?" Our exec spy continues, "The boss yelled when I started to walk away from the work truck, 'Hey, where's your hardhat?'" I answered, "I didn't know hobos had to wear hardhats." He glared at me for a long, hard moment and then chuckled, "Damn if you don't look like a worker!"

The bridge subsurface is idyllic: Dirt embankments, stream, and hobo pastimes. We compete skipping stones across the stream and Pronto wins with five consecutive. Apple flips a thirty second around-the-world yoyo trick. After an hour, our hobo experience depreciates to every instance I've ever known between rides on the rail: Boredom. We steel furtive looks up through the trestle slats at cotton cumulous parading the blue sky. Finally I gust, "Let's go look for the jungle."

To find an hobo jungle, follow a path beaten through the tallest grass near a major yard and listen for the trickle of a brook and voices. The latter was more common when Depression era 'bos covered the cars and jumped down to fill these camps. Nowadays, one may discover a couple tramps in each camp and, if not, always their old cardboard, bottles, food wrappers, and perhaps a lawn chair frame, cutlery, and a cutting board. Often you see weathered plywood over holes scooped in the dirt as shelters, and always campfire rings. Jungles are safe resting places until the catchout, plus now and then an aging tramp-in-resident keeps the spot orderly and gives transients directions and stories.

We heft the packs and follow the tall grass trails—cobweb crossed to indicate no passers-through—from the bridge to just the jungle I've described. It's vacant, but we sit and soak the ambience for a few minutes. In recent memory, twenty years ago, the big summertime jungle a few miles north of here at the red-and-blue Union Pacific sign was a large hobo haunt that has since been paved and overpassed. Spectacular in the past, across the country, a little jungle remains at every division point.

Even so, today we prefer the cozy trestle and return under it at the main to wait out the sun and the repair of the "bad order" track. Down here, unseen, we are able to hear oncoming freights and climb out to hobnob with crews before boarding. Others have waited under here as well. There is 'boxcar art' and monikers scraped or painted all around on the timbers. Pronto carves his initials and the date, and Apple, looking like one and ever the creative contrarian, uses a piece of coal to scratch a Happy Hooligan on a bridge support. I look at my bicep and draw the tattoo I see—a Road Mouse with a smile and a teardrop—signifying the sweet-sour experience of riding the rails.

We pass around books from my backpack library. Apple notices me reading upside-down and requests, "Teach me how to do that." You already know how," I reply. "Try it." He succeeds at once. I suggest the advantages of reading print right-to-left: enhanced tracking of objects such as a tennis ball, boxing glove, or a freight car moving from right to left, less neck strain, and greater reading stamina. "You read one chapter one direction, and the next the other," I explain. Apple practices reading upside-down Ayn Rand's *Fountainhead* until distracted by flies landing right-to-left on the bridge cross-pieces. He springs and swats at least a dozen flat dead with the Morning Tribune. "Now the newspaper is black and white and red all over," I tease.

Apple this morn is a bit buggy himself. Under the bridge he switches between reading, harmonica repetitions, yoyo slaps at water-walkers, and in due course sighs, "I'm sorry, guys, but I can't take it any more." We watch stunned as he reaches into his pocket for a cigarette pack and lighter. "The roots of tobacco plants go to hell," I instantly quote Edison. Apple gazes in indecision at the stream with an unlit ciggie between his lips. "Listen to me," intrudes Pronto. He relates how his identical twin brother and he were paid $500 each a few years ago to participate in a medical experiment. They were given short nicotine or saline drips daily for a week to monitor the comparative reactions. "One of us got the placebo; I don't remember who. But listen, brother. I was maniacal for a month after, and never will smoke."

Yet, after a pause, Apple flicks the lighter. "Throw it in the stream," I shout. He draws deeply three times, crushes it, and stuffs the long butt into his pocket. "That was lovely, but I'm cutting back."

The temperature soon climbs under the trestle to 95-degrees as registered on the thermometer leashed to Pronto's pack. Flies materialize out of thin air. We sip the last of the motel ice water and listen to our stomach cacophonies.

Tramps in camp frequently pool coins in a strange way to produce a meal. Someone drops a hat or a circle is drawn in the dirt, and everyone throws in the change he can afford. Two people are usually charged to watch each other and take the sum for the makin's, and the rest guard the camp. After the return to the jungle, customarily everything's thrown into one pot and cooked, then shared equally by each contributor. The hobo meal is called Mulligan stew.

The flush execs each toss a Hamilton into my hat, and then debate who should go to town. Everyone wants out from under the damned bridge. Apple stands feebly to argue on two heels blistered raw from new boots, but we sit him back down to take the shoes off. We see his heels could peel before he reaches a sidewalk. Pronto, the ex-EMT, unzips a first-aid kit and cleans them with brook water, dabs antiseptic, and leaves them bare to dry. "You're not walking anywhere," orders the hobo 'croaker,' and his patient nods dejectedly.

So Pronto and I walk the tracks a mile toward a 7-11 store kicking coal dribbled from cars along the ballast. I tell him that people in poorer times collected the lumps and sometimes raided stationary coal cars for fuel. We enter the store and buy the makings for cheese-and-cucumber sandwiches, plus six-packs of cold juices and sodas. We exit, check the radio at mid-return and tell Apple lunch is being delivered.

Two loaves of wheat bread and all the fixings disappear into open mouths, and the remaining drinks are dragged in the river upstream from Apple's feet. He, still hungry, determines to open a can of Pork-n-Beans with a sharp rock. "This is an added thrill to the meal," he says, but after five minutes hitting the can without success accepts a P-38 can-opener from Pronto. They share the beans and tap their feet on the stream to Persian music on Apple's Walkman. I meditate.

Soon asleep, the timbers rattle and a whistle blows high. I jump, but it's the imitator Pronto pounding the rafters while teething a perfect train whistle. I pay back with a salvo of contingency plans, my practice from years of chess playing and outdoor survival. What if... shoots tingles up-and-down my spine, but not theirs: what if the bull drives up? "What if we get separated?" The shelling irks them but I know that at one zero hour the execs will cover my ass in an emergency. Today, everyone wants to get out, but "What if..."

The earth shakes and dirt clods rain on us through the bridge cracks. A passing freight overhead brakes and parks on the main. Apples jets into his boots as Pronto leaps out the bridge and shouts back down, "It's a coal train!" He walks a quarter-mile to the head to talk to the crew, and returns to inform. "The engineer says it's a mile-long unit coal train—all coal hoppers. He begs us not to ride since it's dangerous as the bottom trapdoors can pop open on the roll. He doesn't know when the next eastbound is due." I curse the news, "Anthracite is a dirty ride anyway." We retreat under the bridge like annoyed trolls.

We fill our hats like paddlewheels with stream water and wear them for hours. The grunt of yard hogs overhead pushing strings settles into the hot culvert. Flies buzz about us like vultures. Freight hopping is long waits interrupted by flurries of activity, all part of hobo life in America.

In an hour, another train chugs overhead. Cinders drop and we pop our heads out to behold a mile-long unit train hauling an unknown substance. Gondola after gondola, I've never seen the likes of those beans. I mount a ladder for an appraisal and realize in a tick this train will be a tough sell to the execs. "Well, I've never seen anything like it," I holler down. "It's a carload of heavy gray peas. I'll jump on..." I bounce a bit on landing. "It's elastic!" I yell fantastically over the side.

They mount ladders hesitating on the top rungs. Then, as at a pool, they gulp breaths and leap at once. Both land on the bowl of beans and bounce giggling like schoolchildren. "I don't know what these are, but if they hatch we're in trouble," warns Pronto. "Possibly they're pellets for some type of mold." offers Apple. "Look," I stop jumping to say gravely. "Normally I'd pass up this ride because it has V-bottom hatches like the coal train that can jar open and empty the contents onto the track. But that's unlikely and, besides, this gondola is piled almost to the top, so we can rope our bodies to the ladders."

"I'm in. We've been waiting a long time for this," affirms Pronto. "Count me in," weds Apple. We grab our gear, monkey up the ladders and settle on cushy top. Pronto shows us a fireman's bowline to rope our waists to the rear ladders. Far ahead, the engines growl for a new crew. They arrive, the horn blows, the couplers beat from there to our car to the tail, and, laboriously, the long heavy freight pulls away.

We fill our hats like paddlewheels with stream water and wear them for hours. The grunt of yard hogs overhead pushing strings settles into the hot culvert. Flies buzz about us like vultures. Freight hopping is long waits interrupted by flurries of activity, all part of hobo life in America.

The train rattles south out Salt Lake City and bends on many overpasses until the straightaway on the outskirts, and five minutes later reaches 40-mph cruising speed. The track slices the Salt Lake Valley nosing the eastern ranges in search of a low pass into the Rockies. Early on, the trio huddles in a back corner on the strange load to calculate the odds of a bottom-hatch of our car jarring open at 1-in-100,000; a frightfully small chance, so we break the bowlines about our waists. I tell the others our present concern is being sifted to the bottom of the tall gondola like heavy raisons in cereal. They test dance on the spongy surface for one minute springing without sinking and shout, "Amazing!"

Five units blow smoke as Sol sinks to our right. City lights fade behind, farmland envelopes the train and flashlights routinely are brought out. Then a half-moon arcs from the east as we sit rocking on incalculable thousands of tons of mystery pebbles at a new running speed of 50 mph.

"Actually," challenges the lightning calculator Apple, "it is possible to roughly estimate the number of pebbles in this whole train." We challenge him, "Have at it." He rests chin on a hand, eyes shut, and in seconds asks without opening, "Can I use a slide rule?" I offer him instead a pencil. He scribbles rapidly on his cardboard seat with a penlight in his teeth mumbling, "Half-inch diameter pebble; need a ciggy, an 8-ft. x 15-ft. x 50-ft. car; each is 90% full; need a ciggy, a one-mile train ignoring couplers..." He finally totals a line, and concludes, "About 300,000,000 pebbles." "Correct!" shouts Pronto. "The prize is a look over the side to see the city emptying."

The track shears the Valley in half paralleling a busy Interstate. Excitedly, Apple rummages his pack and pulls a one-foot wand. Presto, it flashes neon-green! He twirls the baton over the gondola side describing fantastic equations that pop into his head. "Who knows what a smart fellow thinks?" Pronto asks near me. Interstate drivers must also see the green stick dance in the black for a mile distant. The wand cuts the night for twenty minutes before fading, and he ends with a green signature: APPLE. Then the exhausted author sits and pants, "It's a chemical stick. A capsule of hydrogen peroxide broke when I bent the rod. It mixed with other chemicals that fluoresce."

Pronto elbows him and bursts, "Fantastic graffiti! Thousands from this hour forth shall call you the Green Ghost." Out of hardship and the sweetness and antics of vagabonds arise legends. Tomorrow morning, thousands of tonight's drivers will slam-dunk their alarms and climb from warm beds to hot breakfasts speaking and phoning others of what they witnessed the prior night. But what became of the execs on that fast freight?

Night falls with cold air rushing over the gondola lead lip. We unroll the sleeping bags onto the best bed money can't buy, and fall asleep under the Utah starlight and moon. Sometime in the night the track angles from the highway into darkened farmland and decelerates, alerting us. "What!" I alarm the others. "There's no reason for a unit freight to dawdle on a double-track main unless something's awry." Pronto bellows from his sleeping bag, "Not another contingency lecture!" and pretends to snore. Yet the train continues to slow until it stops smack on the main.

Out of hardship and the sweetness and antics of vagabonds arise legends. It jerks backward with portent. It stops again. "Peek over either side," I croak, gathering the ropes. "A switchman is throwing a switch on this side about ten cars back, but it's too dark to figure why," Apple reports. "Nothing happening on this side," replies Pronto. The horn sounds three short blasts meaning back up, odds on a mainline. Nevertheless, the freight jolts backward, gaining speed.

31

"We're entering some kind of fenced yard," yells Apple. Ancients warn that a smooth path leads to peril. The train backs into a lighted, fenced area. It's a dead-end siding that leaves the mainline and doesn't come back to meet it at the other end.

"Boots on! Stow your bags!" I holler. "What's happening?" questions Apple. "Get out!" I order. A prearranged chain of command snaps to. The freight continues to reverse too fast for novices to debark, and it carries us through a hurricane fence entry into a large yard that is not freight but a colossal industrial plant.

The pebble car passes beneath a walkway with two mounted infrared cameras pointed at our heads. Warm objects are transmitting images to some headquarters. "Everybody take a separate corner." I order. "Now swing your gaze 360-degrees for clues: where we are, where are we rolling to, and how to escape the fence."

"A highway with cars at about four miles toward the north star," yells Apple. "A foundry sign ahead," groans Pronto. "Taconite!" he suddenly recalls. "The pebbles are Taconite for burning molds!"

"Smokestacks!..." I yell. "Dead ahead throwing twenty-story flames!"

The track in two minutes will empty us into the huge foundry door. A vision of the floor hatches opening and the pellets and execs dropping... "Onto the ladders!" I order.

We crouch on three separate corner ladders of the 8mph gondola. Senses heighten, the wheels spin and the flames roar closer. "Abandon ship!" I scream at the portal.

Part 5: Velvet Cushions

The executives drop from three corners of their dark, rolling coffin just before the blazing foundry door. They alight on cinders on both sides of the rail and are separated by the train backing toward the factory door, and by darkness. Beyond the gaping door the huge foundry smokestacks belch smoke and fire, and I moan thanks the execs got off in time. I now gauge quickly: first, locate the others; second, move from the occupied rail; and third, escape the foundry yard.

We are unable to see each other in the night. I flick on the radio and hear the other two reckon in confusion. "Pronto, where are you?" barks Apple. He answers, "I got off the left rear ladder as you descended the right front. So, I must be about a quarter mile behind you on the opposite side of the freight. The last car is passing me..." I horn in, "I got off the right rear, and the last car is coming. In a second, Pronto, you and I will see each other..."

The final car clears, and we wave at each other across the empty rail. Apple, we know, is close by, and we walk toward the retreating train to rendezvous.

The rules of conduct change in an emergency. Each is as terse but set as a chess master before the board. "The foundry yard is ½-mile square with a perimeter fence topped by razor wire and interval spotlights," I depict hastily. "Yes, we're in the center," says Apple. "A worker with a lantern saw me get down," submits Pronto, adding, "He said a camera already spotted us, and no one's happy about it. 'Get out of the yard!' he said, but didn't advise how." Apple takes a deep breath as he breaks into stride from us at the rail: "I saw a break in the fence on a road leading from the foundry."

We strike after him, whispering. "Radios on," but I warn, "try not to use them in case we're monitored." Apple proposes, "I'll lead to the break. We'll angle away from service roads because security will cruise them." Pronto adds, "We'll reach and follow the fence to the break, and exit." I close with, "Apple, lead. Pronto, follow ten yards behind him, and I'll bring up the rear." We file quietly and use hand signals in the shadows of yard lights.

Apple guides us behind some corpse machinery and around darkened outbuildings for ten minutes. A siren cuts the silent night. We reach the chain-link fence and shadow it for five more minutes to the yard gate. There we first must pass on the asphalt a one-story check building and then out the open gate. The executives slither around that watch tower and, with sighs of relief, walk to freedom.

Crickets pound our ears from foliage trimming a country lane. We hike the tarmac without direction for fifteen minutes just to put distance between us and the gate. Pronto halts to explore the issue, "Where are we going?" We can either wander aimlessly the moonless countryside, or... "I think I'll go back to that guardhouse," he proposes. "What!?" cries Apple. Pronto contends, "Disguised as a distressed motorist who ran out of gas, I'll get the facts we need." He dons a baseball cap and asks, "Is my face clean?" Then he leaves his pack, raises his walkie-talkie to indicate it's on, and strides back toward the gate leaving us under a pine copse.

We hunker anxiously under the boughs for thirty minutes. Shortly the radio squawks, "This is radio KHBO with your evening forecast. The break in the clouds you're expecting is on the horizon, but wait for the next report for it will be clear." Pronto has shrewdly coded the message. Five minutes later he steps into the opening wiping his glistening forehead with a pink bandana. "Close call," he breathes heavily, and squats nearby. "I have a feeling the heat is going to come down," he rasps. "So let's get away from here in one minute after I catch my wind."

We exit the woods to jog the rural road for ten minutes to a darkened intersection with a major county road, turn left onto it and dive into thick bushes from oncoming headlights. One sheriff's car screams, another... and a third flies by. The squad cars race to the foundry a good mile away and turn in where the flames climb the stacks to the stars. Hobo Disaster Response Chief Pronto glimpses his wristwatch and says dryly, "Fifteen minutes response time; not bad."

What happened back there?" asks a wide-eyed Apple in the bushes. Pronto describes, "I sneaked inside the gate and sleuthed around the guardhouse looking for a pay phone. Finding none, I peeked in

"I have a feeling the heat is going to come down," he rasps. "So let's get away from here in one minute after I catch my wind."

the front door where a wood desk with monitor screens showed the yard from many angles but the chair was vacant. That explains why we got away clean. I heard a noise down the hall that I followed to a little back room. I walked in and there was a guy with pants at his ankles over a girl reclined on a desk wearing only a brassiere. I pardoned the breach, and told the pair that I'd wait up front until they finished. It's hard to say who was more compromised: security or me. The guard emerged, and I gave the distressed driver alibi. He provided directions to a gas station and was most happy to see me go."

Apple gapes at our partner who shrugs. "The good news," he finishes, "is that we're just two miles from that freeway we spotted earlier atop the pellet car. The bad news is the guy had bigger balls than I thought and got suspicious at my wrinkled clothes." Apple asserts, "Those three cop cars prove that out." We decide to retreat with hasty honor to the freeway.

A 24-hour mom-and-pop gas station sits like an acorn on the entrance ramp. We wash up in the bathroom basin, and Apple, after telling the cashier that we're lost hitchhikers, buys a roadmap and discovers we're still in Utah. "There are no buses, nothing until morning," he laments to us outside on a curb. "The nearest town is five miles south, Provo, where there are Greyhounds and Amtraks, but no major freight yard. It is now 2 a.m."

I obtain change and phone taxis, the local bus company, Greyhound and Amtrak in order to juggle a plan. Then I report, "Let's take Amtrak from Provo to the next freight division point in Grand Junction, Colorado." The pair happily agrees, but the only way to make the 5 a.m. Amtrak departure is to hitch or hike five miles to Provo.

Train hoppers infrequently use the Interstates to get from the spot they're ditched off a freight to the next division point. Nonetheless, our grimy triad cannot hitch I-15, and we're too bone weary to hike. One by one, our heads droop to chests on the curb at the back of the gas station, and we doze.

In about an hour, a Utah Trooper wheels into the parking lot and parks before Pronto. The headlights cordially dim and a rotund but nimble trooper stalks up to him greeting, "I see by your pack that you're a firefighter. I used to be a smoke jumper myself before becoming a patrolman. May I offer you a ride somewhere?"

Pronto grins ear-to-ear and leans against his firefighter pack with his hands clasped behind his crown like an executive. He tells the trooper a hard-luck story of three road brothers hitching and stranded here, and wishing to catch the morning Amtrak through to Colorado. "I'm off duty in ten minutes," responds the officer. "Just hang out while I call my wife and drive home for the family van." True to his word, he returns in a new Ford van and chauffeurs us fifteen minutes to Provo.

He relates en route that 70% of Utahans are Mormon, so "It's a friendly state." I question the smokestacks throwing flames that we can still see from the van. "That's the Geneva Steel Plant. It was the U.S. government's largest WWII construction project and still is one of the biggest producers in the world." We keep mum that that's where the executives almost became crispy critters.

"I see by your pack that you're a firefighter. I used to be a smoke jumper myself before becoming a patrolman. May I offer you a ride somewhere?"

Provo is a whistle-stop, just a hard bench beneath a red-and-blue Amtrak sign. We draw straws where the trooper drops us under an amber streetlamp, and Pronto wins the bench, falling quickly. Apple and I stretch out on the damp earth for thirty winks until passengers start to mill for the departure. A rush from the west and the Amtrak Zephyr screeches to a halt at our feet. "All aboard!" cries the conductor in a starched suit with his hand high, and we enter the silver bullet to take rear seats near the lavatory for smell camouflage. The Zephyr toots and expresses east across the Colorado border and up into the Rockies foothills.

Three business castaways, despite appearance and odor, bring the zest of their specialties to the rail. Pronto protects millions from terrorists and tsunamis as Director of the San Francisco Bay Area Emergency Response Unit; on this hobo trip he heads of our medical, emergency and jungle security. Apple crunches and coaxes financial data worth millions out his computers to launch New York investments; here he is our logistics director and memorizer. I'm a retired veterinarian; and today the hobo schoolmaster. Yet, to the Amtrak passengers, we look like prosaic tramps "riding the velvet" of this passenger train. The conductor stretches his palm... "Tickets please?"

That's an ironic call. The graying conductor raises his bushy eyebrows on seeing us rumpled and stilted on the seat cushions. He looks astutely about and, seeing no witnesses, withdraws the hand to murmur, "Gentlemen, I was a Union Pacific brakie in Grand Junction before coming aboard Amtrak. I still recognize a 'tramp on the posh' (ticket-buying vagabond). I suggest you ask me for the special loophole that allows a 20% discount." We wrangle the tickets at a savings. He steps lively to the intra-car door but turns pinching his nose, "The first-class bathroom is two cars forward and roomy for cleaning up if you please."

We take turns there washing with wonderfully hot water and return to the soft seats to sleep for the remaining six hour run into Grand Junction. "Gentlemen," the conductor suddenly booms as the train brakes. "This is your stop, Grand Junction! And I infer you'll freight east from here, so be smart in the Big (Moffat) Tunnel. Locomotive smoke has digested many hobos there since the tunnel was bored in 1928."

> *"This is your stop, Grand Junction! And I infer you'll freight east from here, so be smart in the Big (Moffat) Tunnel. Locomotive smoke has digested many hobos there since the tunnel was bored in 1928."*

I have nothing yet to report on Grand Junction... I had grown greener and greener by the mile on the Amtrak ride. Not an allergy response, as Apple suggests, but more likely, as Pronto diagnoses, an ill finale to driving leadership through hard times on winks of sleep. My two partners strong-arm me off the Amtrak onto the Grand Junction platform where I cannot stand alone. "Simply, I need medical help or a bed," I echo Wiz's grief three days earlier.

Pronto scouts for a motel or public park but returns shaking his head. "No luck near the yard, however inside the yard is a culvert pipe." With no freight workers about they support me across sundry tracks and around freight cars to the 4-ft. opening of a 20-ft. steel pipe. This is the Motel Tramp—out of sight, weather, and never a no-vacancy sign. I teeter in fever at the mouth and launch a demented speech on the chain of authority. "The group must pass the fallen leader... Get on down the road, boys. I shall catch up!" I collapse like a question mark into the opening. Pronto pulls my ears with concern, "You've got a fever." He shakes my wrist, "Rapid, shallow pulse." He grabs my chin and says softly, "Sleep, and wake up refreshed." They gently stuff me into the pipe so my feet don't show.

Pronto walks off chuckling, "Does he actually think we'd leave him here?" and Apple laughs at his side.

Part 6: Rockies

I awaken in a dark tunnel with a light at the end. Memories flash of the foundry inferno, Amtrak, and my associates trailing from this pipe. The kiss of sleep for five hours has cured the exhaustion of two weeks travel. I feel as healthy as an ape. Medical wisdom would be revamped if tramps, with their filthy habits and superb immunity, visited doctors. I crawl out the pipe into a fresh sunset at Grand Junction.

I stride the high iron—the mainline—to find two scruffy tramps drinking like fish under the RR bridge. They wave me over with a wine jug. I decline but edge up to chat. "What kinda tramp don't drink?" the string bean coaxes as his stubby buddy nods. I lightly tender that I'm a vacationing sub-teacher not wishing to set a bad example. Each smoothes his hair straight away.

"You're educated, can't fool us," says the taller as if deaf. "Why the hell ya ridin' the freights?" I inform, "I like to learn different cultures to teach my students the real facts of life." "Aw, man," Short wines, "I'm sorry, mister. I was one of those snot noses who daydreamed in the back of the room." "Well," I request, "do you have a lesson for me to pass to the alert students?" Short instructs, "Just tell them, kids do the right thing. They know what that means." Tall tutors, "An' listen to your teacher, kids."

"Why do you drink?" I ask earnestly, to which they sit astonished. "Because it's in the bottle, an' it makes a hot day waiting for a freight under the bridge go by quick like Norman Rockwell drew," snickers Tall. "Aw," claims Short, "the booze soothes my working days and cures the wanderlust."

The duo are drywallers awaiting a freight down the line to a job in Glenwood Springs. However, the long bottle has priority and already they've passed up a few. They are good men, good and tough, but drunk. Tipping the jug, Tall argues, "Cheap wine is our drink today like common tramps, but we're working stiffs who deserve and buy better after each paycheck."

Drinking is simply a way of life along the hard road. A shameful brand of liquor is the traveling friend of 70% of men on the rail, deserving or not. However, keen 'bos pack just one bottle and uncork it only after they have safely boarded and pulled out in their car. The life span of one bottle in a boxcar is less than the distance to the next division point, and thus they eschew the foul aspect of freight hopping under the influence—detraining on the fly. There is one other smart way to blend freights and booze: Drink, and then sleep the hangover off under a bridge before the catchout, as this pair alleges they will do.

John Steinbeck writes of paying hobos cash for their real-life stories as the fodder of *The Grapes of Wrath*. Similarly, I oftentimes afford a bottle of Night Train or other cheap wine to bribe my way into jungles, a ruse that has never failed to earn yarns without getting knifed.

But I want to leave the drunks with something special for the day. "I follow a personal Golden Line of Progress through life," I tell them. "Every hour of every day I like to learn or advance on some front. Heaven knows I tried being a hobo, living in the jungles and alleys between rides. But boredom and the Line nipped me onward every time I sat still. For some inner urge, I must continually advance along this Golden Line through life."

"That's pretty," counters a suddenly sobered Tall. "But ain't we all— stripped of romance—just men rolling nowhere?" I retort, "We set our own goals." (Secretly, though, I admit their sad note that home is not a part of many people's lives.)

Short studies my boots—scuff and wear—to dig deeper into my being. "Say, teach, what you got on your ankles." "Ankle weights," I answer. "What for?" "Makes it harder to walk today but easier tomorrow." At that Short snorts, "Like drinkin'... makes sense."

"I follow a personal Golden Line of Progress through life," I tell them. "Every hour of every day I like to learn or advance on some front..."

"Have you seen a couple of other educated guys with packs?" I finally inquire. "Yep, they wouldn't take a drink either," grins Tall. "They were tough dandies," affirms Short. "We directed them to the mission a couple hours ago though it feeds at 7 p.m., about now." I instantly know where to find my partners.

Apple and Pronto stand near the end of a chain of forty men anchored expectantly to the mission door. "Soup's on!" rings Apple spotting me. "Come an' get it!" adds Pronto, diagnostically scanning my frame for signs of health. "Let's eat!" I enthuse, and the door unbolts.

"Follow my cue," I tell the execs for they've never taken this first step. We enter and are greeted by a sturdy gatekeeper with friendly eyes. "First time?" he asks. "Yes," we respond. "Sign the register. No need to show IDs. The sermon begins promptly and supper after."

Feed the soul and then the stomach. This is the hobo lament through history, but no one has figured a better way to yoke converts. Tonight, fifty hungry folks in thin, clean threads file and sit patiently on metal folding chairs in an 80-ft.-square room with a concrete floor and tiny windows. The speaker, a scrubbed man with a hard jaw, mounts a wood platform in front of us for the 'ear pounding' sermon. I whisper to my cohorts, "The preacher looks like anyone in the audience, which is auspicious."

"Folks," the man with the hard chin starts out slow like a train ready to roar. "You know me. I'm Alley Abe." A murmur from the corner, "You look good shaved, Abe." He nods and hollers, "Thank you, Jesus!"

"I hit rock bottom! You saw me puking in the alleys. I worshiped Satan and the bottle!"

Quietly, "And now you see me sober for the first time in two decades."

The giddy man describes Jesus walking on water out of a storm. After that, how easy it was for Abe to take Jesus' hand and walk out of alcoholism. Now he is an upright citizen with a job at the supermarket and a date this Friday.

The speech is impassioned and, in the call afterward for sinners "Who tonight give their hearts to the Lord and be saved?" produces one, no two... now three hands thrust high. A lady sobbing joy and two men likely in need of clothes vouchers are sided instantly by the sturdy doorman and his helpers. Each wins a new Bible, and the laymen lead them with many "Bless you, brothers" into a back room for secret counsel.

The executives grip their chairs and sit upright. "I've never witnessed anything like it," erupts Apple. "A five-percent hit rate is very high," counts Pronto. "Nothing works like a recovered peer," I proffer.

Soon the podium is wheeled aside and, surprisingly for the first time, warm food wafts on the air throughout the room. The folding chairs are bellied up to tables slid to the room center and all sit with renewed vigilance. I insert between the execs and elbow them. "Look around at the people before you put your faces in the stew." It is a typical group of fifty broken down by these pieces: short stakers (itinerant workers who stay on jobs long enough to amass traveling money)—20%; simple transients (just passing through)—20%; local color (street people)—20%; welfare and disability cases (who augment doles with food lines)—20%; stew bums (alcoholics and meth freaks)—10%; working for Jesus (mission staff and traveling stiffs who live off the church)—5%; get into the world quick kids (children possessed at an early age of wanderlust)—3%; kings of the road (train hoppers like the executives)—2%.

We're seated across from a husband-wife couple of short stakers, the brawn and brains, respectively. "I'll stay in Grand Junction as long as the painting job holds out, maybe a month," he says affably. "Ain't he great?" the plump young wife leans against his hard ribs. "My problem as a nurse's aid is I can't take paid work because of SSI (disability pension for an unclear reason), and cash jobs are rare as hen's teeth." I ask, "Do you take the freights or hitchhike?" He answers, "I used to ride boxcars, but with a lady it's easier to hitch the highways and sometimes we freight." They are time-honored Weary Willies who headquarter in a division town using the mission and shelter and working a stint before moving on to the next town. "We just like to jump ruts and travel," she declares.

Supper is undecipherable but no one complains and I go back for seconds. Apple, used to better, chews slowly, peeps frequently under the toast, and whispers, "The chunks in the gravy are green and smell like yesterday." Pronto masticates with a fixed grin, "It's been soup and hardy toast."

Both executives scope the room and catch bits of conversation while discounting the food. Apple appears to be trying to figure out, based on the facts before him, what to do with his own wild and precious life. He finishes the Sh** on a Shingle and rises to clean up at the far counter at three bins labeled: #1 Cutlery, #2 Cup, and #3... ***Crash!***

Plates and pieces fly everywhere. Everyone in the room swivels to see a red Apple balanced on one foot reaching out to steady the top plate of a stack of fifty leaning like Pisa. Finally, he stabilizes the column and turns to face the strangers. The nail that sticks out is usually hammered down, but not this one. He coolly states, "I simply put my plate on top and they all began falling. I'll be happy to replace the broken ones. Is there a mop in the house?"

The big doorkeeper giggles and brushes Apple aside. "Don't worry about it, son," he bolsters. "It's not the first time it's happened." Big Apple owns an inner calm: "Calm as virtue," Shakespeare wrote. And he did clean up. The doorkeeper glows at our leave and asks if we got enough. Pronto smacks his lips, "It's horsehide and liver pieces, tasty!"

The streets outside the mission all the way to the railroad bridge glisten with a fresh rain. I request the execs' reactions to their first mission visit. Apple bids, "I felt fine with the people in consideration of the past days on the rails and cardboard. It was fascinating to hear a former Satanist speak of Christianity, but I have issues with the Judeo-Christian theory. It brought a bit of joy to them and, for many, takes them off the streets into self-respect so it helps the community for life. The meal was hardy, though I was disappointed they thought me clumsy. I was surprised no one knocked you at the sermon for holding the Holy Book upside-down, Doc."

Plates and pieces fly everywhere. Everyone in the room swivels to see a red Apple balanced on one foot reaching out to steady the top plate of a stack of fifty leaning like Pisa.

Pronto appends, "I felt comfortable with the people though I haven't struggled enough to call them peers. They're all there for reasons they know, and understand the drill. I admire the mission exuberance and there are lessons in overall efficiency to take home to my business."

I summarize, "The sermon is a prime example of the church's freedom of speech and acumen to coax a man to give up the street and bottle for the church and Bible. The sword is double-edged, though. Several 'mission stiffs' travel the circuit and stand up at sermon last calls to wash clean their souls by accepting a viewpoint. In exchange for their false promises, they get four days of food and lodging as a free step toward the better life, plus a Bible. I side with the ancient train hopper who said, 'There ain't no pie in the sky.' Though the most convincing sermons in the world are heard at missions and the food is never bad for a tramp's soul and stomach that always seem empty."

The execs are anxious to swing back onto the freights. "The Amtrak ride was a nice break, but sitting inside a bubble without the wind, smells and noise get tedious. The freight is the only way to go," contends Apple. Pronto concurs, "I like the greater freedom of movement of the freight versus a passenger train, better view, and I can pee into a Gatorade bottle."

A splendid rainbow rises over the track in the east, our portal to the Rockies. The old RR bridge is the common catch point in an active yard. The earlier drunks are vacated leaving 'dead soldiers'—empty liquor bottles—and precious cardboard. I tell the pair that these bridges are cardboard cities, so better grab handfuls for the impending ride. Pronto drums his knees. Apple pulls a yoyo from a pocket and flips through some prize tricks including a round-the-world that can knock a bug off a jug.

Yet it galls me after a short discussion that they decide to await a freight under this bridge. I rise tall to expound the options: "Quickly, pick the best answer and let's move in that direction." I insist that camping here calls for all-night rotating watches if a freight sneaks up during sleep. Or, if one cannonballs out the yard, there will be one scant minute to select a ride and get on. In contrast, we can now creep deeper from the bridge into the yard to kip in an empty car next to the main, or right onto the Amtrak platform as sleeping actors for the morning passenger train.

They frown at me at sunset. This rustic bridge is truly beguiling with old monikers tagging the abutments—Slow Motion Shorty, Boxcar Maniac, Jerusalem Slim—the dead soldiers, fast-food wrappers, and see the ubiquitous cardboard. Further, we learned earlier that on average four daily eastbounds pause near here to change crew, plus another two freights are built in the make-up yard. I consider all this under the RR bridge, as thousands of tramps over the past century stood in the same shelter calculating the best odds and place to catch the Denver Man. Our modern joker, however, is Apple's midnight flight in just over 48 hours.

"You guys decide," I ultimately tell them and stand at wait.

The execs are champion problem solvers in a maze of new territory—the rails—and seem drunk on hobo nostalgia. Apple speaks first, "I say wait here under the dry bridge so nobody bothers us, there's cardboard to sleep on, the units will head up near the bridge, and we'll hear them in time to board." Pronto nods heartily. They also figure on no night watch, so we three fall to the ground and—no hard-traveling tramp requires longer—sleep in a minute.

Hours later, the worst scenario unfolds. Late in the night, the ground shakes and there's thunder under the bridge. I leap up next to four smoking engines rolling past. The others are up too dancing in the reflected headlights. "Tramps!" I scream, "Let's get on."

We have a slim chance if the freight departs slowly—unlikely with the four units blowing hard. The businessmen had taken off their boots against my advice, and now struggle to lace them up. In this golden minute, I watch car-after-car tumble by looking for the right one to board. My partners, shirttails a-hanging, soon join me at the 15-mph steel filament... too fast. Our curses are drowned under the bridge clamor.

I scold them after the last car, "You seem to have forgotten the Colorado deadlines, falling asleep on watch, the dangers of boarding on the fly, and an otherwise sure ride from the Amtrak platform in picking this cute spot to flop. Now look at us staring at the damned blinking FRED shrinking down the track." (Or, maybe, I harbor, they're concerned with their Mensa scoutmaster's health and the group need for a night's sleep.)

Still they cavort like keystone cops under the bridge, so I sit with my back to them. Abruptly, there's a bellow behind my ears "Mooo..." but it's only Pronto. Apple hits me on the head with cardboard. "A tough lesson is not repeated," they conciliate. "Let's go to the platform."

We stomp out the bridge to reach the Amtrak ramp and plunk down between a hurricane fence and the high iron. This is a strategic spot under a clear night sky to sleep in wait of a through freight to change crew and board. Out with the cardboard, unroll the bags, and the triad lays on the cushioned cement in harmony.

Maybe out of a punitive dream, hours later, I awaken and lie in the black considering our plight. The exec tramps are still green, mistake prone, and need dress rehearsal. We must catch the next freight or miss our deadlines. "Pronto!" I prod the sleeping bagpipe player. "Let's go inside the yard to learn how it works." He jumps up at once.

"Freight jumping begins before you're aboard," I tell him inside the main yard that's as quiet as an operating room between emergencies.

We identify and climb on various parked freight cars, step up and down ladders for the muscle memory, observe mock "silent rollers"—car strings sliding silently without engines—play cat-and-mouse with mock bulls, and ask one live yardman for train info to no avail.

On the return an hour later to the platform, I ask the final exam question: "What are the four dangers to watch for inside the yard?" "Thugs, silent rollers, bumped strings, and the bull," he answers, adding, "and one's own stupidity." "How do you know that?" I ask. "I read it in your Hobo Training Manual." "You're graduated," I praise. "Get some shuteye."

I nudge a cold trembling Apple sleeping on the cardboard. "Let's go learn about freights." He rises eagerly. At twenty-five, he's an empty page struggling hard to be filled. My main concern is not his athleticism but naivety. His groundwork emails for this trip were speckled with inquiries like, "What should I do if I'm running in Central park and a shadow moves up behind me?"

Tower lamps fling yellow funnels onto the grit and a dozen black irons that we hop across to a derelict string of flatcars, and stop. "Let's pretend," I prompt. "These cars are moving and you are going to 'flip,' get on one. First, check the forward ballast for rough spots and signals. Next, here comes your flatcar at 5 mph. Then, focus on the ladder at the car front; not the rear ladder where the cookie-cutter wheels trail. Don't board if you're drunk. Don't be enticed by a ladder traveling faster than a trot—there are enough variables without throwing in speed. Now, climb aboard." He does with alacrity, and replies "I understand. You are saying favorable traits are preserved on the rails via burying of the less fit under the wheels." After that statement I worry less. Nonetheless, he insists we drill ten times more running alongside the car, looking, hooking, and stepping on.

There are a hundred other little hobo tricks that I pass along during our hour inside the yard: Look both ways at rails, monkey over cars, don't touch seals on boxcars or containers, don't step on couplers, listen for bumped cars, avoid trips through the hump yard, keep the radios muted, stay focused always, keep in shadows or along strings, repeat: *stay focused always*, be alert for bulls and rattlesnakes, and have a good story ready if tagged.

Nothing has moved the whole time inside the yard except grazing bats, cricket legs and our own hard-working minds. Apple gushes, "I had no idea it was so complex, and yet so simple when approached systematically. I feel a lot better knowing what's ahead." We retreat to the platform to sleep, perchance to dream.

It seems like my head just hit the cement platform when there sounds, "Cock-a-doodle... DOO!" I poke my nose out to see Pronto standing over my sleeping bag facing the rising sun with head thrust back.

I ask the final exam question: "What are the four dangers to watch for inside the yard?" "Thugs, silent rollers, bumped strings, and the bull," he answers, adding, "and one's own stupidity."

"Donut?" offers Apple, opening a sack. "Coffee?" Pronto extends a steaming cup. My associates look eager-eyed to taste the rails. "Sinkers!" I insist, taking one and the coffee. 'bos call these 'sinkers' and 'mud.' The hooked duo has visited Starbucks this morning.

Pronto asks if everyone is finished with the Wall Street Journal he has tucked tightly under his wing. Then he greedily stuffs it into his pack citing a hard lesson learned in the cold night before. "Tonight will be different in the Rockies," and he quotes a rail adage. "I will demonstrate the difference between a tramp and a hobo. Both use the Wall Street Journal for insulation inside the pants and sleeves, but a hobo reads it first."

Cleverly showing tough guys don't complain but get resourceful, Apple pulls out a needle and thread to stitch cardboard pads inside his britches seat. "This replaces the need to search constantly for cardboard," he avers.

Next, Apple studies Pronto dry shaving and reddens, waits and asks, "Does it hurt?" "Nah, you get used to it. I don't use antiseptic either. Want to try?" "No," he pats a week-old shadow on his chin. "I started it in New York. I'd never gone two days without shaving since I was a child. Is it hoboesque?" "Yep," I kid, and take the same old razor and dry shave without a nick, telling him some tramps use a broken catsup bottle. Then Pronto reveals a miraculous cowboy trick, twirling a plastic sack into a string and flossing his teeth with it. Apple grins and finishes the group bathroom by brushing his teeth with an index finger dipped in caffeinated coffee.

Apple—ever-ready—and Pronto—steady and experienced—are fast forming a bond based, oddly enough, on Arabic Music. Apple lived his early childhood in the Middle East, whereas Pronto grew up milking cows and beating drums in Northern California. Pronto and his twin brother were world champion dueling drummers, and now he alone heads the San Francisco drum-and-pipe band, plus playing bagpipes at weddings. The pair sits on the cement pad tapping notes from the Persian musician Moein, as I look far, far up the empty inbound rail.

Apple draws a harmonica from his pack. "I bought it new at Barnes and Noble attached to a How-To-Play book at the same time I let my beard go. Listen." He wants to honor the rich hobo tradition of music, despite one-hour practice on the cement car across the Great Basin. "I'm going to play a little tune from the instruction book called *Train Whistle.*

It's bad but it's free. While Apple blows, Pronto sketches the RR yard and salient features—bridge, mission, Starbucks, and our catchout platform—details that will blur in memory after a hundred similar division towns, into a small spiral notebook. This record shall be a treasure and timesaver that every early sharp tramp keeps until, like the network of lines on an old 'bos face, they become firm in recall.

"Train Whistle" ends and, hearing no requests for more rail songs from Barnes and Noble, Apple disposes his harp and frowns into the sunshine. "Last night I hit rock bottom."

We brace for a certain-to-come revelation. "The cardboard bed after bucking the rails across the desert made me think while laying there shivering after we missed the freight. This metaphorically is my fire walking experience. I've just walked on hobo fire and now I can go into the world and do anything." Apple lifts his head. "I can do anything!"

I tell the duo about Todd "Adman" Waters, the millionaire Minneapolis advertising mogul. "He flies around the country to business meetings and rides the freight trains home to his wife. Adman hires employees after they've ridden a freight train or spent one night on the streets. He thinks a person must hit rock bottom too before reaching his potential."

Pronto nods grimly. "A Nobel Prize winner once proved a cell grows or alters after it goes through a period of vulnerability, and it was called the Rock-Bottom Theory. After you hit rock-bottom you acquire the strength and confidence to grow and advance in any endeavor."

Waiting and patience are also large wedges of the hobo pie. We perch on the concrete pad for hours.

At long last, an eastbound train slides in and parks on the mainline before us. It's a stretchy 'unit freight' of all the same gondolas hauling the same goods: a mystery. We leave our packs and step from the concrete platform to the nearest car. "What do these plaques mean?" asks Apple, pointing at two-ft.-square signs up and down the line repeating in bold black: Warning—Hazardous Materials!

I mount the ladder and gaze down at tons of what appears and smells to be dry fertilizer. So simple to spread a tarp and ride the stinky cushion. Instead, I announce down, "This load falls under the authority of chemical spill expert Pronto." He scales the ladder, glances and states, "No good. It's shit! It'll blow in our eyes, and heat under the sun to produce gases. I'll pass."

Curious Apple climbs up, pinches his nose and howls, "It's manure! And there are bugs and flies crawling in it. I'd rather miss my flight." So, I'm out-muscled on the vote again and we retire with hung chins to the passenger platform.

"We need intelligence," grumps Pronto after the manure train pulls out. He firmly knots his green bandana at the throat, and leaves the fireman's pack with us to more freely penetrate the yard for facts. Twenty minutes later, our radios bark, "A shack advises us to forsake the main and try the East make-up yard one mile up the track. I'm on my way back for the pack." He arrives, adding hopefully, "Eastbounds depart twice-a-day."

The forced march is the foundation of hoboing as much as the riding. That, with hearty mission food and outdoor air and bed, tone the shaggy subculture fit as community-college athletes. Walk, walk, you must walk to the main yard, climb strings to the right track, 'frisk the drag' to find a proper car, locate the jungle and rest until the freight pulls out, or maybe catch it on the fly. All that under a 40-pound pack. I used to take a jump rope to skip inside the boxcars, but after the initial strenuous outings traded it for a hammock. Hoboettes—female riders—especially love the regimen and complementary 'hobo diet' of being trapped day and night on a moving train with only what little they brought aboard.

We march the steel ribbons under the bridge and toward the rising sun. I speed ahead of the others with my own thoughts and faults. The illness plus last night's miscalculations nip my heels for a quarter-mile until my trance is torn free by a blast on the left from a building door of rap music. I glance up protectively only to see a lady in a tight red dress and a three-foot purple beehive hairdo jitterbug out the back door. She tilts her head and utters, "Come to the party, darling tramp!" She has enough hair for a hayride, but I shake my head no! and hasten by. Fleet footsteps by my partners catch me, and together we decide it was an Alice in Wonderland party still swinging from the prior night.

We trudge eastward like cart-horses for thirty sweating minutes to the Last Chance Liquor Store. The shack has named it as the landmark along the mainline next to the make-up yard. We enter to buy juice, coffee and milk—the execs are no boozers—and then exit to sip them against the warming back store wall.

Across two mainlines from us lies a bowl of some twenty tracks comprising the Grand Junction mile-long East makeup yard. Here, car strings are clanged together by yard hogs to form entire trains that, twice a day in each direction, pull out. Freights are built on minimal parameters, so after a few yards you start to notice patterns. An old timer uses these to paint a canvas of the yard in his mind with the sounds, images, and feelings in order to make his own move onto it. We face the stock-still morning bowl until Apple finishes his coffee, and then all straighten. "We need info," he says. "Radios on," and off he marches with a resolute jaw. Our programmer has tremendous people skills, knows the questions to ask—time, track, direction, destination, cars, cuts—and a razor memory.

I glance up protectively only to see a lady in a tight red dress and a three-foot purple beehive hairdo jitterbug out the back door. She tilts her head and utters, "Come to the party, darling tramp!" She has enough hair for a hayride...

The procedure when one peels from the base camp is for the mates to wait patiently with their radios on as the scout probes the yard with his off so it doesn't tweak and stir a worker. When Apple wants to talk, he'll buzz us. But today he returns on a lope in twenty minutes. "There was no time to radio. The twelfth track over... They're backing units onto our Denver Man!"

We collect the gear and hump into the yard, scale a couple car strings, and hike to the correct rail where our freight sits in wait. Apple, the youngest at twenty-five and strongest, hands us his pack and jogs to the tail to engage a brakie, as Pronto and I turn toward the head so that the team will soon evaluate the entire train. "Radios still on," I shout after him.

With no bulls about and time on our hands, Pronto and I 'frisk the drag' walking the mile-freight to select a ride. A boxcar is best in ill weather, but today's is perfect. We stride past empty hoppers that would be energetic, but are seeking a container or piggyback for a smoother, longer, faster haul. Thwarted, we finally focus on one battered gondola at mid-train. It is a metal shoebox on wheels with 5-ft.-sides to cut the wind and see over. We spring up, over, and in. The floor is clean of dirt with a few scraps of wood to sit on. In minutes, the walkie-talkies ring in our pockets.

"It's going to leave!" pants Apple by radio. "I'm running!" The brakes test now and the units rev. "Faster!" Pronto screams into the mike. "Can you see me?" huffs Apple.

Closing swiftly at an eighth-mile, we crane over the gondola to spot our sprinting pal. Pronto waves and shouts directly, "We see you!"

The locos roar and tug hard up front, the gondola shocks and it rolls. The scenario then becomes an algebra problem, and this is what's going through Apple's mind, I'm sure: Man running 12 mph is 1/8-mile from the target accelerating away at 1/8-mph/second. Will Apple reach the gondola or miss it by fingertips?... What I forgot to factor in is the unplumbed depths of the man's heart, and perhaps his fear of missing the train and flight to New York. Incredibly, though winded, he accelerates and in one minute touches the tail of our 10-mph car.

I stare hard down at him and say evenly, "Apple, pick a ladder rung. Grab it." He latches and the train pulls him away, feet dangling. "Now swing your feet up." His boots touch the bottom rung. Pronto exhales and I rub my eyes.

We pull his arms over the top. He flops with a heaving chest onto the metal floor, encircled by smiling mid-husbands as over a newborn. "What a way to land a train!" he gasps. He had run for two months in Central Park for this one stellar moment on the rails. A new light takes Apple's eyes: he's changed in one death-defying leap into a man. "Welcome aboard, bro!" Pronto claps him strongly on the back as the freight chugs up the Rockies.

Part 7: Rolling Classroom

A hobo's next-to-finest moment is sitting on a sure ride and watching the scenery glide by after working his tail off to get there. Wind sweeps over the orange gondola conveying the three executives as hundreds of 4-ft.-steel wheels beneath our eastbound train from Grand Junction roll slowly and climb up into the Rockies. The peak experience of hoboing becomes what's around the bend, the unexpected.

Our afternoon freight boasts one mile of mixed carriages drawn by three struggling diesel-electric engines. Our personal gondola, judging by the twigs and bark wind swept into the corners, recently hauled lumber, though this car type also transports pipes, machinery, and anything else—including executives—that can be hoisted over the chin high sides. The length is about the same as a boxcar, fifteen paces, and six hobo steps wide. We spread across the back inner wall out of the air stream sitting on the packs, lying on bags, or standing and peeking over the walls. I yell across to the pair, "We're making fair time. Plus, up the line, 'helpers'—extra engines—will be added to scale the Continental Divide. The prospect of Apple making his New York jet and the rest of us the Eris conference increases by the mile."

Grand Junction was only the foothills... The majestic Rocky Mountains loom ahead. The dirt heaps higher along the tracks, flat browns change to tilting greens, and the car rears as the rail charges up the first major canyon. A stream leaps at the right where pines march up and gains depth and speed behind us as the train's three chugging units slowly acquiesce to the incline.

At dusk, the helpers arrive. Six mighty diesel-electrics—three at the front and three in the rear—are tacked to the long train. In the 80s, my hobo heyday, no one thought of boarding a Rockies freight having less than four engines. Those coveted hotshots had four, up to nine engines, just pulling out the yards before helpers were added at the steep portions. Each modern locomotive, however, runs 20% stronger with 6000 horsepower, but what an evolution to reach it.

"Horsepower" came from horses straining at the bit between 15th-century wooden rails that hauled freight and passengers. Later, the early steam engines that replaced the animals were ridiculed as plodders alongside 10-mph stagecoaches. Horse vs. engine-drawn stage races were thrown and, by the mid-1800s, the steam engines started winning. Their velocities soon doubled the stages, and still there were doubters about the use of mechanical trains to transport humans. One college professor predicted that rail travel at high speed was impossible since travelers, unable to breathe, would die of asphyxiation. By WWII, locomotives set 140-mph speed records, and faster, to the turn of the century as Japan, France, and German high-speed diesel trains now reach 200 mph. Considering their rapid progress, the future holds great things for railroads.

On the road, there's a foretaste to hoboing that embraces the landscapes. This Rockies segment depicts the romantic hobos busting the breeze through treetops who are responsible to nothing nor anyone, free to wander the earth. Yet with responsibility may advance danger.

"Should we be thinking about the Moffat Tunnel?" Pronto questions as the rail slashes an uphill crag. "We'll hit it in the dark," I reply. "And I plan to sleep through it. However, you two should keep awake for the spectacle—the sixth-longest train tunnel in earth at 6.2 miles." Apple wonders, "Should we prepare in some way?" I warn, "Be ready with flashlights, bandanas and water for your mouths. You're safe here a half-mile at mid-train from the locomotives. You may get dizzy, but unless it halts no one should pass out."

One [19ᵗʰ-century] college professor predicted that rail travel at high speed was impossible since travelers, unable to breathe, would die of asphyxiation.

My associates won't sit, refuse to sleep through the afternoon and evening hours. "There's too much to see," says Pronto wryly. "I catnap at sidings." Likewise, Apple misses not an inch of scenery and waves fanatically over the side at tiny mountain town crossings until the first stars twinkle. We continue to stand without speaking under a rising moon. Finally, Pronto sighs, "This is the only way to travel. I can do it alone now."

Dead on my feet at midnight, I fall to the joggling floor and roll up into my bag. I look up like when I was an Idaho kid on a backyard sleep watching the stars sweep over the fence. "Stars scribble mysteries across the galaxy," I repeat to myself, and turn my face to Pronto and Apple keeping the vigil like statues peering over the gondola sides at the progression of peaks. Then I tuck in like a turtle, and sleep.

I awaken in the wee hours to pee through a short rip in the floor. Shaking free, I see the other two on sailors' legs, have been standing for hours, under a star blanket at the passing craggy silhouettes of mountains and drop-offs. I join them to ask, "How was the Moffat tunnel?" "No big deal!" utters Apple, glimpsing Pronto who explains, "I put on a fireman's mask at the portal that made Apple nervous. But I wet a handkerchief for him and we ducked our heads inside our shirts just in case. Turns out the fumes were minimal." "About like in the old days," coughs Apple, "when fleabag tramps rode this track to kill vermin in that extermination tunnel." "Beautiful evening," Pronto closes the night. soon the two finally dig deep into their bags.

Daylight cracks my eyes. The others stir also, and we cloister in a slat of sunshine at the rear of the wobbling shoebox along the rail. The last of the beef jerky is brought out and we chew the fat. Apple beams, "This gondola is a classroom leaving you learning wherever it rolls." Consequently the dialogue becomes a morning show. I hold a tape recorder before the execs and ask, "I wish the answers to five questions: Your Bio, Philosophy, Motivation, Reaction, and Application." Click...

Pronto (Byron Mulver): "I was a rodeo hand in '88-9 working for a northern California stock company. I've always been a clown, but not when it comes to rodeo bulls; they're serious business. I roped and worked in the timed events trying to save the real cowboys from getting gored by horns. I retired from rodeoing to lasso my fiancée on a San Francisco sidewalk, and ask her to marry me. I was a U.S. Mint guard and EMT by then, had been a firefighter and 4-star hotel detective. After it all, I find married life quietly appealing. It's different from the rodeo days for a few compromises. I must practice bagpipes in a cemetery at midnight because my wife can't stand the daily in-and-out. I moonlight as head of the San Francisco Drum and Pipe Band and play for weddings and funerals. I was the star with a medley of Irish tunes at the wake of a racehorse named Dublin Bay. Now, as head of the Bay Area Disaster Response Unit, I figure there's no place higher to go. This is the World Series of Life."

"My philosophy on life is to live well with as many concepts and feelings as one can muster, adding as ready to the ball-of-wax. When one remains in familiar territory—that's surviving, not living. The excitement I've gotten from hopping freights doesn't compare with any past experiences, and that's living."

"From that outlook, it's easy to see why I boarded this hobo freight. I hadn't been on a vacation in two years, so this was such a rare opportunity to unwind. My pop rode freights in the 30s. But most of all, I remember seeing a hobo in central Oregon in the 70s, and he waved to me.... I said to myself, 'I wonder what that's like?' I needed the hobo experience in me for decision-making for the rest of my life. It's predictably proving true."

"The first catchout in Roseville a few days ago captured me. Stepping up onto that freight in minimal time after so long and cold a night was intense. The bull was probably onto us because of our large group, so we had to wish the freight to pull out soon. Then the brake air let out, and I was on it. In the first five rolling minutes, I was in awe of riding something so big, heavy, and stalwart while being at its will. That sensation of being whisked off is what I'm most enthused about and is the draw back to the rail."

"The things I learned train jumping I can sum in a heartbeat... Awesome! To be on a big rolling animal with water dropping from tunnel ceilings reaches the soul. Then there's the spectacular and proverbial light at the end of the tunnel coming out. The amount of force we've been riding on, witnessed by the derailment with shredded cars, and the unpredictability of the ride is etched in my memory. From that main lesson grow many branches. Imagine the awareness of new corridors of travel and lifestyle. Conjure over the decades the tens of thousands of tramps, brimming with yarns, who've experienced the same. The whole journey has been a great reawakening of my traveling days in rodeo. I have learned a greater itch for wanderlust. There are new experiences out there where the rails run. That compulsion makes me grateful for pressing obligations in my 'real' life."

"There are myriad hobo applications to business. The basic elements of making it on the rail and missions are nearly exact to those as an executive. It's just another type of work—our business in the past week has been to get from point A to B safely, just as in my profession of managing people to reach business goals. Mental rehearsal sticks out in my mind. That is, trying it in advance when it's safe so you'll do it right when it isn't. And, backup plans—we got so sick of hearing 'If this happens then...' and 'If that happens do...' But, listen, one in ten of those potentialities is going to pan out, and save your ass."

Apple (Omid Malekan): "I was born and raised in Tehran, Iran, and remember the oppressiveness at school and from listening to my family talk around the supper table. Of course, I didn't grasp the extent of being stifled until at age ten, in 1990, the family moved via Austria to New York and I discovered a whole new ball game. Coming to America was difficult at first for me. Its openness was intimidating to someone who had grown up in an oppressive theocracy. I learned to love the relative freedom this country offers and say, from a deep perspective, that it's by far the greatest place on earth. I soon enrolled in business at Columbia University, and with a knack for computers concurrently helped develop a small online brokerage and market company. Those were busy years, like being the bat boy in the big leagues. All I ever wanted to do was trade, but I understood it all began with a job at the periphery of trading. Ultimately, I became the manager of my own and my clients' money.

"My motivation for joining this trip is deeply rooted. I always seem alone with my soul in a barrel, even when with others. Why doesn't everyone else think and inquire constantly as a sun, delight and wonder what's about him in trying to figure out himself? There I was following the discussion of the upcoming executive hobo trip at *dailyspeculations.com* when the open invitation was posted, so I jumped at it. Here was a chance to explore the country, a new lifestyle, and myself. I went into training immediately with weights and running and gave my girlfriend notice. I was entrenched in a relationship and wanted to do something I wouldn't ordinarily consider.

"Life philosophy? The day I find a concrete one is the day I'll bore myself to death. But I can offer this. First and foremost, there is never a best answer. Second, there is always a better answer. Third, the things I fear in life are squandered opportunities because of their emptiness. I can handle everything else, the pleasures and pains, but not the emptiness that could result from missing an opening. People say I gauge them like a giant electronic mechanism, and answer them with an overwhelming attempt of power of reason. I argue that. Mostly, at the core of my being, is heart.

"My reaction to the first California catchout was an initial relief after spending a dark night hiding and prowling the yard, and then suddenly our train showed and we waltzed to the mainline and got on easy as can be. What a succession of contrasts in a short frame. When the train started I was hyped for a minute followed by a sudden and complete realization that scenery was flowing past my face, and with it the memories of my life. I've always found clarity on a moving train because of the sharp twist of perspective, but nothing as staggering as the scenes of hoboing.

> *"Life philosophy? The day I find a concrete one is the day I'll bore myself to death. But I can offer this: First and foremost, there is never a best answer. Second, there is always a better answer..." — Apple*

"I'm enriched by the lessons from the rails in a short a period. The most dramatic incident was yesterday—jumping on the fly into this gondola. I lost the world for a moment and gained an identity for a lifetime. The hobo lifestyle is addicting but not particularly romantic. I learned about cigarettes, and I'm down to one-a-day and will quit by the end of the trip in a few hours. I've also decided to leave my girl. Freights are better. The scenery is fantastic, the exercise worthwhile, and the road characters step right out of a book. I now have greater recall for a warm bed, my ex-girlfriend, Starbucks in the morning, and the soft office chair. I had a really good time sleeping in the dirt, eating mission food, and having the cold wind whistle in my ears on the go, but I want to celebrate once I get home. I'm going to collect the lessons from this trip for the rest of my life.

"There is one profound application of hoboing to my profession of computer programming and speculation. It's the realization that one must continually make quick decisions under pressure of time and circumstance with limited information in order to get along. I feel like I've had a crash course on focus. I've never sustained such concentration for so long, but it's worth it because I'm well. There is no lesson above that from this trip. Now all I want to do is crawl into a nice bed.

"The other related tip is information gathering, and then assigning probability to conclusions to make decisions. Think of it like quantum theory. At the most fundamental levels, there is no causality, there is no certainty about anything, just certain equations that yield probability distributions. Sort of like the Wild West, or the stock market, or the process of the mind. There is no law, no explanations why things happen, but somehow everything works itself out. Retrospectively, it's all angles."

"Finally, the great lesson of humility. I've discovered new angles into my personality, with some added self-respect. The rich can afford to plan for tomorrow, the poor for today, but the tramp only for the next moment. I'll honor people who work for me, appreciate simple food, a bed... the list goes on. I figure down-the-line that this experience will serve as a model for other ventures. If I can hobo, I can do anything!"

Doc (Bo Keeley):

In the Big Rock Candy Mountains,
There's a land that's fair and bright,
Where the handouts grow on bushes
And you sleep out every night.
Where the boxcars all are empty
And the sun shines every day
And the birds and the bees
And the cigarette trees
The lemonade springs
Where the bluebird sings
In the Big Rock Candy Mountains.
("In the Big Rock Candy Mountains" by Harry McClintock)

I click off the recorder. This has been my peak hour on the rail forever. We peer over the sides of the gondola and are surprised to view Denver coming into line. The track flattens with the land and eventually straightens through the canyons to valleys to mesas and finally onto the foothills of the Mile High City.

A healthy civilization spreads slowly under and around us like roots of a living tree. Some folks this minute may be looking out their farmhouse and neighborhood windows at the shaky train and see three Kilroy heads protruding from the orange wall: "Gee, Martha, I wish we were young again, I'd jump a train," and they turn to chores or supper. We pass the town limits almost to the last tie of the trip wondering, What's life for? This late afternoon freight ultimately slows in a manicured suburb and halts across from a green field alive with a baseball game. The players are uniformed and the freight becomes their centerfield fence. We wave from our bleacher seats but a hundred rooters seated along the first and third base lines are rooted to the game.

Pronto announces into a stick: "There's a fly ball deep to center field... Back, back pedals the center fielder... He pulls it in at the right-of-way!" Apple gleefully pounds the sides of the gondola. No one out there is aware; it's a Them-and-Us game. Two innings later, no runs have scored and the freight has not moved an inch.

Pronto rises proclaiming, "Seventh inning stretch—radios on." He scales the rear corner, descends the ladder and walks boldly toward the ball diamond like a relief pitcher muttering, "Game will be over before we get home." Simultaneously, I climb the front corner, alight on the gravel and yawp to both, "I'm hoofing to the units to see about the train delay." Apple stays to guard our equipment. All the radios are on, and over them while walking away we devise to ditch the freight should it move out with any team member unable to board.

Five minutes later, absurdly, I find no one in the locomotives. The abandoned diesels idle, but fresh tire marks tear the adjacent dirt road clueing that the crew was just snatched to be relieved. "Nobody's at home in the units," I boom over the radio. So our options are to hijack, forsake, or wait." Pronto sounds with dismay, "I have a radio report too. It's tied at 3-3 in the bottom of the ninth. Nobody will let me use their cell phone. They stare at me like a mascot, an ape. I'm returning to the train." Then Apple reports, "I'm waiting on-deck in the gondola for both of you."

Once the triad is back within those walls, it's surmised this freight is 'tied down' or holding on line for a fresh crew's arrival. The old shift legally ran out short of the Denver yard. We decide rather than wait for relief to hike to a highway to hitch or bus into the city. "Hurray!" cheer the spectators at the baseball field over our wall. We peek over to see handshakes around the diamond and that game adjourns... the bleachers empty.

Apple fidgets with his wristwatch. "Evil device! I should have left it at home." Minutes tick to his midnight departure. "Let's move out then," suggests Pronto. We collect the packs, scale the rolling classroom wall and drop from the hobo game.

Think yesterday! Act now! is the pilot trait of all executives, but you can't hurry old Dirty Face for any amount of money. We tread the vacated diamond turf and along asphalt county roads in search of a phone. An Erisian contact, if we can reach him, may fetch us. An hour later, we discover a phone booth in a cow pasture and pool our change to dial.

In thirty minutes, Mark Mahoney, a Denver speculator, jumps out his Jeep and warmly grasps our hands. "I just returned from a fishing trip and am now at your service." Pronto responds for us all, "I just came from a ball game. They treated me like an invading bear, so I left after an inning. I forgot how I look, like my pals. Thanks so much for rescuing us."

It's the end of the smoky line in Denver with our conclusion that the great American pastime for a century has been seeing the country firsthand from a boxcar.

Think yesterday! Act now! is the pilot trait of all executives, but you can't hurry old Dirty Face for any amount of money.

Part 8: Eris

This Executive Hobo Trip was born two months earlier when a casual email to a friend that I was planning a freight trip from the Pacific to Colorado for the Eris Society was posted on a speculator's Website. Surprisingly, eight businessmen asked if seats were available. They didn't quite grasp the hobo pageant. Three execs (Wiz, Pronto, and Apple) actually showed at the San Francisco catchout as the rest—two-hundred speculators and three million monthly hits at the website—followed our progress via satellite emails from the rail cars until we lost Wiz in the Great Basin. Then, on the day when Apple, Pronto, and I arrived in Denver, there was a scurry to get each of us to different vital destinations. Big Apple had priority to catch a flight from the Denver airport back to New York.

I shake his hand at the departure lounge noting with mitigated sadness that Apple's soul has opened like a rose; he'll carry the experience to benefit myriad avenues. "I wonder what my father will think?" he asks. I reply firmly, "You'll be the curiosity and mock of everyone you left behind. Dabbling in alternative lifestyles sifts your friends, and now the right few will pick you. The family will think you less crazy with each step further from the womb, and in the future your dad will push you out the door in order to receive more postcards and exciting yarns." He steps back and smiles. "You have the right answer to everything even if it isn't accurate. I'm ready for the next trip before this one's over. I'm going to leave my girl. Freights are better. Thanks for the satori, Doc."

Next stop is the Burlington Northern Santa Fe yard. Pronto wants to try a new railroad company solo out of Denver through Montana and back to San Francisco. Union Pacific's chief competitor is the Burlington Santa Fe Railway. Both UP and BNSF cover the central and western USA 'Open Road,' the system of railroads that can take you anywhere you like. He puts on a yellow bandana inside the yard. "It was a thrilling expedition, but I want to try the rails alone. The freedom is amazing: No appointments, no phone, no plans. Just the open road, and, of course, thinking about the next meal. I don't remember a time when I saw so much new and extreme data while getting my muscles so sore. I'm rough and ready like in the rodeo days, able to get up at 5 a.m. day-after-day to face another brute or train."

A hot spot in Denver is the BNSF yard about a half-mile south of Coors Field where citizens may stroll wide sidewalks to a viaduct to watch freights 24-hours-a-day pull in and out. The locals refer to this spot as the Mouse Trap. This particular evening some observe one stocky tramp in a yellow headband separate from two other men in a Jeep. He looks like a worker and enters a brick building for train information. Finding no one, he returns to the vehicle and pulls out a fireman's pack. The BNSF locomotive color scheme all about is forest green, orange, and yellow. Depending on the freight he boards, Pronto could end up in Omaha or Cheyenne.

"Dabbling in alternative lifestyles sifts your friends, and now the right few will pick you."

"I don't care," enthuses Pronto at the sendoff. "I just want to ride out my vacation." We shake hands and I counsel, "There's nothing more I can tell you about hoboing that you haven't heard with your damned perfect memory except to keep practicing contingencies." Pronto is relatively unchanged by the outbound trip, just more certain of what he was sure he was before the onset—'blowed-in-the-glass,' born to be a hobo. "I've kept a logbook of the yards and missions, and prefer the low-tech style of travel—no walkie-talkie, scanner, or cell phone—just the logbook and railroad map. Oh yeah! I'll ride again. Always!" He saunters like Hercules between a string of cars and waves back, "Lessons gleaned for a lifetime. Thanks Doc Bo!"

I catch a Greyhound bus to Aspen in the heart of the Rockies for Eris and to pick up a fresh batch of executives for the run back to the West Coast.

The mid-point and turnaround of the overall rail trip is Aspen, Colorado, where each August the Eris Society convenes. Eris is my perennial siding, a unique group—if a society of individualists is possible—since it is without a formal structure. It is neither incorporated, partnership, nor owned by anyone. There are no dues, bylaws, or voting. Rather, it belongs annually to the invitees. Eris began in 1981 when Doug Casey, a best-selling financial writer and daredevil, decided to invite a few of his friends to a party at his Aspen home to exchange ideas in the spirit of Ben Franklin's Junto. In subsequent years, the original invitees expanded the gathering by inviting other individualists to share ideas on a wide range of topics.

Eris draws a broad spectrum of people who have distinguished themselves in their fields, and over fifty percent are published authors. There are scientists, film producers, doctors, historians, artists, philosophers, educators, multimillionaires, swamis… and even hobos. The three-day weekend conference consists of hourly presentations by individuals or panels with ample Q&As after each. A discordant, non-mainstream bent is maintained throughout the weekend in the spirit of Eris, the Greek goddess of discord whose golden apple marked 'to the fairest' was thrown into a party that sparked the jealousy that started the Trojan War.

Eris freethinkers seek out speakers with unconventional or controversial ideas they are willing to defend in front of two hundred excellent listeners and skeptics. I first arrived by freight in 1985 to speak about the freight underground and hobos. After the talk, I issued an open invitation to ride the rails with me. One stepped forward, the Eris founder Doug Casey. He had raced cars, parachuted, globe-trotted, even tried to buy a country, and this year thrilled to ride the freight train from Denver to Portland, Oregon, to examine investment opportunities in gold mines and zeppelins. "I ride freights to be reminded of another reality," avows the world's richest hobo.

Casey must drop from this year's trip for personal reasons. However, a similar invitation to the 2001 Eris Society bears Toronto stockbroker and professional comic Lise Bradley, who quickly announces, "I want to find myself on the rails, baby!" She will become history's first executive hoboette.

Wiz also dashes up after speaking at Eris frothing for the freights. "Good to see you! I'm sorry I had to get off that unstable car in the desert on the rail trip out. It was creating harmonics that wracked me. I checked into a hotel and woke up the next morning refreshed. So I struck solo southwest through Nevada checking out the mines and Area 51. I discovered no aliens but did eat lunch with some businessmen a mile underground in a silver mine. Now I'm ready to ride the rails again!"

On August 4, 2001, the Eris Society adjourns in Aspen, and now we are three—Wiz, Clown, and Doc Bo. We huddle in an Aspen underground pizza parlor to await the bus to Grand Junction, Co., for the freight catchout. Here we attempt to hit upon camaraderie, but first the 'fish,' or green hoboette, retrieves lunch per the hobo custom.

We watch Clown, a slight blonde with an anatomically correct walk and cheerleader glow, weave the patrons leaving a wake of smiles and laughs back to our table. "She plays the field like a pro," remarks Wiz. Surely, the Canadian libertarian comic shows aggression, asks the right questions, has the correct answers, and raises everyone's spirit. "She thinks she's Eris," I groan. But, Wiz questions, "Can she carry it off in the railroad yard with that nail polish and city-girl smile?" She prances to the table with the pizza-to-go in case the bus is premature. "Boxy but hot, boys. Dig in!"

Wiz and I wear standard overalls and flannels while Clown sports embroidered jeans with halter top and a head of two-foot rainbow dreadlocks. "This undertaking won't be easy," I forewarn as we chew. "The outbound execs last week rode hard metal, slept in the dirt, and loved it after it was all over." She leans forward and blows pizza breath, "Do it the right way even if it's the hard way, right?" "Clown," I rejoin, "That crayon-box on your head will fetch information on the rails, but can get caught in moving machinery. Tie the dreads up and double-knot those platform tennis shoes before we reach the Grand Junction yard." She eyes me evenly, "I'll do fine on the railroad, Doc. You'll see."

The basement cafe is not an Exec Hobos but there is the sense of the same, breaking bread and talking while awaiting the catchout. We swap stories for an hour that reveal character and traits that will serve and may save each other on the rails. These experiences, if quantified, are worth millions.

Lise 'Clown' Bradley discloses a personal history of achievement and rebellion. She won high school honors and math prizes, but after graduation submerged into the Toronto street life. "I was a born rebel out of high school. I slept places you wouldn't pee in and did things you might not imagine. There were many fights and I once got nicked in the tummy by a knife; is my face marred? I ultimately quit the street scene because of bad grammar. My constant corrections to peers produced fights like punctuation marks. I was surrounded one day for a 'her to she' redress, and six filthy-mouthed girls pounded the crap outa me."

She matriculated from the tough streets to college for a bachelor's in clinical psychology—because she liked mice. She then earned a masters in English while studying French in Paris. Back again to Canada, she became a stockbroker with a side-interest in libertarianism. "The most recent pivotal day in my life was one year ago when I rose from my market desk and quit to move to Guatemala. I learned Spanish there and self-defense from the jungle guerrillas. I chucked everything Latin three months ago to go to comedy school in Toronto. I want humor to be a part of the rest of my life.

"I had a pet pig once. We lived in an apartment above my Toronto leather shop. He was jealous of customers and defecated on the top step when they entered, pushing little balls off with his nose. Business declined and the relationship grew strained, so I gave him to my boyfriend's mother."

"If there's time, I want to sample every lifestyle including hobos. Maybe I'm gathering pieces of a puzzle about myself. I grew up the middle-class daughter of a Toronto construction foreman, lived with skinheads, did the gold thing with the Royal Bank, studied in Paris, lived with Guatemalan peasants, and ultimately chose comedy for the dividends of investing in people. The only group I identify with are the Erisians because they're individualists, and rationalism turns a good girl on."

She expresses herself with clarity and charm under the colorful if chaotic hair. "The hairdo is part of an experiment to study people's reactions to facade and to set the comedy stage. There's nothing like having an edge," and she glances at Wiz's throat as he clears it to speak.

Arthur 'Wiz' Tyde III is an egghead on a strapping frame with an eager walk. "You carry less physical and emotional baggage if you live each day as though it were the last. More is almost always preferable to not enough. Never underestimate the stimulating value of eccentricity." He doesn't smile below the eyes when he talks but the corners of his mouth twitch speedily with each understanding, and he is an excellent listener. Today, in rare animation, he breaks the yolk of his youth to reveal how he became a self-made nerd.

"If there's time, I want to sample every lifestyle including hobos. Maybe I'm gathering pieces of a puzzle ..." — Clown

"My parents nearly dropped me off on the doorstep when I was twelve. A little bastard named Jimmy next door taunted me so in a fit of revenge I invented

Pooh Juice. I took a bushel basket and scooped the neighborhood dog and cat poop. I slid it into a big steel pot and put on a layer of Brewer's Yeast, then added water. I then wired the pot to the backyard transformer to ferment for a month. One morning, I carefully transported the pot to evil Jimmy's doorstep so he would get the blame, lifted the lid, and ran. In a matter of minutes, all the pet dogs and cats in the neighborhood started choking because Pooh Juice is slightly heavier than air. People ran screaming from their homes and the police yellow taped off a square-block. My parents found out and grounded me for a month in the basement, a mistake because it was my workshop."

"I developed an early collective consciousness with robots. I built a fleet to help my parents with chores. A maid named Red cleaned the basement for mom. It was built from a vacuum cleaner, car battery, electric eye, ice pick, and waste basket. It patrolled the basement whirring and blinked when it spotted trash. Then the pick went up-and-down with a tenacity I hadn't imagined possible until it stuck the trash and tossed it over its shoulder into a basket. One day mother went into the basement in bright high heels and the power went out. She apparently locked the door. The robot chased her high heels with the pick for five minutes until the lights went back on. Those were robotic grandchildren a father could be proud of."

"With dad, it was ball lightning that chased him from the basement office. I fabricated a ball lightning generator in my downstairs laboratory that rivaled nature. It's a luminous sphere appearing out of nowhere that moves parallel to the ground but jumps and can enter a nonmetallic opening before disappearing into thin air. In nature, it's normally only a foot in diameter but I beefed up my generator to prove that the greater the size the longer the duration. I went outside to mow the lawn, a chore I disliked, and must have left the dynamo on. Dad was in the basement office doing taxes when the four-foot ball entered the door sealing the exit. I heard father scream my name over and over and the basement windows began to shudder. I looked in and there was a blue-orange ball traveling around the basement and my dad dodging it. After I ran down and turned off the dynamo and opened the windows to dissipate the ball, he made me dismantle it and promise never to do it again."

"Those were mistakes a kid makes, and no one can blame me for trying. My hobo life also has deep roots. As a kid in Texas, I had a tree house that was my retreat from the world. There was a library of Playboy and other girlie magazines up there that I viewed to unwind. I still remember the 1979 Penthouse spread on hobos. (Peter Spielmann, "Hobos," pp. 138-45, *Penthouse*, May 1979.) The sturdy hobos carrying water bottles were making their way across the nation's rails to Britt, Iowa, for the National Hobo Convention. It was incredible! The article got dog-eared and hobos were the only thing that pulled me away from the foldouts."

"I grew up thinking about it and went to university at Michigan State. In the senior year, I saw a yellow flier on a phone pole advertising a course "Hobo Life in America" and enrolled. After the final exam I promised myself I'd ride boxcars cross-country without a cent in my pockets, and to that end went into Doc Bo's office for advice. You encouraged me but said it was illegal and to be careful getting on and off moving freights. I did it and discovered a new America!"

"My big break at Eris was at the 1985 kickoff party when the robot that served drinks went on the blink. I tinkered with my screwdriver in its back for a few minutes until it served again to everyone's delight. After Eris that year, Doug Casey, you (Doc Bo), and I rode the rails west that opened new life windows. With eventual financial success I still hopped freights. Nowadays, I love the high-tech aspect of hoboing. What could be better than waltzing into a yard with a timetable, preprogrammed scanner to listen to the engineers and bulls, cell phone to call the yardmaster for departures, walkie-talkies to talk to buddies, night-vision goggles for the real hobo hour, and satellite contact to post trip updates on a website?"

"I recently bought an airplane and leaflet Doc Bo's desert digs by air since he's become hard to get hold of for an outing. Incidentally, you were right not to tell my parents about the early hobo trips. You advised me to report instead uplifting stories after the quest. But I think their biggest worry would have been when I hopped my first freight with you after taking your sociology class."

A pause follows around the table to digest Wiz's spicy biography. "In contrast," I then tell the pair, "I was raised slowly in Idaho where kids were released from family and school one week annually for potato picking vacation that kept the state economy going. I was uncommonly bookish and coordinated, and worked summer jobs including cleaning dog kennels, factory work, winter construction, and on to veterinarian, publisher, pro jock, world adventurer, and, for the past two years, desert hermit in a burrow. My philosophy is that life is not a dress rehearsal."

"My big break at Eris was at the 1985 kickoff party when the robot that served drinks went on the blink. I tinkered with my screwdriver in its back for a few minutes until it served again to everyone's delight..." — Wiz

The table is cleared. In final preparations, Wiz sorts his collection of hobo-tech instruments. Clown crams leftover pizza into her white suitcase, and I observe with ambivalence the arrival of the Sunday afternoon bus. Aspen disappears behind us like an overdue sigh.

Part 9: Independence

Grand Junction, Colorado, is Hobo Heaven in the Rockies. The freights roll lazily in and out all day long, the bull looks the other way, and a mission serves chow nightly at the tracks. We step down from the bus knowing that cardboard, the tramp staple for a clean, smooth ride to the Pacific, also will be found in abundance on the ground.

Under the bridge where on the outbound trip a week earlier I spoke to the drunks, Wiz lifts a lumpy cardboard square like a trapdoor and unexpectedly dances. "Bottled water! Free, with the hot desert ahead!" We pull out twenty new 12-ounce bottles, the buried booty from an engineer's cab either discarded or acquired by a tramp, and stash the treasure better than the prior holder in deep weeds for our tomorrow's catchout.

Unlike the outbound trip with Pronto, Apple, and Wiz, this return to the West Coast has no pressing commitments. This is the proper and hobo way, free and easy, taking a turn as it comes. Nonetheless, at twilight, I offer to take Clown into the yard to learn a hobo trick or two. She jumps up from her personal square and we leave Wiz guarding the gear under the bridge.

At the first string of cars I explain, "The freight train is like a string of elephants that can help or hurt you depending on how you treat it." I show her the different cars to ride and their ladders—boxcar, gondola, grain car, and lumber car ends in a jam... where to sit and how to get off.

I quiz her with myriad scenario contingencies: "What would we do if this flatcar is stranded here?" She quips, "Too many variables." I persist, "What do you do if separated from the group?" She pipes, "First, try the radio. Debark at the next division point, and wait. Contact the man with the cell phone. Call our emergency number"—Wiz's wife. "Perhaps, at worst, carry on alone."

We walk up to a yard worker whose eyes bob at the dancing dreadlocks and ask him when the Cali Man (California train) is due. He answers that the building yard won't make one for some time, but hotshots roll through on the main and change crew every few hours, especially in afternoons. The hardhat moseys off, and we penetrate deeper over and around more car strings.

Probability is the essence of train hopping, a sure appeal to a math prodigy turned stock broker. I claim, "The likelihood of catching out in the east building yard is twice that of the west main yard 'til noon, then the probability reverses." "Don't fog me," she scoffs. "I know stats." "And I know trains," I sigh. I tell her things will iron out between us since probability is the key to any reasonable door in life.

In the next hour, we dodge make-believe 'silent rollers' in the yard, scale every variety of actual car, and hook a ladder on a pretend moving grain car. Physical drill is superior to lecture or mental rehearsal for athletics, and she is a quick study. After an hour, Clown saunters back to her pack under the bridge knowing how to think and react in the top dozen recurring hobo scenarios.

We three leave the bridge and stroll the streets north of the tracks after sunset. At the height of train riding during the Great Depression, you could buy a bed for a nickel and a meal for the same in this or any of the string of division towns. Ironically, now government or church free shelters and Sallies replace the old skid row flophouses but with less gratitude from the patrons. We reach the mission to discover it's too late for the sermon, meal, and bed, but a teenage girl on roller skates sides Clown under a streetlamp to gander at the kaleidoscopic braids. "Why don't you stay at the women's shelter tonight," the girl exhorts. "Maybe I will," replies our partner. There is no walk-in men's shelter.

The teen asks for nothing in return for an encyclopedic lowdown of the area. "We call it Grand Dumption. We got everything: Sally, Goody, Shelter, the bread line." She provides the street skinny for ten minutes until I hold up a palm to inquire, "Why are you helping us?" "Because I'm bored, and you're good people." I tell her that performance deserves reward and fork over a Lincoln ($5). She clenches it with growing eyes and skates off humming.

As we proceed I footnote, "The tip couldn't have occurred if we were to be in town long because she'd 'adopt' us daily, or mark us by telling others. Did you see her move out? A hobo once said, 'I got me a philosophy: Yesterday is a cancelled check, tomorrow is a promissory note, but today is cash in hand.'"

"I don't care where we stay as long as it costs at least $50 and I pay," chirps Wiz as we pad along. We check into a luxury hotel and the sugar daddy gets first shower. As water runs in the bathroom I tell Clown she has earned the second shower and toss her a towel. She shuts off the lights and I hear clothes drop to the floor. The night vision goggles are in Wiz's pack, and I pull them. Suddenly the room lights up to my eyes only. There stands a body as perfect and thrilling as Steinbeck's prose. Once you see that, I ponder, you're a slave until you get hit hard on the head.

"Hey, who turned out the light?" calls Wiz. I flip off the goggles and on the light, and confess. She gives a Mona Lisa titter and steps bundled in a towel into the bathroom. A vibrating noise elicits under the door crack and in a minute Clown peeks out with an electric toothbrush in her mouth. "Ebery gal who trabels with hobos shoot hab one!"

When she announces a bit later that she prefers for novelty a woman's shelter over a posh hotel, we encourage the option. I accompany her through a rough-and-tumble neighborhood to the Grand Junction Women's Shelter where a sign on the front door advises, 'Closed,' and knock. The matron in curlers answers, stares at the cascade of colored pigtails, and admits her, while physically blocking me. Clown cheeps, "See you bright and early at the mission for breakfast, Doc," and the door locks behind them.

I jog back through the impoverished neighborhood for warmth and safety, and return to the hotel where already Wiz snores with frogs up his nostrils. I sink wearily an inch into the other twin bed only to hear a clicking from my pants over a chair. I forgot to turn off the radio. I key the mike expectantly. "Yes?" She answers softly, "I am your hobo goddess singing you to sleep. Lullaby and good night..."

"Clown is a loner and that's fine," mutters Wiz now wide awake. "But if she comes out of that shelter in the morning scratching gray soldiers (body lice) there's little pity." "Don't worry," I counsel. "We'll sneak a piece of urinal soap into her pants to get rid of them like any other tramp."

I awaken the next morning to see Wiz operating over his backpack. He looks up and beams, "The pack is effectively loaded now." He opens the top to proudly display a layering method for access as well as protection of the sundry electronics: There's a tier of clean socks, underwear and T-shirt for each of the anticipated three days to the coast—with the gadgets sandwiched between them. He will pull a fresh clothes layer nightly after showering and stuff the dirty clothes under the bed for the maid to find in the morning, and neatly fold a fresh motel towel in the pack in stead of the old layer. "Thus," he explains, "Karma in the universe is maintained."

We check-out and depart the hotel and walk briskly across town to the chow line for our breakfast appointment with Clown. Early risers en route to jobs study our packs and gaits and Wiz surveys them back with, "It's delicious how people look at us so funny when we're outside the railroad influence, but measure up to us at the missions and Sallies." I respond, "Cultures should be fascinated by their subcultures as spice to the meal. These citizens can't guess we're their peers half the time."

We meet Clown a-sparkle in the center of the breakfast line where I query, "Last night was your first in a shelter. How was it?" She replies, "The shelter was buggy with interesting women to talk to. Lights went out at 11pm, but three young ladies kept me up half the night talking about life on the road. I slept a few scant hours, and woke up with one of them staring at my feet."

The mission door swings open and about fifty souls, a linear slice at this hour of similar haunts across the nation, file in and sit down on hard benches. An old alcoholic chews corn flakes like a Clydesdale, kids with runny yolks on their chins fly between the tables, a crackhead gulps coffee to stay awake for food, many muscled laborers return for seconds before the long day's work, and a few scattered hobos munch philosophically while observing the others as if apart of a movie.

The main course is SOS (sh**-on-a-shingle) that hobos call "graveyard," a meaty hash on toast. I close my nose over it for savor but Clown interrupts, "You eat like a pig," and provides a napkin. I take it, chuckle and return for seconds. Soon we shove from the table and Wiz offers, "That was the best breakfast I've had in near memory. No onion, which is important."

We exit into morning sunshine and retrieve the cardboard and water from the bridge, and mosey east along the tracks past homes and little warehouses to the Last Chance Liquor Store. The boys purchase milk and bread, sardines

An old alcoholic chews corn flakes like a Clydesdale, kids with runny yolks on their chins fly between the tables, a crackhead gulps coffee to stay awake for food...

and tomatoes for sandwiches, while Clown buys a month's store of beef jerky, pickles and vitamins.

On the way out, an hourglass lady in a string bikini advances bit by bit along the pavement talking to herself. "Marilyn Monroe, you look gorgeous today!" Then, turning to face where she stood, the same lady retorts, "Don't get fresh, mister!" Clown halts before the lady and says, "It's delusional, sir." We wheel down the sidewalk and Clown utters, "'Whoa. A bisexual split-personality. I've never seen it before!" I nudge Wiz that suddenly our companion is more interesting.

When government funding is tightened the first product squeezed is mental health with released patients from hospitals in droves hitting the rails. Most are "cabbage heads" who have used so many drugs in a lifetime that physical recovery is difficult. "A thesis could be written on tramping crazies," I suggest to the pair.

"Execs, let's hit the rails!" and I lead them from the sidewalk to the back of the liquor store right on the main. We set up temporary headquarters in a weed patch where I describe the setup. Grand Junction is divided into the main yard next to the Amtrak office where periodic through freights on the mainline change crews; and the 'makeup' or building yard now across from us where car strings are parked in a bowl of two dozen tracks. New trains for west or east are constructed on these rails like beads on strings. Rarely, a through train stops in this building bowl to add or cut cars before rushing on. It's a twenty-minute walk between the makeup and main yards. This overview is the normal layout for most railroads across the country, but larger ones have a building yard at both ends.

Our two options are axiomatic: To wait for a newly-built freight at the makeup yard but have no chance to catch a through freight on the mainline, or to hike a mile to the main yard to bet on a through freight stopping before any westbound is built. Clown rebukes, "You told me that last night, Doc. Let's wait here and eat."

We sit in the patch like weeds, Wiz in dark coveralls, me in bib overalls, and she gliding about us like an ice-skater swallowing vitamins in jeans, pink halter-top, and a white floppy cap with fishing lures to hold back the hair. A burly tramp in green camouflage angles across the building yard stepping lightly at us under a sparse pack—he is the archetypal Viet Nam veteran.

74

"Mornin', Flintstone Kids," he greets in a gravelly voice twixt missing incisors. Clown demands, "What's that mean?" He utters, "It's people who ride with plastic... ya know, credit cards. It's easy to see you ain't rail vets." The early morning insects buzz to fill a long silence.

"Say, lady, why don't you take a ride with a real train tramp to places that don't exist in your imagination." "Nah," she replies, "but thanks, buddy. I'm with these other Flintstones." The geezer examines her like a Belle Starr. "I'm the oldest hobo in the country!" he cries abruptly, but from his heart I hear great pride pulse. "Hey you," he hooks a finger at me. "Stand up so I can see what you're made of." At that Wiz fingers a screwdriver in his breast pocket for emergencies. I gaze back and reply, "I'm sitting comfortably." The Vet shrugs, "Don't get lost on the American gridiron, Flintstones. Good day!"

War veterans have formed a strong contingent of rail riders beginning with the Civil War when soldiers, accustomed to camping out, foraging and traveling by trains, hoboed west after the battles' end on the same right-of-way as the executives take. The railroads give today's vet, who sifts for himself as well as his predecessors, the type of thrill he came to expect in Nam. Future wars will fill out the boxcar fraternity for as long as freights run.

Furthermore, a lone wolf's dream is to hobo with a woman for many reasons: Yard workers are freer with train information, the bull doesn't cause so many headaches, hitchhiking off the railroads is faster, shelters admit a husband or boyfriend together, families get firsts in food lines, and there's no end to the advantages. The catch-22 is that females profess the opposite view. A quick way to about-face a lady is to ask her if all this is true. The consequent issue is, is it safe for a female to jump freights alone? They're safer than males on the road because people ease their ways. A slight worry of rape exists, improbable, with so many worse things than that happening on the rails. So, I tell women the first time out to travel with a companion, and then she can go alone as many I've known have with flying colors.

"He's right, you know," I post my partners in the patch. "We're hobby hobos next to him."

Part 10: Long Road Home

We twiddle our thumbs in tall weeds until three hardhats working strings across the yard appear fleetingly into view. Clown pops up to pursue them, vowing over her shoulder to radio intelligence every fifteen minutes. She traipses merrily out the trampled circle into the lengthy makeup yard.

Fifteen minutes later, Wiz carps, "Why hasn't she radioed?" I mutter waving my hand, "Give her ten minutes more." We sweat, look, and listen to units rumble toward the spot where she vanished. Car string after car string bang together there into one train that surely is our ride out of town. "Let's get out of these weeds," I finally urge, and we stand with our packs and hers. "Soon that freight will highball."

I lug two packs following Wiz with his across a dozen vacant tracks toward the clamor. Nearing, we hear singing between car clashes, and stoop to peek under a gondola. Behold, Clown with crayon-hair flowing over a pink halter top giggles within a ring of hardhats. They help her place coin after coin on a rail beneath the three locomotives' wheels, and the engineer rocks back-and-forth over them to make "hobo jewelry." (Later, one may drills holes in the twice-sized, flattened coins that retain a faint outline of the head and tail to fashion trinkets or earrings.) She now holds up beautiful pieces—nickels, dimes, and quarters—to reflect sunlight. Wiz collapses his pocket telescope and cusses.

"You know what?" he questions, brushing a bee from his face. "First of all, I'm allergic to bee stings. Second, I don't think she's in danger. In fact, she seems to be enjoying herself. Third, I'm so irate this is what I'm going to do..." He keys the radio and bawls, "My name is Clown and I like trainmen!" In the distance, Clown grabs her pants for the walkie-talkie. I yank my radio and yell, "After the finale, gentlemen, get her on this California Man." The hardhats recoil that words could pour so angrily from a hoboette's jeans. She jerks out her radio and transmits, "Oh. It's you, boys. This is your train. All aboard!"

Wiz and I shake our heads, and rise from our haunches. We climb six rungs over the blue gondola wall and, with no inside ladder, drop the packs five feet and tumble to the hot floor ourselves. Then we peer over the gondola like Kilroys. Men watch her. They can't take their eyes off the Medusa with a sharp tongue. "She'll leave a trail of erections all the way to Sacramento," I curse. "Train information is the sole determinant of a successful hobo," Wiz abates. "She gets it better than all my gadgets."

Moments later, Clown mounts and drops to the gondola floor and we squat in the shared sunshine smelling the diesel of two growling engines about to connect up front. We brace in the car center for the inevitable jolt and, though the power joins ½-mile away, the couplers pair-by-pair jam in a staccato beat—our car rocks as if hit by a wave—that washes by and to the rear end. In seconds the brakes hiss, the horn trumpets, and our freight charges out the rail.

"I found it stimulating to talk to the yard workers," says Clown as the car waggles down the track. "There aren't a lot of men in these parts. I convinced them with the rail lingo you taught me, Doc, that I knew what I was doing. So, they said, 'Hold the train!' After you spoiled it with that radio slot they joked, 'Your guys are better equipped than us,' and finally let me go."

I grin and pull out another L'Amour book. Wiz tunes his scanner to crew chatter in the lead unit, and Clown, smiling mysteriously, eats a whole jar of pickles before we reach the town limit.

This mile-long mixed freight draws boxcars, grainers, oilers, gondolas including our blue one, but no pigs or containers. This is called a 'dog' for low priority that'll side for hotshots having boxes and pigs zooming past *Men watch her. They can't take their eyes off the Medusa with a sharp tongue. "She'll leave a trail of erections all the way to Sacramento," I curse.* from either direction all day. But no one complains because our train is shambling toward the Pacific. The track parallels I-70 for a few hours across high, flat desert and on into canyon land past the Arches National Park.

The afternoon journey becomes a string of knots—sidings for faster freights—but we knew it would be slow going when we made our play in Grand Junction. At one pause, we switch from the gondola to the shaded back porch of a grain car.

Most freight hoppers watch the scenery flow until it blends with their personal past, and then they drowse. Conversely, I've never seen Wiz without something to do, and now he tinkers with various electronic gadgets from his pack for miles on end. Clown always has a book in hand, and prefers it to the landscape sliding past the freight. I, with a deep reserve for introspection, am my best own company in one corner of the platform.

Suddenly Wiz holds high his cell phone and blurts, "That's it! We are, as far as I know, the first hobos ever to send an email from a moving freight." On request for particulars and he replies, "It went to the Wiley Publisher Chief Pam VanGiessen and reported what I just told you, that this is the first hobo email. I promised to try to update her via the *dailyspeculations.com* Website with daily progress reports."

The freight lumbers constantly at 40 mph until the rail picks up a parallel river with sporadic rapids. Our hopper overtakes a boat of rafters traveling the same direction, but they're intent on their ride and miss ours. Clown asks if a hobo ever rides atop a car, and I reply, "Yes, that's called decking, a safe maneuver when done with sensitivity." Wordlessly she zips up the ladder of our rolling porch and, as Wiz shakes his head over a gadget, I trail her like a worrying father.

A two-ft. steel catwalk runs the length of the car top that she crabs to the center and sits on. Now, with one hand clutching the bucking grate like a cowgirl, the train breeze punches her dreadlocks horizontally and she whoops "Yahoo!" She leans back and unbuttons and strips off her blouse and bra with the free hand, and waves them high at the boatload. The rafters hoot approval for a quarter-mile before ebbing.

Satisfied, she dresses and brushes by me on the catwalk to the ladder with, "It must have been the excitement of the locomotives and the first ride." We descend to the platform and to Wiz engrossed in electronics without knowing the better.

The region flattens in the hot part of the day, and a Zen quality clutches the slowest train on earth. Freight hopping ultimately becomes sitting on a large vibrating rock and living inside one's self. We're grateful for the hopper shade and each makes the best of his passing hours. Wiz declares he's out of Internet range, Clown reads, an opportunist dragonfly pinches insects on the wing in our car draft, and I catnap. Several hours later, the countryside turns agricultural checkerboard green and brown, with lofty red barns.

There's an old hobo depiction where a slow freight stops at every house except when it comes to a two-family house it stops twice. That's probably exaggeration, but I've seen tramps climb off milk-run drags like this one to pick oranges in an orchard, rob vegetables from gardens, 'gooseberry pick' (clothes from lines), and catch trackside pigeons for supper—and board in time.

We side off the main yet again for a double-stack hotshot to race by to Salt Lake City. That faster horse gets the inside rail, the enduring theme in our scenic pilgrimage.

Part 11: SNAFU in the Global Village

The long train glides weightlessly through the heat. Wiz dabs his brow over the glorified cell phone near occasional towns that collects the Internet. "I'm not going to hide that I'm hot under the collar," he swears. "but the consolation is that we certainly are the first hobos to use the railroad's own website to consult a RR system map while on the road. I'm checking the bigger towns ahead in hope that we can get off this miserable dog and onto a hotshot." In minutes he answers himself, "It's dismal. There's no big yard for 150 miles until Salt Lake City."

He expounds further while typing little buttons as the freight trudges through the Wasatch Range on the eastern hot lip of the Great Basin. "It's clear that the rails run through the Global Village. Technology contracts the world into a tiny village where remote events are instantly communicated and experienced by everyone, and the gridiron becomes a basement toy train set."

It's a powerful image, one most hobos wouldn't care for, but thumbs up to Wiz Kid. Years ago, he was the first 'bo on the block to take a scanner onto the freights. Then, in the nineties, he was among the vanguard of hi-tech hobos with state-of-art electronics who revolutionized freight hopping. We now have aboard:

☐ cell phone

☐ walkie-talkies

☐ police scanner

☐ infra-red goggles

☐ global positioning system

☐ satellite connection to the Internet

We also carry Rand McNally's *Handy Railroad Atlas* and The Automated Timetables.

The irony is that technology in agriculture knocked off the greatest waves of freight riders in history. By the start of WWII, one after another innovation each replaced a dozen straining backs in the fields across the nation. Mechanization all but killed the working American hobo.

Now, high-tech hobos, though not the rule on the rails, crop up often enough. They are usually boxcar tourists, like us, rather than *bona fide* long-haul train tramps. Their instruments take a little magic out of the freight riding experience, but they get us on more trains easier, faster, and safer. Wiz concludes, "I wouldn't leave home without at minimum a cell phone and a two-way radio."

Wiz irritably snatches the scanner after our freight stops a third time within one track mile with nothing passing us by. "Let's investigate this holdup," he gripes. He selects the next yard's frequency and we listen in to discover that many trains are 'staged' (stacked) in line because the entry rail to the yard is blocked with a building freight. It's going to be thirty minutes before the track clears.

"Let's go on a hobo Easter Egg hunt," I suggest from the platform. "Are you daft?" Wiz pleads, "it's not Easter." Clown adds, "What's up, Doc?" I propose, having noticed periodic dry, cracked ties in the roadbed that cue valuable hobo date nails, that we walk the rail to search for them. Wiz opts to remain with the gear, so she and I drop and amble toward the train rear while peering under cars at older ties. We're searching for three–in. nails with thick, flat heads stamped with the year the tie was laid. Theoretically, 20-30 years after a tie is laid—its lifespan—the date nail is noticed by a worker and the tie is replaced. Hobos collect loosened or pulled nails to trade or make lucky charms (with the wearer's birth date) by silver-plating the dated head. The hobo nails are often found in older sidetracks out west in 'veins' of years, but today Clown and I discover a sole '58 date nail that remains stuck tight in the long tie and between our birthdays.

Further back along the train, a red-faced tramp and his long-tongued dog stand on a hopper platform and, at our approach, a gnarled hand reaches out with an upside-down canteen. "Sorry, buddy, we're out too," Clown replies honestly. "Trains are stacked on the main," I inform, "and they won't release for thirty minutes." He rubs a scraggly chin, looks up and fixates on an object across the way. "Ya know, I figured as much."

I follow his gaze. "It's a water spigot," he finally says. "I've been staring at it on the outside of that white building for ten minutes. That's a bramble patch between the rail and house." I read his thoughts and roll my own dry tongue. "It's five minutes each way through the thorns, a minute to fill your jug... You can be back in eleven minutes, with luck and by leaving the dog."

He, followed closely by the dog, bounds down to the roadbed rising with heat waves. He is sinewy, tattooed, and dehydrated; the pet is a Heinz variety with a long pink tongue. "I'll watch him till you get back," I offer, but he gently declines, "Naw. He knows his business." The mutt rests a chin on the old army pack and the tramp nods quietly at us before turning to face the patch. "Here goes nothin'" he yells, and scampers down the bank.

"The water will taste better for the thorns," I call, and the dog's concerned gaze follows him.

We watch until he wanes in the patch. "Love it!" I exclaim. The major types of riders are boxcar vacationers like myself, the homeless or those too poor to afford bus fare (though the freight is usually faster and more comfortable than Greyhound), migrant workers, the unemployed looking for work, immigrants, loony bin rejects, antisocials and outcasts, men on the lam, marriage fallouts, runaway teens, veterans, the curious, and now executives and pet owners.

Clown and I continue to walk the train identifying the different cars: gondolas, tankers, other hoppers, flatcars and, at the very end, a solitary boxcar. The dog grows smaller in the distance even as the tramp has disappeared in the briars. "I can't let go the feeling of freedom of the man and dog," declares Clown. "Yes," I agree. "They are a living example of hobo life and of the American pursuit of happiness. It's what this one country on the big globe stands for. The collective doesn't decide the purpose of the individual. Every person, hobo, and dog has a right to try different paths, pick one, and live it for himself."

"A boy and his dog on the open road makes me want to click my heels," pulses Clown. "Meanwhile," I remind her, "Free clicks demand vigil. This freight may pull away any second." "Doc," she warms, "give me the benefit of the doubt of knowing exactly where our next ride is if this train pulls out." I clam up. We round the last boxcar with FRED blinking red over and over, and beyond a sweeping view of the empty back track for miles.

Hiss. Click. Bang. The freight suddenly hiccups forward.

"For Pete's sake!" cries Clown, sprinting around FRED. "How do we know if the door on the other side of this boxcar is open?" "It's high on the springs—an empty," I spur. (Railroads often leave one side door open for the next load that may be hobos.) "It's open!" she soon verifies.

We race to overtake the door, then slow to match pace at a walk. Now the hardest part is getting up and on. The boxcar floor is five feet off the cinders—at Clown's nose. The ballast is angled and slippery, plus the freight gains speed each tick. "Follow my lead," I instruct, and trot to the moving ledge, bend swiftly and slap my thigh. She steps on and vaults into the car. The door passes but I regain it and belly flop in myself, scratching nails on the hardwood to keep from sliding out. She yelps and grabs my shirt to tug me through the opening. Safe and panting, we retire to opposite ends of the boxcar.

Remembering the tramp, I peek through a wall crack on the closed side. "I guess the timing was off," I report. "The dog is sitting with its back to the freight watching the master with a jug of water stuck in the patch." She antes, "That's the American way."

"They [man and dog] are a living example of hobo life and of the American pursuit of happiness. It's what this one country on the big globe stands for. The collective doesn't decide the purpose of the individual. Every person, hobo, and dog has a right to try different paths, pick one, and live it for himself."

The world changes once you enter a boxcar door. The outside and your past are left behind with the gentle shake and roll. Though the 'window' (open door) provides light and a god-like imperviousness it takes a good minute for your eyes to adjust to the dim. It's a rare old boxcar with a wood floor that cushions and muffles the rail travel to make conversation possible. Locked boxcars, like some lives, are sealed shut until the right moment when a worker breaks the seal to admit light and unload them into a yard. Empties, like this one, are seal-less with one 'window' left open after the last cargo was off-loaded. That door becomes a wide-screen TV featuring the local nature channel. It measures 15-ft.-wide and 9-ft.-tall and slides on a horizontal floor track that I stake with an 8–in. railroad spike to prevent it from vibrating shut on rough track. We sit in opposite ends of this side-door Pullman chewing fingernails over the next move.

Clown stands, prances the shaky floor, and sits close by me. The boxcar reaches speed and the inside movement progresses from jiggle to sway to rock-and-roll all the way. "I feel like a hoboette for the first time," she murmurs snuggling closer. "Are there many girl riders?" I answer, "Hoboettes are the rarest, about 2%, and almost always with a man in tow."

My breast pocket jumps. "You're morons! If you hear me, I assume no responsibility for you." I key my radio and she answers in it, "Morons must be the last hobo type. Thanks for your concern. We're on the last boxcar: Doc, me, and FRED!" He roars back, "Wave through the door so I know you're alive." She warily rises and reaches out the door. "Rock on Wilma Flintstone!" fires Wiz, "what's your plan?"

That plan takes action in thirty minutes as the train slows and parks on the mainline. We leap out the door and gallop the half-mile toward Wiz waiving at us off the hopper. "The trick here," I puff behind the lady, "is to look ahead for the next possible ride while recalling the last nearest one in case the freight starts." She tugs my hand hard as I continue, "Give greater weight to the one behind because if the train starts that car will catch us while the one ahead will..." At this instant the freight lurches and we are caught in a no-man's land between no real cars to ride. She drops my hand, screams "Goddamn baggage!" and sprints to the first oil tanker car ahead. I dash and grab the same moving ladder in the nick of time.

An oil car is a black bottle with a two-foot thin grate at the end called a bumper that rides over the wheels. They twirl faster and faster below our bird perch. "Where the Hades are you?" sounds Wiz on the radios. "On an oil tanker," I shout with one hand on the grate and the other the receiver. "What!?" he gasps. "I'll phone the next yard and tell them to radio this train to make an emergency stop." However, I urge patience that an emergency stop might throw us off.

"Give me a minute to think," and he signs off. Momentarily, the walkie-talkie blurts, "The mileposts cross-reference the railroad map to show the freight seventy miles outside Salt Lake City. We'll arrive in a smaller yard sooner, but the scanner reports that the mainline is clear so we'll sail through. If you can hold on, there are many small towns in the next two hours before Salt Lake, so just..." I complete the sentence, "...work forward whenever the train stops." He requests, "I can still radio the next yard to contact the engineer." "No," I answer, "the danger doesn't equal the embarrassment."

We fasten like ivy to the mesh platform. "You stepped out of the Eris crowd, the only person willing to ride a freight. Why?" I ask close to her face. "It's another lifestyle sampler to figure out myself," she replies, and scoots closer on the bumper. "I'm hard to get to know."

I coax her, "We're sitting on a narrow mesh inches above racing wheels and can't get off. If the train emergency stops we fall. If the local police see us, we're nabbed. In an hour our fingers will cramp like sticks. After sundown it gets nippy. Are you nervous, Clown?" She retorts, "Not unless I should be."

"Why are you on this trip?" she counters. I am instantly carried away from the tiny stage to the mightiest autobiography. "Did you ever read John Griffin's *Black like Me*?" I ask. She twinkles, "One of my favorites. What happens, it begins, if a white man becomes a Negro in the deep South? What adjustments must he make, what changes occur within him, and what are the sensations of being different. How else would he know except by becoming a Negro?" "Exactly," I echo, appending, "the story haunted me for years until I became a hobo. Unlike Griffin's transformation to a black using dyes, oral chemicals, and shoe polish, I only avoided shaving three days, donned old clothes with empty pockets, and walked into a railroad yard."

We ramble at 40 mph down the rail over bumpy crossings and through little burgs where passersby wave incredulously, but we can't let go of the bumper to wave back. I glance at Clown, as a teacher to a student, proud that she doesn't quiver or puke. "This," I tell her, "is your moment in the sun. You are a hoboette!" After twenty minutes ride on the dodgy tanker, the freight pauses on the main, we jump down and race to our hopper before it trundles.

Wiz pulls his hair and stamps his feet on the steel porch. "Don't do that again at the risk of death!" he screams. "You needn't have worried," I console him, "we had you watching over us."

Wise tramps slow down—slower than the train go their minds. In jail this is called doing 'easy time,' and doing train time is the same to make long hours pass easier. Spread ideas out, taste one at a time, and let conclusions arrive like maestro piano keys. I pull out and read L'Amour upside-down to decelerate after the tanker. "Doc Bo," quips Wiz, "you're the Zen master of the 21st century, with an upside-down book in one hand and a thumb up your ass with the other."

Later, a sky of lights ahead. The freight train, truly the greatest technological wonder of time, pulls into the Mormon capital after dark with three heathen hobos.

Part 12: Railroad Indicators

In a dark corner of the Salt Lake City railroad yard we find our land legs and exit quickly to the wee-hour city streets like weary slugs under heavy shells. Wiz wheels into an all-night donut shop announcing, "I must phone my wife!" "Are the brownies finally kicking in?" I jibe. "Not that. She'll be anxious for the epiphany."

Clown and I look at each other in vexation. He stalks without further word to a private corner, so we order coffee. Later the trio, red-eyed and wrinkled after the cups and call, leaves to locate a hotel. Wiz wears along the sidewalks a Masonic Lodge shirt to 'capture local sentiment,' and she a T-shirt striped 'Gametes Spawn or Die' to argue it.

We sleep until noon the next morning with Clown the first to rise and trampoline on Wiz's hotel bed. He flings oaths, and she walks up and down my sleeping bag on the floor. "Let's go eat," she prompts us. We check out the hotel and proceed toward the city center where Clown pauses in a thrift shop doorway saying, "I need to outfit for the trip," and ducks in.

The 'Goodies and Sallies,' or Goodwill and Salvation Army thrift stores, are favorite haunts for Wiz and me too. He scrounges computer parts and I look for 'Railroad Indicators.' Moreover, the shops are ports of call for all train hoppers who score free clothes vouchers from the local mission to trade for threads at these stores. The Utah Goodies and Sallies are rich digs for tramps because Mormons waste not. "Someone could make a fortune buying this thrift stuff for pennies and selling it for dollars on e-Bay," perceives Wiz, strolling the hard goods aisle of racks of old plates, utensils, salt shakers, and archaic computers.

The 'Goodies and Sallies,' or Goodwill and Salvation Army thrift stores, are favorite haunts for Wiz and me too.

Clown breaks down in the bedding section and explains why she arrived in Aspen so ill-equipped for the hobo trip. "A year ago, I crossed from Canada into the USA with a newspaper clipping on immigration with circled items and comments in the margins for a standup comedy skit on why borders shouldn't exist. U.S. Immigration found it, put me in the computer, and makes it tough to enter since. I must bring just a small suitcase indicating a short stay."

"Also, the matter of no sleeping bag," she blushes. In the rush to catch the bus out of Aspen, she'd left behind a green bag kindly donated by the favorite mule-riding candidate for U.S. Representative of Colorado (since elected), Wes McKinley, who had it wrapped around buffalo meat in the trunk of his sedan at Eris. Now in the SLC thrift store we unearth a five-buck sleeping bag to replace the dirty little blanket that's been binding her white suitcase and keeping her warm nights.

She dons skinny sunglasses and sashays the clothes aisle looking like Hunter Thompson's hip daughter. "There's so much I'd like to take to change into, but so little room to carry it." Miss Thompson finally settles on the sleeping bag and one purple bandana. The latter is strategic for a buck that, with a quick knot, draws all those rainbow dreadlocks safely underneath.

I scrutinize every aisle in the store for economic indicators. Speculator Victor Niederhoffer and I formulated RR Indicators in the late 80s when Victor termed them Low-Life Indicators. The gist of the system is that business is always moving between high and low, and lower currents may determine the whole. Everywhere fish flip their tails and flick their fins. Can economic tides be predicted by observing the fishes' behavior? We thought so.

Some of the RR Indicators include:

☐ the length and frequency of freight trains

☐ the flux of the hobo population plus the hobo (worker)/tramp (non-worker) ratio

☐ the length of discarded cigarette butts (in the worst economic times smoked to the bitter end)

☐ and, at the bottom of Low-Life Indicators, the price and activity of prostitutes

Freight loads are qualified and quantified such as coal and autos (sticker price on the windows) to determine specific markets. The downtown 'slave markets' (agencies that place temp workers) have stretched queues during rising unemployment.

So, I monitor and every so often relay these and other indicators to Victor who directs his computer staff to factor in sophisticated analysis to determine if there's an investment edge. If so, he buys, as he once nationally cited, Turkish bonds on the tip of an explosion of non-smoking, English-speaking youths in the business sector, and Brazilian stocks on the increasing prevalence of long butts on the ground.

Likewise, in thrift stores one discerns for indications the amount and wear of apparel donated to the institutions during economic shifts, as well as the numbers and types of patrons. Hobos shop smart for clothes more comfortable than those they wear from former busy owners who stretched them out of shape. Clown offers new angles to all citizens to beware of endeavors that require the purchase of new clothes. Moreover, she claims, personality can improve by outfitting yourself in someone's discarded clothes. "The proper way to advance as a new man among great men who look past the exterior is through a person's internal makeup. Most socialized people are cowards on this point."

We three would like to buy additional clothes this morning but the pack space is limited, and we reject the street people style of wearing their entire wardrobes layered—second-hands from the Sally and all too large—in the dead of summer.

The executive trio strolls out of the thrift store to nearby Pioneer Park, an oasis of freshly cut grass on the only square block in Salt Lake City without a parking lot. The park predated the first transcontinental rail as a campsite and later was an early employment center for trucks to pick up day laborers. It's easy to envision century-old tramps recently fallen from the freights and resting here for the next job, sandwich or ride along the nearby track. Dozens of vagabonds today sprawl in little knots of their own types under uncaring trees. Clown pulls lobes off a fallen maple leaf on the lawn and asks, "Who is the traditional American hobo?"

I wave feverishly. "You see a few of them with water jugs and packs in this park. Look closer at their calloused hands, quick eyes and sturdy feet. The escort of American expansion through history has been the working stiffs carrying bindles. They built the nation's roads, canals, and railroads, felled lumber, drilled oil, dug mines, harvested wheat and ice, and picked crops everywhere. Their mobility on freights answered periodic manpower demands where no other existed. Each train rider often carried his tools, per one derivation of the name from 'hoe-boy.' The traditional 'bo was homeless, unmarried, and unburdened with cares, ready to hop a freight at the drop of a hat to a rumor of a job.

Between services, he was a freeloader at city street corners and was seen in the soup lines next to non-working bums. He was an American product who rode the freights into history books and music, half slave-worker, half adventure hero that's conjured every time a food line forms or a train whistle blows."

We heft our packs from the park to places at the end of a block-long food line in front of a square pink building across the street. "This is Mormon Town," I promise. "They won't run out of chow." A food line is worth careful study for the following treasures: Erect men with semi-clenched fists and hard stares, unwed mothers with one on the hand and another at the breast, drug crazies who don't cotton to insults, rubber legged 'stew bums,' Mexican laborers straight from the fields of toil and sleep, a handful of introspective train hoppers, awkward businessmen who've shed ties and wristwatches for the noon hour, and a sprinkling of street people with so much time on their hands.

"...The escort of American expansion through history has been the working stiffs carrying bindles. They built the nation's roads, canals, and railroads, felled lumber, drilled oil, dug mines, harvested wheat and ice, and picked crops everywhere. Their mobility on freights answered periodic manpower demands where no other existed..."

The savvy 'bo has a junkyard dog's set of eyes for their dress, body language, mannerisms, and accents from places afar. Most look down at the pavement, so the trick is to catch rare individuals who do the same thing—look up, catch eyes, and devise excuses to talk. Though we are quickly tagged in line as "Gentlemen (and woman) of the Road"— hobos who show signs of having worn the white collar—Clown sparks a dialogue with two Mexican laborers who speak hardly a lick of English and grin sheepishly at her torn Spanish... "How did you cross the border? Did you ride the freight train here? Is work easy to get in this town?"

We learn that Mexican illegals in great daily volumes cross the border by foot. Some continue within the USA by bus, but those familiar with freight riding (widespread in Mexico) take the rails to uncounted American destinations and secure false drivers licenses (about $100) to get hired to assorted jobs. The lion's share of their paychecks are often sent home to pueblos to sponsor more mushrooming illegals. The Mexicans tend to club together within the USA working and sleeping in the agriculture fields, and are bad-mouthed by 'native' white workers for stooping for lower wages.

The food line offers more economic indicators than fleas on a dog tail. The length is an historic dial with short ones meaning good times. Soup lines absurdly offer indices of food stamps too, plus their cash street price (hovering at half-face value). Dumpster diving increases in better times with nicer food and articles tossed and rescued therein.

The mission door crack enlarges and all other thoughts drop as our team prematurely sniffs the air. The porter admits groups of ten from the line with no ID check until, finally, we enter a spacious dining hall where 150 people chat amicably while devouring a five-course meal at picnic tables. It's smorgasbord style, as usual, with drinks served by church volunteers wearing ever-sincere smiles. The few residual women diners, given earlier front-line preference, finish pears for desert just as men return for entree seconds, indicating a bounty.

The execs gobble salad, chicken, mashed potatoes, and peas, then rise for seconds as well... Wiz returns without the trendy cookies. He seats and justifies, "These sugar cookies, according to my Cub Scout campfire test, burn brighter than anything but baby diapers. I advise everyone here not to eat them." Those within earshot push the cookies away.

Except Boxcar Clown. "Being with a lady changes the whole hobo complexion," I explain to our table as she grinds another. There are a hundred examples along the way: Yard workers are freer with information, the bull is appeased, outside tramps don't pick as many fights unless they're envious, hitchhiking is a breeze, homeless shelters admit you solo or with a spouse, and food lines lead with women. There's no end to the advantages of having an extra X chromosome on the road. However, try to get a gal to admit it and you'll get your face slapped. "Or worse!" jokes Wiz.

Clown stops chewing to pay him a sharp look. "When I was in Guatemala I climbed the jungle hills daily to practice hand-to-hand combat with guerrillas..." Suddenly she lunges from her chair for Wiz's throat with a guerrilla death grip that just misses the Adam's apple. He rises in defense. "Just kidding," she apologizes.

For clear security reasons, a buxom lady wearing a nametag 'Counselor' looms near to ask Clown and me, as a presumed couple, if we need assistance. "Yes," and I speak for the two of us on the further ease of traveling with a female companion. The lady cuts me off wagging a finger in my face. "You shouldn't waste the time others could use if you don't have domestic problems." However, she winks at Wiz on leaving.

We three remain at the picnic table. Wiz sighs, "I loved today's meal, clientele, and conversation. By contrast, $500-a-plate dinners are unappetizing. The portions are small and look odd. The speeches are long and boring compared to a mission sermon. But it's true the other man's bread is sweeter, plus I'm hungrier coming off the rails."

"I'm ambivalent on American welfare," he continues. "On one hand, people have to eat and simply cannot afford it otherwise; on the other hand it's abused. In San Francisco a guy can get two, three hundred a month plus food stamps for having an address under an overpass. The more wily ones ride freights around using different IDs to collect more welfare in different places. One brute had 20 welfare accounts across the country and a book to keep them straight, murdering people for their IDs until he was caught. The pity is most of these 'circle tramps' spend the extra money on booze and drugs. There should be a way to stop the bilking of the system of tens of millions of dollars while spending tens of thousands keeping the deserving fed."

"I'm not for welfare," he restates, "But these missions bring progress to many lives. There's a fine line between sanctioning a victim and helping a deserving guy get on his feet. A fellow who's down and out through no fault of his own can get clean, fed, and on his feet again for a job interview. Nine out of ten won't, but one will. I've seen enough to know it's a judgment call, but I don't have time to go around being the nice guy to individuals. I reckon certain missions do better jobs than others, so when I enter one and get a free meal or shower, I give back. That keeps it simple."

Clown crinkles her face into an intellectual vent and leans forward. He concludes, "I've weighed both sides of the welfare question until I can't stand looking at the fulcrum any more. People don't advance in life with handouts. On the other hand, some people cannot get necessities otherwise. I throw my philanthropy where it's absolutely needed."

He spots Counselor, rises with a pleased look, and chases her across the room. After a short huddle he returns grinning. "What happened," asks Clown with an upturned lip. "Oh, I got the address of this place. I didn't get a date, but she'll be happy with what comes in the mail." He clarifies, "As a matter of fact, since making 'big money' some years ago I've been sending a check for a grand to each mission that treats me well across the country. Some things come against the grain, but don't have to be taken that way."

I tell them of a predecessor philanthropist Eads How, dubbed in the early 1900s, the Millionaire Hobo, for donating much of the family fortune made from the St. Louis Railroad to sponsor hobo colleges and conventions. Now that's faith with action.

We walk out of the mission door and across the road to Pioneer Park. It's a clear, sunny afternoon for sharing secrets on the grass, even among a habitual incommunicado trio each holding the key to his heart. I suggest we sit and digest in the shade of a tree.

"A lump has kept me up nights," I confess, and reach around the back of my bib overalls to release a safety pin securing a hidden pocket sewn in the small of the back. "Pull out the wallet," I direct Wiz. He does, and I yank it with frustration. I open it and finger the uncounted hundreds, thinking back to the discovery in Aspen. "One bill can block out the sun if you hold it close enough, even distract you to lose a billfold," I offer lowering one. "I have a story to tell..."

"I'm sitting in the Aspen Lodge reading a glossy magazine waiting for you two to come downstairs for the bus to Grand Junction. I sink into a cushion and scan the lounge to justify my sense of disaffiliation. I like to think I'm what Roger Miller sings, 'A man of means, by no means... King of the Road.' Yet, here I sit among 'bums on the plush,' the idle rich. These vacationers will soon check out and return to homes and high-paying jobs and try to match pace with each other in the work world. I glance under a couch and reach for a dropped puke (leather wallet). I crack it and see the New Mexico driver's license, Sports Illustrated staff card and, in the back fold, a sheaf of crisp 100-dollar bills. I quit counting them at eight-hundred with tears in my eyes, knowing I must find and return the billfold to the rightful owner.

"I pocket the wallet and pace to the hotel front desk to discover he's gone home. The hobo bus is ready. So, I safety-pin the wallet inside a secret pocket in my overalls and try to forget it. But I'm disaffiliated, you see. A financial basis of travel is that people can get by with sum-little money. This wallet has been an irritating bump on my back for 600 miles since Aspen."

"What are you going to do?" asks Clown. "Go back and give it to the mission," proposes Wiz. "The moral issue is secondary," I respond. "What do I tell a bull down the line who searches and finds two IDs and all that cash... 'Son, here's a free Go-to-Jail ticket.' Hell, let's discuss it on the way to the post office."

In line at the P.O., the other patrons must think our yak zany. "There's a labyrinth of options," I gather. "We can splurge part or all of it, climb a tree in Pioneer Park and drop the bills like leaves to the needy, or return the intact billfold to the owner."

As the queue progresses I enter a solitude of thoughts, listening to echoes of my father, mother, scoutmasters, teachers, past businessmen, and road partners. Their verdict is that dishonesty digs a hole where habit's the spade. When you get deep enough in, people discern you. Now, any option with the wallet is correct but individual honesty recognizes another in all reaches of life and I'm still a young man.

"Virtue is a slow path!" I explode. But no one in line seems to understand except Wiz and Clown. "My conclusion is to take $20 for postage and handling, and another $20 for our trouble and supper. I think recklessness should be punished, not rewarded. Mail the rest back... That's my decision!"

There's no peep except Wiz volunteers to call the owner at the number on the Sports Illustrated staff card. He returns from that call as I reach

> *"The moral issue is secondary," I respond. "What do I tell a bull down the line who searches and finds two IDs and all that cash... 'Son, here's a free Go-to-Jail ticket.' Hell, let's discuss it on the way to the post office."*

the front of the queue, saying, "I spoke to the man who is very anxious to get the wallet. The driver's license address is confirmed and he prefers priority mail. He offered no reward but many hearty thanks."

I drop the puke into the priority envelope, seal it and sigh relief.

Outside the Salt Lake post office, Wiz backs up against the sun-baked concrete and tugs his earlobe. He's been sidetracked for some time. "We've had a wonderful day," he opens. "A day of surprises. And now I want to reveal what I told my wife last night." We lean toward him at the hot wall. "Honey," I yelled on the cell. "I've reached an epiphany... I'll see you tonight!"

"But she's in San Francisco," Clown protests. "Days away," I add, but he talks on among deaf ears.

"Yesterday I had an epiphany," he continues solemnly. "First, there was a hot flashback while crossing the desert. My life before hoboing had been narrow and sheltered. Fifteen years ago, I rode my first freight after taking Doc's hobo course. I jumped a dozen trains since and saw so many new things in tasting the hobo life without grasping it. Each trip ended with an itch for more. Each unfolding scenario made me a better-qualified human. One angle I learned was that a person with ingenuity can work just three months out of the year and put money in the bank to travel. One tramp I met worked odd jobs until he squirreled $200, and then took $100 of it and rode the rails for six months, ending back in California to start the cycle over with the other $100. My thought is that the best executive takes a drastic pay cut to delegate authority to a few trusted colleagues and evolves his life on other fronts except for those three working months each year. The difference between the best tramp and executive is a few zeroes in their bank accounts.

"Then, yesterday, came the second part of my big change of heart. I love the adrenalin flush when we catch out and the relaxation of the ride that follows. But I don't like the heat and sleepless nights. I'm used to the job stress of a $40 million budget with 130 employees; freight hopping is supposed to cut that like a holiday. The itch to ride—I'm not sure why—quit yesterday after I scrambled for an hour glimpsing mileposts, flipping timetables and listening to the scanner while you guys rode stranded on the tanker. I was worried as hell. When you arrived safely back it zinged me: Hopping freights doesn't move me anymore. The sightseeing and subculture studies are a watershed behind yesterday's tanker bumper. So, we arrived last night in SLC and I went into the donut shop and first called the airport and then my wife. I've milked the hobo experience to a point of diminishing return, I notified her. I deeply conclude that I know Hobo Life in America. I don't need to ride again. Excuse me, I'm flying to San Francisco later today."

His radiant face is transformed. Our jaws drop like anvils. This is Wiz's longest speech, and the most sincere ever. "We'll miss you," sobs Clown with a big hug. "And your devices," I shake his hand. So Wiz turns on a dime commemorating a moment's insight is worth a life's exploration, and walks off. He has done the whole Pacific to Colorado run like Pronto and Big Apple, only in two segments.

He calls an airport limo from the post office for the 6 p.m. plane. Yet, I suspect, watching him step into the stretch limo, once a train tramp always a train tramp as long as the freights run. Each person has a unique set of values and reacts to them. For now, he waves at us through the back window taking away all the electronics.

Now we are two.

Part 13: Soot and Grit

Finding a safe bed is a nightly dilemma for the tramp on the road. At a poorly chosen spot, the router is a mugger, cop, or nosey citizen. Hobos evade them by sleeping in jungles, missions, 'carry the banner' walking all night, or in a RR yard. The sunset after Wiz flies to San Francisco, Clown and I enter the SLC Roper yard on the east city edge to search for a bed.

We discover an empty boxcar in a string on a track near the main. This empty is clean, older with a wood floor, and offers in one corner the inevitable thousand-mile-paper or cardboard from previous riders. We climb through the door confident of a night's repose and unroll the bedding onto thick cardboard. No passers-by can see two stretched-out people on the inside wall. Fresh air and moonlight enter the wide open door, and with the shared dream that we shall hear a freight pause on the main during the night and awaken to board for the Pacific.

Instead, daybreak floods the door as couplers clang a few tracks over in the building yard. Clown yawns, stretches, and purrs, "Railcars are the best beds in the world." She stuffs the crayon braids under the purple bandana and tops it with a white fisherman cap, then bounds out the door. "I'm going to reconnoiter... Radios on." She climbs our car's end bumper and munches across ballast on the boxcar blind side toward the building yard. I stow the packs except for a L'Amour western.

This old Roper Yard of the former Denver & Rio Grande RR is one of the prettiest and smallest of the big town yards. Two mainlines steadily shovel freights east and west. Crews change here on every through train. Freights also build on a bowl of twenty tracks just west of the mains. There is activity in the bowl this morn as hogs (yard engines) shove strings to build the hotshot the hobo sees in his mind's eye. Light towers peek over the many rows of cars but the old, tallest yardmaster citadel has been flattened. Years ago, I sneaked up to it behind an uprooted 7-ft. pine tree held in front of me and planted, closer and closer, until I reached the tower base to secure train info from a genial crew who thought the scene hilarious. As in the days of old, a stream bubbles through an Exec Hobos under dwarf willows, and passes beneath the Roper mainlines.

Three chapters of my novel later, Clown belly flops into the boxcar grinning ear-to-ear. "They're building our Man in the west yard. A shack advised me to watch for lead unit [#]465 to back onto a set of mixed cars in about an hour. We're good to go, Doc!"

We jump to the gravel and hike with the packs to the building yard. On the way, I insist she practice getting on and off a stationary flatcar on the mock 'fly,' a dicey operation. "In fact," I advise, "tramps take names like Fingers, Lefty, and Stump, then try to shake your hand or kick your butt to prove these monikers don't annoy them since their accidents."

Freights don't keep exact schedules like Amtrak or Greyhound. There may be a morning and evening freight built for each direction inside a big yard, but it varies depending on how the cars stack up on the holding tracks. Likewise, through trains on the high irons that change crews but neither cut nor add cars during their long hauls across the country can be hours early or late. This all amounts to the hobo's patience.

We wave down a young shack in orange coveralls to ask particulars and he trots over like the early morning rooster. "See those cameras? The bull is watching us talk. I can't give out information." We look skyward to the four-story light-cluster but pick out no camera.

"Rats," I inform the ill-tempered shack, "comfortable in great numbers in most railroad yards, may aid the bull one day. Did you know scientists are controlling rat movements by remote control up to a quarter-mile away with brain electrode implants? They also talk of tacking small video cameras to rat collars, originally conceived for ferreting live people out of the rubble. Don't you see these could pose a threat to future hobos who smell like cheese in the first place?"

"Tramps take names like Fingers, Lefty, and Stump, then try to shake your hand or kick your butt to prove these monikers don't annoy them since their accidents."

The shack stares with beady eyes and hisses, "Go ask the old guy at the west yard shed."

Deeper in the building yard we find the shed. Any sizeable yard in cold climes has a hut at either end for the workers—shacks and brakies—to warm, read, and chat down time. Sometimes they invite you in for fresh coffee before your train departs. In summertime, the workers hang outside. "Good morning," booms a voice on the far side of the shanty. (He has sensitive ears or was radioed by the other.) We circle to find an ash-stubble gent in overalls on a cushion chair in the sunshine. He points a dirty boney finger to the near rail, and advises, "The Cali Man heads up here in thirty minutes. Lie low until then." Then he pulls a pinstripe RR cap over his eyes, leans back, and waves us away.

The noises, odors, and circulation within a RR yard are clockwork to the old worker and hobo alike. Today, an engine set advances along a track pushing a string and shaking the ground to a twenty-yard radius. The cars slam into our building train. The engines back up and blast smoke high into the air. They whine and snort off to the building rails to fetch another string, and another, with recurring racket. Thirty minutes later, when our freight is complete—except the locos—the ballast crunches all alongside the headless string with workers' strides to check for hot journals and fizzing brake leaks. Now the engines, with lead $^{#}465$, tap on and the crew van arrives, then the engineer and conductor step out and right up onto the units. They check the cab instruments and sit with bronzed arms on open window frames to await the yardmaster order: "Cannonball!"

At that word, Clown and I are aboard. We cram at mid-train into the cubbyhole of a hopper car eating each other's elbows. The whistle toots an adrenalin push. The units gulp diesel, roar, and blow smoke. We hunker on pins-and-needles on the outside chance the insistent shack was correct that cameras spy the out-rolling stock. Sixty sets of couplers strain from the front car to ours... until the big tug. The freight clears Roper and SLC.

The track leaves the city and rounds the Great Salt Lake south shore, the largest saline lake in the Americas. The 2,500 square-mile water body has two arms, a north and south, created by the railroad causeway (that the outbound execs traversed ten days ago into Ogden). Because there is little water mix, this creates two separate ecosystems. The south is a half-foot higher, slighter fresher and provides more wildlife in the arid region. For miles on both sides of our rail, the shallows support a hundred bird species standing, fishing, and sunning. The train pierces vast white fields of seagulls like Moses parting the sea with thousands winging away before our eyes.

The lake recedes and time rolls on and on, until the noon zenith over a great open sand, and the train trudges through. The hopper is low on the springs—with America's breadbasket grain bound for the Pacific—and it's possible sitting up front on the quaking porch to read (but not write) or to converse (via a cupped hand). We perch at mid-train of the three-quarter-mile string of ominously mixed cars and, instinctively, I caution Clown inside this Great Basin lest we get cut out in some isolated siding. This is called getting 'ditched' and may lead to unspoken misery.

The train sides and sets off frequently. This is a 'bird-dog' freight whose dirty job is to pick up and deliver loaded cars, and to fetch and return unloaded ones. It stops at every puny town, grain elevator, industrial park, and sides for every other train on the rail, and takes four times as long to reach the next division point. "But it's progress," Clown sings.

When the freight deliberates at a desert silo with illusive reason, I instruct Clown to look up and down her side of the freight for another car to board. It's better to ride near the units or the FRED since both ends must continue when the train starts again. "I see nothing fore or aft," she reports. I spot on my side a few cars ahead on a curve an unsavory, beaten gondola, but before we can attempt it the train resumes.

While on the roll, Clown hails, "I have to poop," prompting the oldest hobo impasse. "Look, just hang it over the side and remember which way the wind blows," I warn. "I'll blow up before I try that!" she rebuts. I won't discuss it and point to the cubby portal—a two-foot opening—into a steel pup tent. She crawls inside the great bulwark and squeals with delight at sighting the six-inch drain hole in the floor above the racing ties. "You just got lucky," I shout and turn away from the lady's toilet. Two minutes later she emerges grinning like the first person to defecate in high cotton. "That's a fine potty!" she calls.

The life-quickening horn blares at desert crossings where unfailingly at each the driver of the lead auto blocked by the RR gate reaches and waves at us. "Look at us, riding the rails across the greatest nation on earth!" she fires back joyfully. Small towns generally detest the hourly blasts. However, Florida in a recent test banned train horns after dark and crossing accidents instantly doubled, so the cross-town toots were revived. Train sounds can be reckoned like animal grunts. The horn signal uses two characters like Morse code: short and long. Two longs says the train releases brakes and proceeds from a standstill; three shorts is back up; long-long-short-long signals the approach to a public crossing; and a succession of shorts broadcasts an emergency on the rail.

Night falls over us sliding the Great Basin rail with the infrequent blink and clang of tiny town intersections. Each appears as an advancing soft light in the black that enlarges over miles to swallow the train for a fleeting moment, and then the freight erupts out the other side. The Doppler of the crossing fades, too, and—until the next town—peace reigns on the jiggling steel platform.

Later, with earplugs in a deaf sleep, I sense the wheels decelerate... and stop. I tap sleeping Clown on the shoulder and warn, "Be alert!" We peep around the car sides for clues. The train rests in a small desert yard only four tracks wide with no lights in view. Extraordinarily, the conductor strides back from the units with a lantern to uncouple the car right at our feet. He jumps on hearing Clown, "What's happening?" He gapes up at us specters but convalesces to retort, "Be quick! This and the next dozen cars are being cut. The nearest ride is the battered gondola ten cars forward. Be careful of leftover scrap on the floor." He stalks off clutching the 'manifest' or list of cars before there's a chance to ask if any more will set off.

We trot to the gondola to discover inordinately high walls—ten feet— with a ladder at one outside corner. She scales eight rungs to pose on top for me to pass up our gear, then drops it like tossing stones into a deep well. Hearing the far-off thud but unable to see the floor, she returns to the roadbed to report. I scale to replace her on the six-inch gondola ledge even as the string jolts to life when the units rejoin far ahead. I eagle-claw the gondola lip and lower myself inch-by-inch until the boots dangle, let go, and drop a foot to the floor. She follows over the top, standing like a totem-pole on my shoulders, until I curtsy like a dutiful elephant and let her down. Instantly the train shakes into action.

The freight accelerates and in five minutes reaches a cruising speed of 50 mph. The Great Basin, encompassing western Utah and all of Nevada, is called a cool desert due to the northern latitude and the night air whistling cold above the gondola and blowing off our hats where we stand. We retrieve them as the high-side box waddles the rail and rattles us silly with metallic echoes. I stick a penlight in my mouth to clear a few jangling scrap metals to the back corner where the wind pummels the walls making little tornados, and to look around with increasing horror.

We're in a rolling cigar box as if a fire raged across the floor and left soot everywhere. Already our packs and hands are dusted charcoal. Her face gets blacker every time I look at her. She returns my look and grimaces, "Riding freights is still fun," and then drops bushed to the floor. She wraps up in a blanket like a burrito and bounces like dirty laundry.

I stand braced against the roll and rock, shivering in mid-car as the wind whips the cowboy hat off and catches my neck by the strap this time. I slap thighs and do jumping-jacks, and walk circles inside the 15-yard box to bring up the circulation. I warm to crawl inside the bag near my sleeping partner ten feet from the front wall, and lay on my back rhythmically popping an inch off the floor. Satisfied that we won't break our necks in an emergency stop, I finally sleep. We jiggle over the miles throughout the night and gradually to the middle of the car leaving worm tracks across the soot.

First light shows two tramps vibrated together in the center of a rolling box across Nevada. I look at her black face and the white eyes pop open with red gums and teeth. "I like black men," she says snuggling forward. It strikes us almost at once—the freight is stationary!

Our snooze must have deepened when the train decelerated, but absolutely nothing sleeps through the sharp WHOOSH of locos 'dynamiting' the brakes that carries for miles through the countryside. "Jump! Our car is cut!" I scream... forgetting. We're trapped inside high walls. We listen helplessly to the engines detach and trail west never to be heard again. She whispers, "It's a new day, but where are we?"

We peek through a bullet hole in the gondola side The aperture shows a generic siding on a narrow asphalt strip that leads both ways into isolation. The Canadian peeps and mutters, "This is what Americans call 'Nowhere USA.'"

We sit on the packs with chins held forlornly in hands looking about. Our world is a black floor, four ten-foot walls and a bright blue sky. "It's a metaphor of life," she avers. "Where are we? How do we get out? Where are we going into that blue?" I stare at the scorched floor, a diary of our night perambulations, and then up at the light.

"Did you ever see the Twilight Zone episode "In Search of an Exit?" I ask. "Yes!" she whoops rising. "A hobo, clown, and three other characters, a collection of question marks, are stuck together in a dark pit with sides just above their reach. There's no reason or logic, just a prolonged nightmare of fear and the unexplainable. They stay there for what seems forever philosophizing until one day the clown looks up and for the first time notices the blue sky. She points it out and..." "...the Hobo boosts the Clown out of the box!" I finish for her.

I bend like a camel at the corner and she stands on my shoulders. Rising, she touches the gondola lip and chins herself to the ledge. I toss up a rope coil from the packs, she ropes them to the top, and drops them over the wall. She fastens the end to the outside ladder and I skinny the rope. We perch on the wall edge surveying the countryside and she shouts, "I am not afraid!"

We leap down. The train has disappeared on a steel ribbon through a flat land. Two silos stick up like sore thumbs next to a hedge paralleling the track. The worst hobo scenario is to be sided in the middle of nowhere. Our families wouldn't recognize us by sight or smell. "I wish I had a mirror," she titters nervously. You scratch your head and gauge the possibilities.

We could walk the rail to the empty west or east, burn a silo as a signal that no one will see, or look no *Two silos stick up like sore thumbs next to a hedge paralleling the track. The worst hobo scenario is to be sided in the middle of nowhere.* farther than the track hedge now at sunrise. So we lay out one blanket behind the thicket and nap with our boots on and laced. In a few hours, we awaken to a deafening mechanical storm. "It's a pig train!" she jigs on the blanket.

"Get down," I caution gently. "If it stops, some RR crews don't like to see dirty tramps board pigs because of their valuable cargos." We stuff the blanket and duck behind the hedgerow as the train decelerates and halts on the main. A 'piggyback' or pig, is the semi-truck van mounted on a flatcar. Before us stands a mile-long unit train of pigs and containers. The engines break with twenty cars from the rest of the train and push them into the diminutive yard siding. "We want this train," I drool, "And there's five minutes to board before the units rejoin."

The best ride for us this morning, given the latest setbacks, is very near FRED on the last couple. The anthropomorphized FRED is one the unasked change by hobos to modern railroading. He is the F***ing Rear End Device, a little black box affixed like a taillight to the last car couple that replaces the caboose. FRED sends radio signals to the units to tell the engineer everything's hooked and running smoothly. Hobos may no longer beg rides in lousy weather from the conductor in a caboose. Yet by keeping close to FRED the rider ensures he will not be cut out because the device is required for transport.

While the units are away, we walk toward the end of the pig line and climb onto one and squirm between the trailer wheels as shields. The engines soon affix and the train sits long and lovely and nosed at the RR switch waiting for green. The light switches and whistle blows. "It's like a toy train set!" she explodes. Some engineers are expert and know, even at a distance, how couplers tenderly tighten during a smooth pullout. Other engineers, like this, are not.

Green tramps learn the hard way when the freight starts with jerks to brace and watch the soft head. Our car lurches as I fawn over Clown's safety, and I take a hit in the temple by a steel wedge. Dazed for thirty seconds, I slump... then things clear up. "No knowledge is better than one's own frame of mind," I tell her. "It won't happen again."

The freight barrels out from the little yard. "Tie everything down the wind could take!" I bellow under the pig. It has four-foot tires that shelter us as pillars on both sides, plus the roof. In next to no time we punch a stiff headwind at 60 mph across the desert. "This is the best ride going!" she burbles with a mouthful of wind.

The many benefits of riding under a pig van include the roof shade, a nearly 360-degree view of the terrain, and speed. Piggybacks are being replaced in this century by containers and double-stacks (two-story containers) on flatcars that are harder to ride but just as fast. All, including ours today, are 'hotshots' with priority cargo that will side for no one except Amtrak clear to the next division town: Reno, Nevada.

The mountains and playas—basin bottoms—sweep the rail and train up and down across the Great Basin. The desert is striped by 6000-ft. north-south dividing ranges as the freight roller coasters them toward Reno at the foot of the great Sierra. The vegetation in the Great Basin, in contrast to the country's three other deserts, grows low and homogeneous for miles on both sides of the track before shifting to new species with the elevation and moisture. We see, for example, one region of dominant Sagebrush at one siding followed by one of Greasewood at the higher next. There are few cacti anywhere, and the wide geography over time sets a lazy rhythm.

The openness causes a quiet ride and the better-sprung, loaded flatcar takes a cradle's rhythm and mother's hum along the rail. This hobo 'Mozart effect' is easily felt if you accept the science precept that certain music enriches brain development in children. For growing hobos, the lullaby deposits at rail's end a smarter man and woman.

Later the Reno casino skyline cuts the desert harmony. I turn and speak softly to Clown about detraining on the fly.

A rider without a pack can step from the low rung of a 15 mph ladder safely to the grit. The sensation is striding off an escalator. The deception is that the ground seems to move toward the feet, however the actual force vector is forward. So the proper thought is "I'll stride with the thrust" on touching. Johnny Cash in *Man in Black* describes his Arkansas home along the tracks where the freights daily slowed to 20 mph and men, his father included, returning from work leaped from boxcars down the ditch and rolled into the front yard.

There are four swift considerations in getting off today's moving train: The Reno-Sparks Yard is bull-happy, we're too grimy to step into public, I just spotted a stream north of the main, and she has not yet known the elation of stepping from a moving freight. Hence, we study the wheels, survey the oncoming roadbed, and toss the gear overboard with a clatter on the grit.

She bobs to the ladder, descends and toes the bottom rung. "The first time is risky business," I yell over the top. She smiles sweetly, "I was a hockey player and gold trader..." and steps off.

Part 14: Reno is Hot

Clown alights like a ballerina on the Reno gravel. The white hat blows off and the ornamental locks fall. I follow her off the 8 mph ladder but my inertia, like stepping off a giant escalator, posts me into her. She steadies my head, shouting, "You're my action hero!"

We hike the warm ballast toward the Sparks Yard on the brown fringe of Reno, Nevada. The morning sunshine brings out a waft of creosote and pitch from the tie pores. Our faces and hands are black as spades from last night's ride. Birds twitter good-naturedly at two outlanders walking the main cutting agriculture fields to a culvert that offers a gift sparkling stream.

We smell like something from a February hole, and wash upwind jockeying for position and splashing cold water on each other to stop the heat. We wade out into the miracle pool and raise the packs to continue along the line a mile to a Denny's grease ranch (restaurant). Pancakes go down like silver dollars into a poor man's pocket. We board a local bus for a ten minute ride into Reno, step down and rustle up a motel.

Reno is a hobo's and a gambler's oasis on the final stop before the RR track and highway climb out of the Great Basin into the Sierra. The high-stakes skyline rises sharply around us. Tramps typically alight in such a division town with smirks knowing in the coming hours they'll get clean and fed at a mission, and probably drunk at a skid row bar. Clown, thinking unconventionally, charges scrubbed out of the motel bathroom and shouts into the mirror, "Let's go to a comedy club!"

She dons a Flintstone dress splashed with Fred and Wilma, the Rubbles, the kids and Dino and "Yabba-dabba-do." I wear freshly laundered bib-overalls and a flannel. She takes my tan arm around the block to the Reno Comedy Club. "Isn't it grand!" she bubbles at the front door. "Let's enter my turf," and she sweeps us past the doorman with a joke.

The ensuing show features rising stand-up comics, but Clown is brighter and funnier.

We return to the motel and fall into deep twin beds five feet apart to discuss humor. "I don't enjoy humor, but you're the funniest person I've ever met," I confess. "Stand-up comedy makes you come to grips with yourself in front of others," she replies. "Intellectual humor is your strong suit. It cultivates the mind by making thinking fun," I return. "What should I do, coach?" she asks. "Your humor springs from personal experiences, so the more assorted your future the funnier you become," I respond warmly. "If a person next to me has no vices or weaknesses then I can't make him laugh," she renders, and we both chuckle.

Reno never sleeps, but finally we do, and our relationship is cautious… and platonic throughout the trip.

In the morning, we check out and amble a few blocks to the gambling district to enter Harrah's Casino for breakfast. Inside, ranks of hundreds of people shake hands repeatedly with one-armed slot machines amid a horrid clamor. "This reminds me of a church," she mutters. "How you spend today is how you spend the rest of your life," I chime. "Let's get out of here!" we ring. We take a fashionably late breakfast at Harrah's and board a local bus to the Sparks rail yard.

Sparks was an afterthought of the railroads at the turn of century when a big switchyard was needed to take apart and build trains. Other than the endless banging of cars in the switching yard, and the clang, hiss, and whistle of through trains in and out of the station day and night, everything was quiet in Sparks for fifty years as the small town grew alongside the bowl of tracks. In the 1950s Sparks changed. Subdivisions were planted on pastureland and acre upon acre of tile roofs blossomed over the desert. In the 1970s, the city began to grow in an unexpected direction when the residual family farms sold out to light industry and warehousing connected by an asphalt grid of new streets. In the 21st century Sparks is changing again. We step from the bus with our pack and suitcase and promenade past well-heeled citizens along manicured avenues to the rail yard.

Clown and I sit on a mowed grass strip between the RR mainline and city skyscrapers to discuss today's strategy. We design to enter the medium-sized yard to query workers about building freights, all the while keeping an eye on the main for a through train and for the bull.

On entering the yard, abruptly giant pinchers appear skyward. Whirrr... Boom! A giant crane hoists a 50-ft. container, swings, and drops it onto a flatcar twenty yards in front of us. We watch, box after box, a unit container train being built. But we tarry too long as a bull in a Bronco screeches up; probably the crane operator snitched us out by radio. There is no place to run or hide.

The RR bull is the yard watchdog. He's also the historic nemesis of the hobo, yet as long as the trains have and will run people will jump them despite him. My strategy against the cinder dick is to dodge him with a hundred tricks he's seen a hundred times. That makes it an even contest. A savvy dick with free time on his hands and high-tech equipment—infra-red cameras, ground sensors—plus patrols, fences, and ratting yard workers—catches an experienced 'bo half the time and misses the rest. That's given the bull's dream scenario. Nowadays, however, the little western yards like Sparks are understaffed, unfenced, under-equipped, and the workers rather than turn in the riders usually abet them.

Of the hunting styles, standard is forage-chase-capture. The bull cruises the yard in a white truck with a ubiquitous CB antenna. With the report of an invader off he goes. He also may 'roll' or scrutinize each car for trespassers on special trains like mail, containers, and piggybacks as they enter or exit his yard. He is the yard dog. Yet if he spies an outbound 'bo in an empty boxcar he prefers to look the other way rather than give chase, wishing only the tramp to get along without getting hurt or stealing.

Freight hopping is illegal but downplayed as jaywalking in most RR yards. The dance begins the second the 'bo is nabbed: ID, scratches on a pad, "Don't return on my duty or it's to jail," and "thank you, sir." I am ever genial to special agents whom I consider a cut above local police and county sheriffs. If I can't evade one, I walk straight to him with hands displaying no weapons and blow polysyllables in his face to prove a milieu sans inebriation. I stand upright and vow not to disturb RR property before catching a ride right out of town. We cordially step apart.

There's fun, and there are hurdles to it, so I'm philosophically cheerful when caught.

Yet I tense with Clown at my side; some bulls don't respond to intellectual humor. This Reno special agent is stocky with a no-nonsense crew-cut and cop mustache. Military bearing strengthens his gaze, lower back, and opening argument. "You're trespassing on railroad property." He doesn't blink. "I won't lie," I reply, "my partner and I are trying to leave town without trouble. I work in California." He fires at her, "Where are you from? " "I'm a Toronto University student doing a dissertation on the American hobo phenomenon," she offers daintily.

The bull grunts and extends a meaty palm for our IDs. He jots data from my driver's license into a spiral pad and hands it back. He raises eyebrows at her Canadian passport. "It's the first time in twenty years on the job that I've seen a passport," he mumbles fumbling with it.

"Canadian, huh?" ... "Eh?" ... "It doesn't tell how tall you are." ... "160 centimeters." ... "In English?" ... "I only know metric."

He jots nothing but returns her document with a thread smile. I leap on it.

"If your mother-in-law were to try to catch a freight in this yard, where would she wait so the bull couldn't catch her?" I ask. He snorts laughter despite himself and utters, "I'd tell her to go to the Red Rock Bridge," pointing west along the main. "Wait there with the rest of the godd***ed tramps outside my jurisdiction." He walks off whistling in the morning sunshine.

"If your mother-in-law were to try to catch a freight in this yard, where would she wait so the bull couldn't catch her?" I ask.

The bull proves a rare asset today and we skirt his yard along a mile sidewalk to the Red Rock Bridge.

It is an iron freight overpass with city traffic passing beneath. A sloped dirt waiting area, not quite a jungle next to the mainline, provides the usual carpet of fast-food wrappers and empty bottles. We prop the pack and suitcase against a nearby hurricane fence and swiftly duck under a patchy tree out of the sun.

Clown kicks off her platform Converses, smoothes on cherry ChapStick, and picks at a chin pimple. "All this travel has got me on track to freedom," she starts. "The Erisians sit on their soft chairs and talk about it. Your constitution quotes it often. Every one of us has a small or great opportunity if we'll seize and work hard. God bless America! I'm anti-American, but pro-American ideals. Don't be confused, Doc. The American experiment is the greatest locomotive of change in world history. And hobos are one of or the last free groups in America."

"Don't," I argue, "force liberty on people. There are advantages to being captive to a job or institution. Thoreau thought it rare to meet a person who can be free. 'World-ridden' he called others without having the opportunity to come out of the woods himself to the good company of the rails. Hobos may be going to hell, but at least they're moving right along."

A trim, middle-aged man in a baseball cap with 'War Vet' emblazed in gold across the bill snails along the hurricane fence. He angles toward us presupposing a 'starter' for coins to pool to buy booze. Beggardom is parcel to division points and skid rows, and to freedom. This is a decrepit area where drifters and locals 'throw their feet' or beg. It starts and pushes out from a town's cream business center, decaying the districts like a launch of maggots, expanding to the finger fringes until the bums get tired of bumming each other. "Spare a dollar?" repeats the man.

When a location gets overrun, it's circulated up-and-down the roads and rails that the spot's 'bummed out' and a balancing force exerts as train jumpers avoid it. Beggerdom then shifts to the next division point. "You look like executives in overalls," expresses the man with disquieting perception. "You read folks like a book," I reply without handing him change. He smiles. "I've been a good judge of character since flunking out of the world."

A full-time beggar with the right hat, feigned handicap, sharp opener, and solid 'ghost' story may rake in a hundred dollars a day. That's what I make as a sub-teacher. Exact location is important, too, and where medieval European beggars formed guilds, their modern American counterparts jealously guard a territory or pool their takes with partners.

"Why are you and the Missus awaiting a freight?" he pursues. "We're out to see America and meet its characters," Clown responds, adding, "how about you?" The man stands stock still as a wave as big as life passes over him. "It may come as a surprise to you," he intones, "but a long time ago I was Perfect Timmy."

The tramp got our focus with that in the buzzing flies. "Correction," he purses his lips. "There was a single flaw at eight that I never figured out. So here I am."

"What happened between the flaw and here," Clown pleads.

"I was born and raised over the hump (the Sierra) in Hollywood. Los Angeles was a wonderful spot to grow up in the 50s. When the protagonist in the Lassie TV series grew balls they had to find a replacement boy. In response to an ad, my mom took me at age eight to the studio for an interview. They said, "You are the Perfect Timmy,' and told me to return in a week for the final cut. Mom got drunk the night before and I missed the appointment. Years passed, and I carried that thought to Viet Nam."

Veterans, as after each war's end back to the American Civil, find continued adventure on the rails. They are unafraid, comfortable with travel, could forage, navigate and camp outdoors. Returning Viet vets in the 1970s were familiar sights on the rails but in this new century the surviving proportion is more easily recognized by their age, infirmities, and willingness to face hostility at the drop of a hat. The survivors are also lonely after three decades of freighting, and love a sympathetic ear.

"You know, they hypnotized us troops for better fighting... and it worked. I was a Hypno-Soldier, one of the best. Hypnotists put us under in mass, gave auto-suggestions, and our duty to kill the enemy was clear. After the war, we landed in the States scarred under the under-pressed uniforms, and many Americans shamed us."

"They couldn't shame me!" He springs to his feet like a gymnast after a perfect 10. No jungle soldier walks erect but with a wary roll that at the same time is relaxed, and the movement becomes automatic. Now he reenacts being circled by Charlie, shooting, kicking, and fighting his way to freedom through the jungle. After, he sits and drawls, "It's memories with a spiked postscript. Agent Orange is eatin' up my skin alive. So I ride the trains, stop for fun, ride the trains... It's the best life I know." He fingers a graying stubble, remembers his ulcerating hands and hides them.

"I returned to the States and jumped my first train out of Texas. Made it a lifestyle for a few years... until a close call catching one on the fly in a rainstorm. I picked myself off the ground, smacked my forehead and said, 'Timmy, what the hell, it's time to rejoin society,' and I began working a string of jobs." He scratches the backs of his hands. "Aye, that's the rub. Orange is better than work for a few years, but then the stipend ain't worth the progressive ulcers." He stuffs them into his pockets.

"Instead of me, Tommy Retig got the part as Lassie's faithful companion. I often sit under this tree and ponder what would have happened if Perfect Timmy had become famous instead of growing up to kill gooks I didn't even know in Viet Nam. What do you think? Would I be talking to you with a bellyful of heroin staring at Lady Medusa who asks all the right questions?"

Clown asks for his knife, I tense, but he hands over without hesitation his 6–in. Buck. She kneels at the tree trunk to engrave as he continues.

"I ain't the same man any more," grieves Perfect Tim. "You want to know what's wrong with the world? It's the willingness of the good to serve the bad. Goddamn it, bloody people!" he shakes a fist at the tree crown. "Don't let anyone take advantage of you!"

He blinks slowly. "Today I'm riding heroin too, excuse me." He proffers a tainted cookie from a brown bag that we refuse.

"Now you may be wondering what I'm doing in Reno eating magic cookies in this jungle. This is a good welfare town and even better for panhandling the gambling tourists." He tips his cap, saying, "Don't worry about me. I touched the gamblers for $90 this morning and spent the afternoon high. An' now I'm feeling drowsy." He turns his head heavily to Clown, "That smile could stop a traaain..." and nods off.

In a few minutes Clown finishes, folds the blade, and slides it handle first into the dormant hobo's pocket. Great care has been taken in carving each letter on the trunk: CARPE DIEM. (Seize the Day!)

Carpe Diem is the buried American theme since the Founding Fathers. Life is short. Enjoy it. Seize the day!

Sleeping Timmy misses four diesels growling like dragons at the gate on the mainline. The power rams a string of cars down the rail from us. Clown vaults up and lets the vibrant locks fly. She jogs in platform sneakers out the tree to the yellow lead unit, shouts questions high up to the driver, and sprints back screaming through cupped hands, "All aboard!"

We walk to the lead unit where the grandfatherly engineer waves. "This is a double-stack train, folks. No rides, so hop on the trailing unit. We climb the steps of the second locomotive, walk in the cab and shut the door, the engineer toots, and the regal freight tugs west from the Reno casinos, Perfect Timmy, and our last impression.

Part 15: The Last Westbound

A freight departs with graceful abruptness, and all thoughts are forward.

The Union Pacific engine paint scheme is the oldest in use on the rails. The lower portion of the locomotive is Armour yellow, a thin red band separates it from the Harbor Mist gray upper and roof, and the underside fuel tanks are also gray, making the UP units handsome and sleek along the rail.

Clown has weaseled us aboard the second unit by telling the engineer that her Christian husband and she are trying to get to the Pacific to meet friends who have a painting job for us. It's a rare treat to enter the locomotive with red lettering that dwarfs us, up short stairs to a perimeter platform, then up two more to the cab door, and inside. The vibrating chamber is the size of a small den with two cushy chairs, a front panel of gauges and dials giving off a yellow-white glow, the whistle and throttle. Behind the chairs, illuminated by the soft light of the instruments, sits an electric heater, a refrigerator stocked with bottled water, and a step down to a bathroom.

Now the engine revs and horn blasts.

The track leaves Sparks, slices metro Reno, and starts the desert crossing toward California, an hour away. Then the desert vanishes behind us and the rail tilts into the Sierra Nevada. The train crawls its eastern flank where we shut the sliding windows against the squeals and cold air. The cab is above it all, a small jiggling room with captain's chairs at either side window. We sit back, and peer past the lead loco at the series of oncoming tunnels. The freight noses into short ones and out the other end before the last car enters, but other bores are five minutes—a mile long—as the diesel smoke clouds outside the cab without danger to us inside the sealed units.

The cab is above it all, a small jiggling room with captains' chairs at either side window. We sit back, and peer past the lead loco at the series of oncoming tunnels.

We watch the afternoon sun sink, night fall, and stars spread over the Sierra like a blanket. She flicks on the cab heater and light, and alternately reads *Atlas Shrugged* and the King James Bible, scrawling margin notes for skits in the second. Clown's Bible has

114

more scribbles than my brother Tom's, an Episcopalian minister, only hers are for parodies. Last year, United States Immigration discovered these notes and since has detained her entries. I offer to her tonight that reality beats fiction. "Toss the books out the window and sketch what happens to you."

The lady and the tramp ride that westbound by the heater all through the night. The train adds 'pusher' engines at the steepest ascent. She has Doc Bo in one hand and the Bible in the other when a polite knock at the cab door arouses us. Our engineer pops in from the lead unit, spots the Bible and declares, "Bless you, young Christians, on your life's journey. I just want to let you know that we're adding helpers here and not to get off. It's a downhill run to the Pacific." He looks squarely at Clown. "Glad to see you're holding the Good Book, Ma'am," winks and shuts the door.

The other book she now reads is the "bible" of Objectivism, Ayn Rand's *Atlas Shrugged*. In it, the female protagonist manages a struggling transcontinental railroad tangled in bureaucratic restrictions. What would happen if the world's movers, the CEOs and executives,[3] went on strike? Her encounter with a hobo on the same rail the executives now ride is memorable, as is the later move to a utopia like Sand Valley whose members regard self-determination rather than collective responsibility as the higher ideal. The thousand-page novel provides many readers with a philosophy that rocks their boots. "Like it?" I ask. She nods without glancing up. I grab the thick text and page to the end where Dagny Taggart meets the Hobo:

"When did you eat last?" she asked.

"Yesterday," he said, and added, "I think..."

"Where are you going?"

"I don't know." Then, almost as if he sensed that this could sound too much like an appeal for pity, he added, "I guess I just intended to keep moving 'til I saw some place that looked like there might be a chance to find work there."

This was his attempt to assume the responsibility of a purpose, rather than to throw the burden of his aimlessness upon her mercy—

---

[3] Obviously, these CEOs and executives are of the Ayn Rand 'productive class' variety.

an attempt at the same order as his shirt collar... "Only I think it's a sin to sit down and let your life go, without making a try for it." ...The tramp's last sentence was one of the most profound moral statements she had ever heard, but the man did not know it; he had said it in his impassive, extinguished way, simply, dryly as a matter of fact.

"Don't you know that's what it's all about?" I ask Clown. She takes the book and continues afresh from that page.

After the passage, we shut out the light and roll again through the cold, rich night, slowly shaken asleep on the warm floor. So profound is the slumber that we are not awakened until the freight stops on the Roseville Bridge at sunrise. The kind engineer waits us to put ashore out of the bull's harm.

"These are hobo thrones," I proclaim from one of the tall engineer's seats. "How do you feel?" "Like a queen!" she decrees from the other. "You're my *King!*" and she bends across and kisses me.

Our dream ride ends on the whistle at the bridge, and we bound down to complete the circle.

Part 16: Carpe Diem!

Art "Wiz" Tyde returned to his loving wife after the rail trip, they divorced, and he left Linux-Care to start Sputnik Communications. He bought a condo in the Philippines. Omid "Big Apple" Malekan, in the old American tradition of leaving the girl to hit the rail, returned a bachelor to New York but failed to shake the cigarette habit. He works at a startup fund and trades client money as well. Lise 'Clown' Bradley won All-Canada comedian honors using material from the hobo trip, and quickly took off on a career as a globe-jetting gold broker.

Byron 'Pronto' Mulver awakened me on his San Francisco couch following the Executive Hobo Trip. It was the morning of September 11, 2001, that I was to fly to New York City. "You can go back to sleep," Pronto alarmed. "The office just called me... Terrorists bombed the World Trade Center and your flight's been cancelled. I'll be busy for a while."

September 11 shook the nation as well as hobodom clear to the Roseville, Ca., bridge. Homeland Security police rousted a bridge troll there who told the press, "It's all over! The whole thing. The police want everybody out, and you can blame 9/11 for it." Railroad security clamped down nationwide, bulls proliferated, railroad town newspapers denounced open boxcars as conveyance for terrorists, and tramp numbers plus the good hobo name plummeted to the lowest in decades signaling, some claimed, the end of a hobo epoch. The executives slid in under the wire.

In balance, I tell everyone that as long as trains run executives shall ride. Four years after this grandest hobo trip in history and 9/11, in 2005, two more dynamic executive trips would dawn: One through the Canadian Rockies and another across Mexico's Copper Canyon.

This original story was contracted to a cannonball editor for a glossy national magazine but, as you see, 9/11 derailed that. So read this account in the hobo spirit and, if you get to Sparks as I recently did, check the growing message, America: CARPE DIEM!

We parked in a hospital lot like any other patients and crossed the Pepper Street Bridge over Interstate 10 to scramble down an Aloe Vera carpet into the RR yard at sunset. This is the southern California Eucalyptus fringed hub where in these rough times a mile-long string of some 100 locomotives coupled nose-to-tail gather dust beneath the bloody red sun... now gone.

Two other almost mile-long freights with four and five locomotives huffed near the Pepper Bridge and we slithered between them away from the bulls with infrared camera eyes into a diesel haze trying to fathom which would pull out first. "Whichever it is," I said, "we'll be carried over the San Bernadino hump (mountains), past the Coachella naked people (five hundred ten-story windmills), within twenty miles of my Sand Valley home under the sand, and on to the tramp capital of Yuma, Arizona, in time for morning chow at the mission."

We climbed the metal ladder of a cement hopper car to a 8-ft. x12-ft. steel 'front porch' with a 3-ft. portal to a hobo 'hotel room' within the bulwark and hugged the steel floor ready to spring if the adjacent train highballed first. Gecko marked our spot with a GPS that would become his close companion on the trip as I flashed a disposable camera. An electrical click up and down the train signaled the brake check prior to departure on the line next to next us, so we rose to change rides even as our own freight clamped and strained in a metallic beat from engine to tail, and our platform on America jolted east. Hunkered on packs with a mounting breeze in our hair and not a care in the world the train advanced from one to five mph to... The yard bull accelerated a white Bronco in pursuit nearly alongside our car until the dirt road hit the bridge where he peeled off, and we jiggled the iron road east.

Gecko's analytical jaw dropped in appreciation of his first hobo ride and I peeked around our curved side cement car at the five locos and felt my own whiskers hit lapels at viewing a long intermodal freight perpendicularly blocking our path at Colton Crossing a hundred yards ahead. The crossing is one of the busiest junctions in the United States where the east-west Union Pacific intersects the north-south BNSF rails that also carry Metrolink and Amtrak trains. And if it's a potential headache tonight, it was a bloody scene in the 1882 Frog Wars between the two lines. At the last second our freight swung north, I whistled and admitted, "We just made a rare turn into unknown territory." He punched the GPS, and we settled into the sleeping bags on cardboard on the steel under a star spangled sky. An hour later Gecko whispered to himself, "Average velocity 49 mph north-northeast." I propped on a calloused elbow and confirmed by the bounce and Polaris that we were speeding over 40 mph nearly due north.

We'd packed light for the trip, just the sleepers, quart of water each, granola bars, and reading books stuffed into day packs, with dark clothes on our backs. My new road partner peered over the one-ft. platform lip at house-size boulders rolling past as I slid asleep and the train snaked through mountains striking sharp notes on curves with sparks under a full April moon. The freight chugged into the wee hours beneath a ghostly bridge and crawled under one after another yellow yard lamps popping with moths. Slowly the five locomotives and two human cargo entered a half-mile wide bowl of rails at least four miles long. "No idea where we are," I offered, "but strike the ballast before the yonder yardmaster tower...." The sentence was punctuated by the brake, stop, and release of all cars as the locos ran off. "Ditched in a mysterious yard," I muttered. We scrambled up a dusty bank and broke out a Eucalyptus hedge to scan all horizons for a hint of location but saw only a quiet, darkened desert stretching off to a tiny green stamp that may be an Interstate sign. "It matters less where we are than how to return," Gecko rasped. "Freight hopping is computer programming with grit," I replied shivering in his frosty breath, and adding, "What should we do?" He proposed to drop into the yard to try to catch back to Colton. Down we slid, stepped over a dozen rails capturing starlight, and climbed the rungs of a trundling car string that stopped and reversed. We hopped doggedly to the ballast and delved deeper into the yard.

In the next hour we took stationary or moving posts on a dozen cars as other metal strings entwined about us, and twenty times we bobbed around cars to avoid yard workers' eyes and a circling security truck with bubblegum roof lights. We boarded a slow rolling coal train and squatted atop anthracite like moonstruck cats until the train gathered speed and coal dust blew up and we jumped off the black cloud. So we shrugged and climbed out the yard bowl and slalomed the chaparral toward the far off postage stamp. An hour later Gecko brightly used the GPS to determine our latitude and longitude, and dialed a Florida kin to paste the coordinates onto GoogleMaps and tell us where we are. "Then," assured my road partner, "I'll call Tomorrow, my wife, to pick us up!" However, Florida didn't answer and Tomorrow never arrives.

Approaching the freeway in another hour, five mongrels leaped out an abandoned car and barked our butts to the freeway sign that read 'Interstate 15.' False dawn lit a long arc along the freeway to lead us full circle back to the RR yard far end where we hiked up to yet another sign that broke the suspense, 'Barstow, California.' A nearby all-night diner was assaulted for eggs, bacon, and a plan to get home. The options were to freight that we nixed, Amtrak just left, Greyhound didn't go 'til noon, hitchhike, call the wife, or… I dropped my fork and slapped my head, "Let's rent a car." "Avis is around the corner," chimed our waiter, and in five minutes we had reserved a car with no drop fee from Barstow to Colton for $40, about the same price as one Greyhound ticket.

On the short walk to Avis it was apparent that the hobo bug had drawn blood in Gecko. "I like the ongoing puzzles with the need to remain calm during crises," he gushed. Now it was back to a California condo hidden in roses and a loving wife and high-salary job, with a pain that will forever stab the heart every time a train whistle blows. He had darted from the crowd like other executive hobos who stumble on *bokeelytours.com* and found I was not too mad in the short run. Four hours later Gecko wheeled a '09 Pontiac into the hospital lot near the Colton RR yard and exclaimed, "That's the way to return from a class hobo trip!"

It's all about the trains. They hiss and snort, line nose-to-tail like elephants, and will carry or hurt you.

Part 1 The Rails Sing, eh?

It's all about the trains. They hiss and snort, line nose-to-tail like elephants, and will carry or hurt you.

My road partner is Brit financial journalist Tom 'Diesel' Dyson. Our startup yard is the flat middle of the Saskatchewan prairie, a one-crossing town named Melville, with the goal of Vancouver, B.C., on the Pacific. The mid-May barrier is the snowy hump (Canadian Rockies). It's raining corn and wheat in the Melville freight yard.

We sit on packs in an inch of rainwater on the floor of a container car in a long string of more of the same. An overhang container blocks the hard drops that pool on the floor. A half-mile away, at the head end, two locomotives whistle 'Cannonball,' the couplers catch in a drumbeat back at us, and our car lurches west. Sooner than later, we tire and lay in the jiggling water, he inside a sleeping bag on a sponge mat and me in mine enveloped by a leaking garbage bag. The hobo perspective is that the land rolls by, especially at night. Rivers ice alongside the train during the climb into the Rockies. Diesel peeps at me shivering, grins, and proclaims, "It doesn't get any better than this!"

I'd flown into Calgary, Alberta two days earlier, on May 19, taken a room at a hostel, and inquired about bus transportation to Melville. I'd never met Diesel, as we were hooked up a month prior via email by a mutual freight aficionado who bowed out of this trip. I also checked the Calgary street scene of cordial ruffians bundled in the spring thaw around the 'Sally' or Salvation Army. "You gotta be stupid to catch a Canadian freight these days," a stiff reported. "Since 911," another alleged, "the railroad bulls search each train. It's jail time or a big fine for the first offense." This flew in the face of my wide-ranging experiences in the USA where sympathetic rail workers and bulls help tramps get out of town. I didn't believe him.

Big city Sallies are coast-to-coast clearinghouses for lowbrow travel as is this trip's aim. Through Calgary conversations, I learned about freights, locker storage, missions, thrift stores, jobs, and food lines. These 'homeguard' or local street informants rarely hobo but cruise with weather and caprice for week stints at different Sallies. They know the policies and locations to use the services to the utmost. Sallies and missions are generally religious-run with mandatory sermons before the meal and bed. The best sermons and worst song voices escape their windows. A call for sinners at service end brings forth a handful who 'cry for Christ' for free Bibles and fast supper and bed tickets. Some are truly saved, but most are pretenders. The mission thrust, besides saving sinners, is to clean the man so one morning with dignity he may visit the 'slave market' for a job in working up and out of skid row.

The Mustard Seed food kitchen served chicken and 'Forty-Fives' (beans) that evening to more than 100 Calgary street folks. These were cordial, even intellectual, compared to the USA counterparts. The regular citizens outside on the sidewalks were likewise sharp but oppressed by the chill and politics, white and stagnant as Elmer's Glue. South of the border—Left-Handers, they call us—we Americans are in contrast stupid and exciting.

Greyhound USA had lost my only bag on the short ride to the Phoenix airport to catch the Calgary flight, leaving me just days ago wearing what some call my gay CIA flowered shirt that allows me to walk into any office or country, and shorts. No toothbrush or razor, just a paperback. I spent two hours in 40 calls from the hostel to Greyhound USA but got nowhere. So I went to the zoo, and caught a bus for Melville.

"Canadian politics stinks!" griped a blonde caressing her longhair boyfriend in the seat behind me. "Corrupt to the toenails, eh?" he added. "But it's not so bad in the East." Yesterday the pair got on the bus in Vancouver after being

Sallies and missions are generally religious-run with mandatory sermons before the meal and bed. The best sermons and worst song voices escape their windows.

rousted by a SWAT team from their boarding house. Someone had smelled methamphetamine cooking in the room above theirs; the raid proved it true. The innocents were forced to vacate on the spot, and this couple pointed to the greener pastures of Quebec.

The Dog (Greyhound) in Canada is cleaner, better organized, and the riders and drivers friendlier than in USA. There are no nasal threats of imprisonment for smoking and drinking over the intercom as the bus pulls from stations, and there are videos. Countless, little prairie towns reminiscent of 1950s USA with sniffing dogs, banging mufflers, and Woolworth stores paraded by. I, the 'discard artist,' stepped into one of the omnipresent thrift stores and outfitted with used clothes and a book for $12 USD, and slowly warmed for the first time since alighting in Canada.

The Trans-Canada Highway [#]1 with its green-and-white Maple Leaf highway marker runs 5,000 miles cross-country from Newfoundland to Vancouver Island in British Columbia. Unlike USA Interstates, it varies from two-lane farm road to limited access divided highway, and the scenery runs from boring in the prairie to spectacular in the mountains. This was the prairie, miles and miles of it.

All the while, my mind was on the dream freight ride: I studied the yard layouts and workers and engineers from the distance of the bus. The two rail goliaths are Canadian Pacific Railway (CPR) and Canadian National (CN). The Dog follows the nation's first cross-country rail and stops in freight crew-change towns every six hours or so. As late as the 1960s, people settled in the West along the rail line when there were few schools, so the government created CPR School Cars. A teacher traveled in a rolling schoolroom to prairie stops, got sided for up to a week to teach, and then left for another area. Each car had desks, a blackboard and library. Literacy spread in this manner across the prairie.

Part 2: The Meeting

Diesel and I were to meet at the Regina, Saskatchewan, bus depot at high noon on May 21, and to recognize each other by my shirt and his big blue backpack. I arrived early, toured the streets and museum, waited at the station to no avail, and then walked to the library to email him. "Where are you?" he had written minutes earlier from the same place. "I didn't see you at the station, so thought to go to the library computers. I'm headed back to Greyhound." I dashed off that we were thinking in parallel, and picked for him without success among the rousting library birds, then returned to the station. There I spotted only a young man with a green duffle and small blue pack with whom earlier I had spoken—he owned a Brit accent that I mistook for Canadian. He squinted at my green Thrift jacket over the Hawaiian shirt, smiled like a Cheshire, and extended a big mitt. "Tom 'Diesel' Dyson. You gave me that name by email." "Doc Bo Keeley," I returned. There was a flash rapport. He looks like Dennis the Menace grown up, and thoughtfully brought me the duffle with a sleeping and garbage bag. We caught a Dog to Melville the day before the Queen arrived in Regina.

Rain obscured a theoretical sunset from our container perch in the diminutive Melville yard. The freight jerked, rolled West and the Canadian Rockies drew nigh like a white stripe across the horizon. Diesel scooped freezing water into an inch floor hole and astounded me with, "It's hard to be cold at this moment."

Tom Dyson is the managing editor of *The Daily Reckoning* and the co-author of *The Daily Reckoning Weekend Edition*, a weekly wrap-up of contrarian investment analysis. Before joining that Baltimore team, he worked in London at Salomon Smith Barney and then Citigroup as a CPA on a bond trading desk calculating the traders' daily profits and managing their books. His passions were always finance, writing, and travel. Three years ago, the London straight job dragged him down, he quit and moved to Colorado to work as a bank teller and snowboard. One day a freight train passed that launched a one-month rail odyssey through Mexico, the USA, and Canada. A year ago, he merrily took the

Daily Reckoning job in Baltimore and began weekend freight excursions up and down the East coast, but couldn't find a road partner.

They called me Doc Bo long ago. A moniker is normally bequeathed by another tramp, but my stamp came at a college sociology class "Hobo Life in America." I've caught 280 freight trains, really just a summer boxcar tourist, and all in the USA. My dream has been to hold down a 'rattler' across the Canadian Rockies.

Our gracious host today in Saskatchewan, closing on the Alberta border, is Canadian National Railway. Like other modern corporations, CN is the result of merging numerous—about 200—older and smaller roads. It was government-owned for 75 years until privatized in 1995. Diesel calls it the world's classiest freight system. Everything about it—the yards, rails, workers, and trains—squeaks of clean efficiency. Don't need no ticket to ride.

> **I've caught 280 freight trains, really just a summer boxcar tourist, and all in the USA. My dream has been to hold down a 'rattler' across the Canadian Rockies.**

Our sleeping bags seep last night's Melville rain on the container car across inclining Alberta. The metal platform measures 8-ft. x 10-ft. with 4-ft. walls from prying eyes. It's at the car rear with four stacked containers soaring two stories above and in front of us. The bulwark thwarts wind and faces from approaching trains, and evades a shifting load in an emergency stop—[#]1 killer of hobos. My experience is that a full cross-country journey will have one emergency stop, though the load may remain stationary. We're on a CN main line, with another track for opposing traffic that we duck every 30 minutes from the engineer's gaze.

The caution is because there are two rides that railroads don't like to see hobos on: the intermodal container and the piggy-back (semi-truck vans) trains whose valuable cargos are separated from greedy fingers by one peg the thickness of a penny nail with a seal. Break a seal and it's an automatic six months in the slammer. Ours is a 'unit' intermodal train with a three-quarter-mile string of solely containers. These boxes were no doubt boated from the Orient to a port in Canada or the USA, transferred onto a train, transported to metropolises, unloaded, reloaded with goods bound for the Orient, and the process reversed. It happens that this freight has two hitchhikers secreted in the line of containers. Intermodal freights started to cut into the truck industry in the 80s when my concentrated time on the rails ended, and hence I rely on Diesel for intermodal intelligence.

"Containers become cost-efficient alongside highway trucks when the travel distance is over 300 miles," he notes in a green region east of Edmonton, Alberta. "Hence the rise of... Ulp!" We duck. A freight sitting 'in the hole' on the adjacent track lets our priority train pass, but the engineer has stepped from it to observe our train roll. Diesel groans, "He lifted his radio as we passed. I think we're busted!" A savvy hobo wears his slicks (boots) and can abandon ship in a tick. We jam gear into the packs and sit below the walls. The train rumbles for miles, so we breathe easier. It finally slows, and I peek to see flashing lights at an intersection a quarter-mile ahead. One 'bo with light gear might skip and melt into the woods, however the wet sleeping bags weigh us down like bricks and the Mounties are on us like falcons. We hear them climb the cars ahead, and then up our ladder. "Gentlemen, step off the train!"

Part 3: The Bust

The train halted strictly for us. Bells clang, cop bubble-gum lights twirl, and traffic snarls at the intersection. One frowning CN bull and three spiffy Royal Canadian Mounted Police (RCMP) are the escort. The blue in uniform pipes, "How are you feeling?" He is no gentleman, balding, forlorn, and especially so after driving far out from Edmonton to collar us. "Warmer," I parry. He reddens and mutters, "You're out of my jurisdiction now." In contrast, the three Mounties are professional, cool. "Do you have weapons?" one asks. They aptly search the soggy packs. "Do you grasp the dangers of riding freights," one with a stereotype handlebar mustache questions. "Yes," I reply. "I taught a college sociology course on hobos." They run our IDs and order us into a patrol car: "We're taking you to a transit station for Edmonton."

"We must issue petty trespassing tickets," explains a Mountie en route. It's a hefty $250 USD fine but he postdates the court appearance until after we'll exit the country. They tell us that a warrant will issue if the fine and court appearance are ignored, but the ticket shall be purged in five years. It's on par with a traffic citation and shouldn't show on the immigration computer. The RCMP is Canada's national police service, keen as any in the world, and even a notch above the California Highway Patrol. The railroad bull radios the Mounties, "Tell those two tramps if they're caught on any train in Canada again, it's straight to the magistrate." Railroad police—the bulls or yard dicks—have an historic rep as the bad guys. Yet, in the USA, my opinion is that bulls are capable specialists. The CN cop was just a bad seed or enjoying a poor day. We chat with the RCMP about hobos until reaching the transit station. "Makes me want to try it some day," muses one in dropping us.

Edmonton, Alberta's capital, lies on a green valley carpet protruded by grey buildings. There are galleries, colleges, some fine architecture, and the world's largest mall. The citizens seem bridled by others' beliefs, bowed in their gait, and content to circle about day after day. Collars are looser in the University area that we ply for food and a Laundromat. Diesel steps into a tattoo parlor for directions and emerges minutes later shaken. "The tattooist distinguished me as a hobo off the bat and forced $5 into my hand. I was afraid to refuse it. He wrote an address saying we had a place to stay." Soon, another man exits the door and says huskily, "Don't crash at his place." The eventualities are: The money was an invitation to theft at night, to pander drugs, or sex, or was simply a cordial offer. "I'm not going to chance it," Diesel decides.

Fortunately there's a backup who issued an open invitation years ago. I call Rip McKenzie who cries, "You're welcome!" We find him, coincidentally, deep in a *Railway King* screenplay about his real great-grandfather who founded the Canadian Pacific Railway and, as the story goes, before the old man dies he hobos with his great-grandson the rail he built. We discuss the screenplay late into the night, and it's only family obligations that prevent Rip from joining our journey across Canada.

The next morning Diesel bolts upright in his sleeping bag and announces, "I'm not afraid of CN. The bulls don't scare me. I'm going to ride their train over the Rockies!" I calm him down. The first time a bull nabs a 'bo is a 'gimmie;' the second time, punishment. I explain that though we're tagged in the CN computers, it's unlikely that CPR has heard of us. Only CN runs from Edmonton, so we should switch modes to Greyhound to explore the Northern plains and Yukon before pursuing the dream ride on CPR.

The Edmonton Greyhound men's room end stall offers the only mirror writing graffiti I've seen outside of Leonardo Da Vinci's notebooks:

> ,erif eht ni denrael yeht snossel eht yb deiruB gnitabed sehctaw elihw gnitiaw fo emitefil eritne na koot ti ekil demees ytinretE reverof erusaert dna eruseem ot stnemom hcihW .erusaelp rof rovaedne yreve gnireves elihW

An hour later, and the day after the Queen leaves Edmonton, we buy seven-day Dog passes and launch a marathon tour.

Part 4: The Dog

The bus climbs Yellowhead Highway [#]16 into the snowcapped Rockies where every five minutes a passenger shouts, "Bear... elk... bighorn... bison!" and the rest crane their necks this or that way to watch the animals lick salt from the roadside. Jasper Park, the most northerly and grandest in the Canadian Rockies, is a place I'll return to hike. Only Diesel seems distracted by inner thoughts. In Jasper town, he marches off the bus with pack in hand and sits, chin in hands, repeating, "I hate the bus! I love the train!" a hundred yards from locomotives crashing car strings in a small CN yard. A brakie reports that the first westbound isn't until the next morning, so we reenter the bus as Diesel tears his hair.

The passengers, a mixed lot, are mysteries each from different origins and bound for other destinations. I'm thrown into John Steinbeck's *Wayward Bus* and furtively hope for a breakdown that will reveal us in the wilds. A high school girl is returning home after dancing for the touring Queen in Edmonton; many obese tourists hug the windows in search for beasts; a high ratio of travelers are employees of the Athabasca Oil Sands. Diesel snaps to at that mention, though I can't say why. He questions the blue-jeaned toughs about the worksite, production, and prospects. "There are tens-of-thousands like us," we're told. "Twelve-on-and-twelve-off... draw pay... leave the hellhole... PARTY till the money runs out!"

"I ain't met a Brit before," remarks a stocky welder. "Can you show me a Sterling note?" My good-natured companion grabs under his jeans to the money belt and pulls a fiver. "Keep it close to your balls, eh?" observes the heavyset worker who examines the note, whistles through gold front teeth and hands it back. I gather he's the provincial wrestling champ and outdoor welder at Athabasca. At a Prince George, B.C., stop, in the middle of an endless Spruce forest, Gold Tooth offers to guide us into the woods next to the railroad yard to await a westbounder. But an Athabasca electrician warns us that one year ago, 50 meters from where we stand, he was struck in the head and robbed. I tug Diesel by the elbow and say, "We don't go off with that gorilla after he's seen the money belt. Let's ride on."

Sometime at night, as we nap on the cushions, the bus driver angles the bus northwest toward Prince Rupert, B.C., and awakens us at sunrise at a remote highway T. "Your stop, eh? The Cassiar Highway. It gets lonely, so take care." Diesel's brilliant hatch will have us hitch north from here one day through bear country to avoid a two-day bus ride around a circuitous route. Birds, crickets, and squirrels join a forest symphony around a single gas station—closed—at a bridge at the start of the highway.

Remarkably, a sprite, elderly lady is helping a traveling disc jockey break into his rental car where the keys dangle in the ignition. She gets him underway and sidles to us. No lake in the Rockies is bluer or more reflective than her eyes. My mind shouts, "Maude!" but I stammer, "You aren't the ax murderer?" *Harold and Maude* was an early-70s film about a teen looking for life beyond his yard who hooks up with oldster Maude through their mutual habit of attending funerals. "Heavens no, boys! Climb aboard." she chirps. We jump into a new van and enter the forest-swept Cassiar Mountains.

She sits erect at the wheel as she did a week ago at the San Francisco onset, and is driving the Alaskan Highway to meet her son in the forty-ninth state. She has seen the world, bicycled across China... planning the trips around cemeteries. "They're so interesting, don't you think?" In Egypt, she fell into a crypt. "The ground gave way, and I looked up for an out. I had a flashlight so it wasn't difficult." She touches her shirt collar. "This is the lucky blue flannel. Of course, I've sewn the rips."

The Cassiar Highway [#]37 connects the more northwestern rain forest with the jack pine and spruce forests of the Yukon. It's some of the best mountain scenery on the continent. Out there, away from the gravel and pavement, survive grizzlies and mountain goats though we see only brown and black bears. The road also serves as a landing strip in places. We pass the continental divide at Dease Lake and progress into the

Yukon. The Coast Mountain range grows larger on our left west flank. Maude, entertaining with her travel stories, drives the distance to the Alaskan Highway #1 junction. At sunset, with sadness all around, we part at the road's northern terminus where she nonetheless waves gleefully, and wheels northwest. We stand stranded at another woodsy T.

It rains. Our thumbs catch the breezes of infrequent trucks grunting up the opposite grade. An hour later, a pickup snatches us. The driver is a 'splinter belly' or bridge builder with a Sad Sack face on a grizzly body. He opens caringly, "Better to pick you boys up before the bears do." He soon turns into a dirt lot with a small neon sign sputtering "Roses." No power line comes this far north along the Alaska Highway, so each establishment runs a generator. We enter a cabin-bar where the lady proprietor argues nose-to-nose with a patron about the jukebox selection. They hold half-filled shot glasses like pistols. "Rose," softly interjects Sad Sack, which stops the fray. "These poor boys hitching in our woods don't have much money and want a room. What can you do?" She beams from her loins, and replies, "There's a back cabin I can let go for $40." "Now, Rose, does it have a TV?" "No," she admits. He produces a wad of bills and hands her one. "Give them the best." I protest but his bear chest heaves and the Sad Sack face withers. Canadians have been funny with money, and we take the gift.

On the early road in pine perfume, we walk four hours unable to flag a ride into Watson Lake, B.C. I pull a calf muscle beating the hard pavement, but Diesel slows patiently, in his way, continually waiting ahead for me to catch up. His head swivels at the town limit and he howls, "A signs copse!" We enter two acres of street and town signs and learn this is the world famous Sign Post Forest. It started in 1942 when a homesick U.S. Army G.I. working on the Alaska Highway erected a sign pointing and stating the mileage to his hometown of Danville, Il. Other travelers followed his lead to a present total of 60,000 signs. We exit and get bites at a half-dozen fast food restraints until the Greyhound stop.

At one, a middle-aged Yukon Native Indian, seeing our packs, greets, "Mornin." He's light olive-skinned and tall with sunglasses. "Why do you wear them?" I ask. He removes them and stares with blue eyes into mine. "I'm an albino, as was my great-grandfather. That supposedly makes me special in the tribe, but acts are more significant. When I was six, I rode a bicycle into a stonewall without knowing how to brake. The bike bent but I was unscratched, and that's why they call me Stonewall to this day. We share our snacks and he warms to us. "There's overt friction between the Yukon Indians and Whites. The present policy is separation by putting us on a reservation. Actually, we have a choice of sitting on the reservation with subsidized housing and a few-hundred dollar per month dole, or leaving. I personally live there but come to this town to take odd jobs and out of boredom."

I throw out *Watership Down*. "In this book, a housing development forces a group of rabbits to abandon their warren. The little band strikes across the countryside and encounters obstacles such as a stream, bean field, and iron road. They meet another warren where the rabbits are strangely philosophical, and pass. At a farm they find an Efrafa warren that is ruled like an army camp by a tyrant buck. The rabbits there aren't allowed to leave despite overcrowding. Some of the original band risk their lives to lead members of the philosophical and the oppressed warrens to the safety loft of Watership Down."

"Well," remarks Stonewall, "we have the tribal law and enforcement. The prime law is that each person respect his elder." He looks over my partner and me. "I am his (Diesel's) elder, and you are mine. There are other rules and customs but these are nothing without enforcement. The degree of punishment depends on the crime, but something serious is dealt with by a beating to within an inch of your life." No one blinks. "There is room for mercy. I recently forgave my wife for stabbing me in the femoral artery that nearly killed me after I hugged a female friend. My wife was drunk with sorrow with the knife." We rise to make our bus. "Indians react differently to firewater—alcohol—than Whites," he clarifies. "It makes us crazy. Many newborn have fetal alcohol syndrome." We shake hands whereupon he gazes skyward and utters a guttural thing in his native tongue, then smiles in parting, "I'm happy to share some tribal secrets with you."

We Dog it east into Alberta passing many Alaska-bound vehicles. The Alaska Highway stretches 1,400 miles from Dawson Creek, B.C., through the Yukon to Delta Junction, Alaska. The road opened in 1948 as a muddy, twisting track

"There is room for mercy. I recently forgave my wife for stabbing me in the femoral artery that nearly killed me after I hugged a female friend. My wife was drunk with sorrow with the knife."

bulldozed by the US Army Corp of Engineers. Our day's section is asphalt interrupted by one-mile gravel gaps. The bus pushes south through Dawson City, and onto a spur route to Ft. McMurry, Alberta, in the center of the Athabasca Oil Sands.

Part 5: His Secret Itinerary

Diesel squirms as we pull into the Ft. McMurry terminal and step down. He finally explains, "A small reason for the Canadian trip is to find investments for my newsletter *The Bull Hunter*. I've struck a deal with the publisher where I use alternative transportation to locate opportunities around the world. Freight trains are just one mode. The next issue may be "Latin Like Me" where I—and you if desired—trek Mexico disguised as Mexicans and sneak across the Rio Grande as illegal aliens. The following issue could be bicycling the jungle Transamazon Highway to locate a trade route from Brazil to China to supplant the Panama Canal. It's anecdotal, of course, but the financial tips are my signature—quirky and sound."

The town of Fort McMurray grew recently and rapidly to 40,000 atop the largest oil deposit in the world. The biggest machines work 24 hours a day, 365 days a year, to dig and separate the oil from sand. We breakfast in a all-night café where a representative slice of the tens-of-thousands of hardnosed workers provide a Wild West charm. A thin electrician cocks his ear at Diesel's accent and asks why we're here, and then offers to drive us around. He tells us that Athabasca black gold doesn't geyser up but is bonded with sand within a sandbox twice the size of Lake Ontario. Great machines transport, crush, and separate two tons of sand per barrel of oil—160,000 barrels daily—that's piped mostly to the USA. The generous driver bids us adieu at the Greyhound with, "You missed the Queen in Ft. McMurray by two days!"

The bus spills out with workers with fat wallets leaving the pits. They work 12-hour, 14-day stints and then vacation two-weeks, often in international junkets blowing their wallets on booze and girls. The monthly cycle repeats for years. It seems that 10% are married, and an equal number save a fair amount of their princely wages. One welder informs that it's easy to get work at Athabasca but hard to leave until one flunks a piss test. Crack cocaine, and methamphetamine have replaced pot as the drugs of choice because they stay in the urine only a couple days compared to marijuana's one month. "The piss test has caused a meth epidemic here. Of course," he concludes, "a hard hand has the right to live it up during free time."

One young Caterpillar truck driver describes his job: "I sit two-stories up in a queue of Caterpillar dump trucks. When my turn comes, four scoops from the 10-meter jaws of a digging shovel fill the load with 350 tons. The truck engine is 3,400 horsepower (about the size of a locomotive), and I haul the sand at 1 mph on 13-ft. tires to the crushers. As a matter of fact, I quit yesterday. The wages at Ft. Mac are sky-high but the cost of living matches them, and a married man can't make it. I'll take a job elsewhere at half-pay or buy a farm and raise a happy family."

We touch Calgary in time for evening chow at the Mustard Seed. Most major Canadian cities boast a Needle, or 'syringe,' as Diesel deems them—one skyscraper with a pointer. It's the city center and unwitting hobohemia marker. Hobohemia is generally located in its shadow, so we work toward it and shift into a flow of hungry street people. Soon we claim the end of a line stretching around a block into the door of an old brick building. This is the venerable food line, and virtually every North American large city offers at least one. Those ahead, and now behind us, include the homeless, low incomers, addicts, folks on dole, and single mothers with kid strings and one hanging out the blouse.

Cheerful staff smelling of shampoo and sporting nametags serve us. We sit by two Native Indians who, by their strong necks, tattoos, and quick eyes, have held down freights before. Our table becomes a greedy litter since the first finishers earn limited seconds. Diesel, the vegan, slips meat onto my plate, and I pass my rolls to the Natives. One asks, "Passin' through?" "As a matter of fact," I reply, "we hope to catch a freight to Vancouver." "Well," he says, "the bulls climb every car like bugs to rustle the bums. Go to Fort Calgary Park tonight and wait for the first westbound to roll out real slow. Nail it! They all go to Vancouver."

Part 6: To the Rails

Easy as that, we have directions and hump the packs a mile to Fort Calgary Park. We settle in the pines littered with dead soldiers (empty booze bottles) a quarter-mile from the yard tower that is the yard nerve and communication center. It's an ideal spot to wait for the sun to disappear.

The hours drag. One mixed freight steams by too fast. Actually, Diesel hopped adroitly onto a ladder but I couldn't make it with a game leg, and he returned. A seasoned tramp eschews the 'fly catch' for the many pitfalls: uneven ballast, stick-up markers, off-balance backpack, slippery rungs, and the temptation of a fast ladder. We discuss the relative merits of waiting at a mainline vs. infiltrating a yard. He likes to sit in wait, hoping to be awakened by rolling stock or the hobo alarm clock, an automatic switch. I prefer to penetrate, glean info, and board before a freight pulls out. A week ago, CN caught and put our names in their computer, but this is CPR territory where we're unknowns.

We determine to wait thirty minutes before moving, and are rewarded by three advancing units hauling an intermodal train. The fly catch is to trot alongside a ladder until matching its speed, grab iron with one hand, then the other, then a foot and climb aboard. I never board a freight moving faster than my jog, and this quick starter is too fast even for my partner to latch to. We shrug, and start for the yard interior via city streets to skirt the tower where sits the yardmaster who controls traffic, and sometimes the bull.

An overpass spans the 20-track breadth of the CPR yard that becomes our perch above the tower eye for over an hour. It's like overseeing a battlefield. Yard hogs (engines) growl, car couplers bash everywhere, or engineless 'silent roller' strings creep off the hump hill, workers jump on or off quads, and headlights pop up. We try to figure it. The vast yard cannot be fully appreciated from the overpass, so we enter deeper. There are more hours of walking, and once a crew van mistakes us for crew and stops, but we hurry on. Dawn finds us back under the original pines with the dead soldiers. We snooze-in-wait, Diesel's favorite tactic, until he elbows me and points to a long intermodal freight halted at mid-train in front of us.

Before a train pulls out, an electric clicking along the airline signals a brake test that triggers the adrenalin. Within a minute, the loco whistles, there's a shout, 'Cannonball!,' the couplers clash, the car pitches ahead, and it's rock-and-roll. There's nothing like catching a freight—not the first breast nor the last breath. We lay low behind the steel walls until the freight clears the yard. Now we burst out of the city into starlight, and that white swath of mountains is palpated by the increasingly laboring engines and cooling air. At sunrise, the adrenaline has dissipated and we bounce gently on the floors of facing container cars.

The sun in my face awakens me as the freight braces a curve along to a river cutting a valley between white-topped mountains. Bear, deer, elk, and wild horses graze the right-of-way. An eagle darts into the train updraft. Higher still the rail climbs. A sign reads "Glacier National Park—Canada" and the slopes harden and bare under melting glaciers and waterfalls. We live the railroad dream through the Rockies.

Within a minute, the loco whistles, there's a shout, 'Cannonball!,' the couplers clash, the car pitches ahead, and it's rock-and-roll. There's nothing like catching a freight—not the first breast nor the last breath.

The freight threads in-and-out of tunnels and dripping snow sheds. Out of the blue, the tracks aim straight into a towering range. At 14.7 km (9+ miles), the Mount McDonald Tunnel through the B.C. Selkirk Mountains is the longest railway tunnel in North America. We enter a hole and the lights go out. Inside, the sway and gentle grade for twenty minutes isn't unpleasant, and the locomotive smoke bouncing along the ceiling doesn't reach our noses at mid-freight. The locos thunder, a round light appears and we exit. On the west side of the pass, I watch the track join the older line leading around the mountain to the original 1911 Connaught Tunnel. I gaze across the car into Diesel's black face. Soot coats our gear, the car, everything, and he grins thinking (I know), "It doesn't get any better than this!"

Filthy as spades another day, our black heads pop up-and-down at mountain crossings. We drink the last drops and eat the final apples, read through the vibrations, and chat above the steel chime. Somewhere a sign posts 'Continental Divide' and the track descends to the Pacific. The landscape becomes less harsh with rolling hills pocked by farms.

Our carrier is Canadian Pacific Railway, the other of the two RR giants. When CPR completed Canada's first cross-country rail along this very road in 1885, it opened up the Canadian West to settlement and united the nation. Towns sprang up—Millord, Kamloops, Spences Bridge— along the modern densest CPR segment between Montreal to Vancouver. Today, CPR is a national icon and the leader in bulk and intermodal transportation, plus a couple 'bos. Diesel reports that recently the company started using mid-train remote-controlled locomotives to allow their freights to run two miles long, though ours with a string added somewhere after Calgary is about one mile.

The train stops center in a single track along a mountain river. Freight riding is perpetual problem solving, like smudge chess. Why should the train stop on a single line? Diesel vs. Doc Bo—his accountant mind is quick though I have the weight of experience. "Probably something in the track," I submit. "Maybe a yard jam ahead," he counters. Suddenly, the engines 'dynamite' or break with a BANG from the train as the brakeline disconnects releasing pent-up air. The set-off is the hobo nightmare. "They could pick up a string of cars ahead," I proffer. "No. There's mechanical trouble," he asserts. We watch two huffing units pull a few cars out of sight.

We crawl down a slope to the river to drink like thirsty animals. The water takes a bit of smudge too, and then we flop on the sunny shore to continue the game. "Sooner than later they'll return to solve a mechanical problem," Diesel stresses. "Later than sooner," I disagree. He says to sit it out, but I suggest a swim across the river to hitch a rural road to the next yard." We compromise by walking west. A muffled growl comes around a bend and the ground shakes. The two units pass and reconnect to the freight. Caught flatfooted, we sprint to a shaggy-headed engineer in the lead loco. "Seen you earlier, eh?" he yells down. We discover that a split brake hose forced him to drop that 'bad order' down the line. He's generous considering that a rotten tramp may cut an airline for an emergency stop to get off. "Look lively, boys. This train leaves in five minutes!!" That allows us to reboard. We end the dialogue, "If we're nabbed by a bull, we never spoke to you," and the engineer replies in turn, "An' I never seen you boys."

The rails scream and spark from the Rockies to the Pacific. We could hide in hunger behind Yield signs with dirt-n-pores that must grow out. The rails sing my name, or is it Diesel calling?

Part 7: Vancouver

Port yards—where rails meet water—are 'hot' and crawl with bulls. We hop off the freight prior in Pitt Meadows, B.C., five miles east of Vancouver Port, and take a local bus into Vancouver. Canyons of a new type envelop us. Guidebooks praise this "Most livable city in the world" as a hub for art, culture, commerce, and transport including the railroads. Nevertheless, we take the tramps' tour along Grandville St. bohemia where the duties are laundry and a mission.

The sidewalks coast-to-coast across Canada are littered with cigarette butts and pennies as economic indicators. This is the smoking-most country in the world. Discarded long butts mean strong times, but Canadian citizens smoke down to the bitter end. Diesel suggests that the $6-a-pack price undercuts the normal indicator. On the other hand, he collects pennies from the gutters and dozens jingle in his pocket. "It means either good economic times or currency inflation," he claims.

At the 'Gathering Place' Community Centre on Heimcken St. the receptionist suggests the nose bags or free sack suppers at 6 p.m. in the parking lot, but when I thank her cordially someone of discernment in the back orders, "Give them the works!" and we're handed a shower ticket and $5 vouchers each to the in-house café. We figure a Brit accent and tramp's limp go a long ways in raising kindness. We could overnight at one of the many town missions that most hobos shun for potential 'rey soldiers (lice), and a mission stiff may smell of urinal soap in his pocket to kill the 'crumbs.'

Instead, we kip at the West Vancouver beach apartment of our contact Don Osborn, a writer of song and music contracts. We can almost dive from the third-story apartment into the 137-meter Kitsilano Swimming Pool where Diesel, part fish, is overjoyed. We pore over the options for the second half of the trip: CN, CPR, Dog... And I introduce a novel idea of going south into the USA and freighting on the Burlington Northern Santa Fe (BNSF) to the east coast. He nearly jumps out of his boots in response!

Part 8: Back in the USA

We take a Greyhound from Vancouver, B.C., to Washington State because although it's easy to catch a freight from a small to big city, it's thorny to catch out of a metropolis.

Border immigration is a cinch, and afterward the Seattle Greyhound and downtown are shameful. The regular citizens are arrogant zombies for the most part, while the homeless look dangerous and use poor grammar. Diesel glances at the midnight Greyhound station, declares it a butt-hole, then strolls out for a vegetarian restaurant. Trash climbs the terminal walls, only sleeping drunks smile, and my Louis L'Amour western begins to smell. Thirty minutes before the final bus departure—ours—an Amazonian guard yips, "Everyone up against the wall for the next bus. All others out. I'm locking up!" I ignore her, so after lockup she draws near with a compliance to chat. She: "You'll miss the bus." Me: "It doesn't leave for 20 minutes." She: "You must line up for a seat." Me: "The bus hasn't arrived." She: "What if everybody acted like you?" Me: "Would you be out a job?" She: "Are you giving me a hard time?" Me: "My partner isn't back yet." She: "How does he expect to ride the bus?"

I switch on the walkie-talkie but get static. Diesel's vegan grin shows at the terminal window five minutes before departure, and he sneaks in the back bus entry. A stupefied waitress had tried to double-charge him for supper, delaying him. In a jiff, we're eastbound with all but one seat filled. Nobody reads, babies cry, teens curse, students scream into cell phones... this is excitement?

Border immigration is a cinch, and afterward the Seattle Greyhound and downtown are shameful. The regular citizens are arrogant zombies for the most part, while the homeless look dangerous and use poor grammar.

"I got an hour sleep last night. What about you?" Diesel asks as we step off the bus into a Spokane, Washington, sunrise. "I could say the same thing. You talked all night behind me," I retort. "The dude next to me just got out of Washington State Pen. His jacket hatched a genius business plan." We saunter along empty sidewalks as he shares the idea.

141

"It's a counterfeit jail garment business! The jacket with the WSP red embroidery sells for $300 in good condition—$500 new—on the street. The buyers are gang members who wear them for prestige. The outfit includes pants, shirts and shorts each with the WSP. Men are allowed to take one set of clothes on release, and many sell right away to get a stake on a new life. The market is there, so here's my idea. I take a sample set—plus one from the major 'stirs' across the country—to China. They duplicate them to the thread for $5 each. The key the smart buyer looks for is the prisoner's ID number stitched inside each article. A list is available on the net. I sell the counterfeit jail wear on eBay for three-quarter the street price. A tidy import business, indeed!"

That's what I mean about Canada vs. USA demographics. Canada has 'doughnut philosophers,' the stiff who's satisfied with the price of a coffee and feed. USA boasts the variation who doesn't object to the doughnut hole getting bigger because it takes more dough to go around it. Only in USA would a counterfeit jail clothes business crop up. Then, it takes someone like Diesel from London to implement it. "What's the downside?" I lead him. "I get whacked by a gang," he replies. "When do we leave for China?" I say.

Spokane is no more to us than another knot in a string of catchout towns. Diesel is forthcoming in all. He strolls into the Spokane Holiday Inn and asks the concierge to use the guest computer to locate the freight yard. He rushes out with a print of the *East Spokane Yardley Yard*. We take local transit there and scope it from an overpass. According to the printout, BNSF operates fifty freights per day through this behemoth facility. It's active, but where do the trains go?

Our quandary is that eastbound trains take either the High Line northern route via Havre, Mt., while the more southern Low Line goes via Billings, Mt. The High Line is denser with freight and hobos and takes a day, while the more scenic Low Line at twice the length takes three days due extra train changes.

The Yardley hard-hats buzz too fast on ATVs to flag for questions. Diesel is atypically sluggish in hiding from hogs (yard engines). "We'll be tossed out on our ears," I admonish. "They're robots!" he exclaims. Sure enough, I've been ducking unmanned yard engines for a week. Radio controlled locomotives for switching in yards initiated, I'm told, in the early 1990s to reduce the staff. One worker with an electronic gadget strapped to his belt can start, stop, and accelerate diesel engines up to a mile away. Live engineers must still run the point-to-point trains between cities.

We study the yard in a growing heat for a couple of hours and retire to a little grocery store. It isn't hard to finger a train rider. I tell Diesel about my Them-Us hypothesis under the cashier's haughty stare. "Trampdom has customs, a subculture that is grasped only by riding freights. This collides head-on when we step outside the world. Look at us—filthy, happy with homes on our backs." The grocery clerk, though living next to a yard, has never held down a freight and gives us the pariahs' service.

When in doubt, walk to the departure yard and gaze at the yellow headlights of newly assembled freights on the spreading rails like Gatsby picking out the green light at the end of Daisy's dock: "And as I sat there brooding on the old, unknown world...

> "He had come a long way this blue dawn and his dream must have seemed so close that he could hardly fail to grasp it. He did not know that it was already behind him, somewhere back in that vast obscurity beyond the city where the dark fields of the republic rolled on under the night. Gatsby believed in the green light, the orgiastic future that year by year recedes before us. It eluded us then, but that's no matter—tomorrow we will run faster, stretch our arms out farther, and one fine morning... so we beat on, boats against the current, borne back ceaselessly into the past."

We lock onto the moving ladder of a lumber car, and scale 20 ft. of plywood to a cardboard nest. "Good sign," I yell over the rail noise. "This wood is from the West's forests and bound for cities east." The train, a mile long and powered by two units, is a 'rattler' or fast mixed-freight, though not as speedy as intermodals or piggy-backs. We memorize the lead engine [#]5498 in case it leaves the train en route to shuffle cars or refuel.

The view is first-rate up on the lumber where we're sitting ducks for town clowns (constables). At the first siding, we hop down and walk the train back to an empty (boxcar) with one window (open door). Shorter hobos and ones with gimps whom you see waving at crossings from boxcars face chin-high floors on the entry, and here Diesel boosts me from the gravel before himself hurdling in. Once inside, I'm transformed: This is the most ancient boxcar I've ever seen. The corners lean from 90-degrees, the floor is 1–in. hardwood slats, and the open door isn't on a track but hangs from the roof. Normally the door is staked with a railroad spike to prevent it from vibrating shut on hills, but this door is rusted open. The ghosts of hundreds of hobos linger. Cotton bounces and blows as the train picks up speed. "We're bound for the Chicago Cotton Exchange," quips Diesel, reading the freight.

The question of High Line or Low Line became moot the moment we boarded the lumber car since the main track forks east of Spokane. High Line is jargon for a mainline and fast freight, whereas the Low Line carries milk-runs, this morning's destiny. A sign flashes by the rail: "The Last Spike of the Great Northern." In 1893, amid gunshots and cheers, the final spike into the Great Northern track was driven to open the Pacific Northwest to settlement and trade.

A tramp doesn't defecate where he lives, but anything more is acrobatic. Then again, a freight sides for an indeterminate time that challenges analysis. Diesel steps down in the Great Plains to void but the train starts instantly and he staggers after the boxcar with pants-at-the-knees. I pull up my partner who mutters, "I'm finished," and he retires to a corner, "Now I'll wipe."

Any empty car is a bumpy ride, but tramps seek wood boxcar floors for a quiet ride. The track under us is continuous or welded without joints that lulls us to sleep. He chooses the front end where there's more cotton but the danger of being thrown into the wall in an emergency stop, while I take the rear end where the bouncing is horrific. We're like cats in a spin cycle. I grow chilled through the American Rockies and scoop cotton from the corners to make a bed. His boots vibrate past the door and to my nose in the rear corner, and I vow he'll hear about it later. In the morning, our 'side-door Pullman' rocks into the historic railroad town of Laurel, Montana.

Part 9: Long-Haul Tramp

The train dynamites and kicks apart in Laurel. We sit a few calm minutes until the morning chess game opens. Is our train adding or setting off cars, or are the units simply refueling. These and other possibilities in each of our minds are assigned probabilities, and we play one card at a time until there's a winner. His yard strategy is to stick to a train on a main line, whereas my style is to throttle the yard for information or other freights. At loggerheads, we compromise with a 30 minute hiatus before jumping off to explore. We're chagrinned in walking past our train's last car for breakfast to discover FRED is gone.

This Flashing Rear End Device that 'bos call the Fu***ng Rear End Device replaced cabooses in the 1980s. The one-foot flashing red light hung on the last train couple radios telemetry including brake pressure and motion to the engineer in the lead unit. A freight without a FRED goes nowhere.

We hike E. Main St. with the yard at our right elbows and dingy establishments on the left. This is East Laurel, once called Railroad Town. A slimy Mexican Café catches my colleague's eye. I've stretched a gallon of milk for the last two days. He orders fluently having minored in Spanish at university and later worked a year with Mexican peons. I don't know what I eat for breakfast, but it's delicious and meatless.

Rail towns are never uninteresting to anyone with the slightest taste for history, and Laurel illustrates this. These days, it's a main entry to Yellowstone Park for millions of tourists who drone I-90 a mile south of the café. It's the present BNSF crew change, and earlier was one of many RR towns that grew like weeds along the line to supply the workers and trains. During WWII, German prisoners of war constructed buildings in the town park where we can camp in the event there's no train. Chief Joseph led the famous Nez Perce flight of his people through Yellowstone and beat back the U.S. cavalry nearby. Right now, Diesel and I sit on the 'main stem' in the weeds debating whether to wait outside the east yard or to penetrate for information.

"Life is a puzzle," he avers. "Let's kill two birds by watching for an hour and then explore." Nothing shakes in that time so, radios on, I stick with the packs while he hoofs into the yard. Minutes later I hear, "Bo, they're making up an eastbound freight that isn't called yet; a brakie

145

says an intermodal train should pass and change crew soon; plus I'm monitoring our original units that are refueling." We again sit together in the weeds keen that hoboing equals inactive hours chopped by frenzied seconds. He picks a fingernail file from his jeans and carefully cleans his nails. Then a toothbrush. Perhaps the only full towel hauled by a tramp in history scrubs off his soot. "Now I feel like a civvie!" he jabs.

This yard is grand, miles long with about thirty tracks side-to-side packed with car strings either sitting, inbound or outbound for various destinations. Restless, we walk in the direction of travel to the workers' shack at the yard's end where brakies and switchies chat and read between jobs. A call board there lists the eastbound trains with their call times. Freights are assigned calls instead of departure times—a call being when the crew is notified in their rooms that the train is on mainline and ready to man. A crew van picks and drops them at the head locomotive. By watching the van movement, an educated tramp knows when to board a train. The actual departure time after the call varies from a few minutes to an hour or more. The yard workers normally give the inside story after one tosses out a polysyllable word that doesn't stink of alcohol. The crew—engineer and conductor—are tighter lipped but typically don't mind if you climb into an empty boxcar, gondola, or grain car.

The shack confirms Diesel's report without spilling guts to the bull, so we slither between car strings to position between our original sided-freight and the mainline where the intermodal is due. The mountain air is pure except for train diesel. Suddenly, Boom!—our previous units hook to the freight. We board two grain cars with facing platforms to lay in wait. We are found in the same position an hour later when the intermodal chugs up a few lines over. We transfer to it, but the original mixed-freight sudden starts out of the yard first. Ten minutes later, the intermodal dynamites, so we sit at point zero.

On a good day a tramp steps into a yard and right onto his train. On another day, such as this pretty morn in Laurel, he porks fruitlessly about missing trains and dodging the bull until sunset. At that point, I've never had a poor night in a rail yard. It's a time of sneaky rats under the rustler's moon when the deck is stacked for the tramp. In early evening, a worker suggests to wait under an overpass where eastbound locos head up before backing into a train, and he points toward I-90 a half-mile east. The classic hobo lair is under a bridge where the wide stage of the yard is previewed, the multiple lines converge to two outbound mains, and the train theoretically rolls by slowly to step onto. The bridge provides shelter from sun or rain, booze drinking is hidden as well, and town clowns don't molest the goddamned tramp because the space appears to be railroad property, while rail workers tell you it's town property free of the bull. I once invited a supreme court judge to speak at my sociology class on hobo legalities and, though he spoke eloquently on miscellaneous laws, when it came to bridges he said, "My researcher turned up that the jurisdiction of the property under highway bridges is confusing. I'm sorry." If for no other reason, we hike to the Laurel overpass.

On a good day a tramp steps into a yard and right onto his train. On another day, such as this pretty morn in Laurel, he porks fruitlessly about missing trains and dodging the bull until sunset.

"I don't like this tactic," I notify Diesel under the bridge. "For these reasons: It's better to walk a train or at least scope it before trying to board to know which cars are rideable. It's a quarter-mile dash for the initial cars from under here, and we'll be seen by the engineer. Usually it must be taken on the fly, and sometimes it's too fast for that." He grunts, and I conclude. "However, the cheery fact is just knowing where the units head up in front of us." A plan brews to wait for the power and then sprint obliquely into the yard, snake between strings, and board the slow roller. He urges, "Let's do it."

A strapping Irish tramp under a tall frame-pack and chugging a Bud-Light invades our shade. He paws another can, hands it over, and plops to the dirt. "You're not going to believe it, but I just came down from I-90 trying to hitch a ride. Nobody so much as looked at me for two hours. The hitchhiker's day is over. F*** 'em! I'll stick to the rails." His merry eyes scan us and, satisfied, he relaxes with the beer. He's surprised that we came in on the same early morning train. He'd nailed a grain car on it in Helena.

"My name's Long-Haul Tramp," and his big mitt engulfs first Diesel's and then my hand. Slowly, his life unwinds. He left home after a standard childhood at age seventeen with itchy feet. "An' they still itch!" he bellows, kicking himself. Now he's thirty-four and forever on the road, often by freight. "There aren't many of us long-haul tramps left," he claims. "We're a dying breed." He's clean, ruddy, ready, and slowly getting drunk. "I know it," he picks up. "I'm half-exhausted and half-drunk, a combination for an accident. But hell, I work so I can drink, and when I drink I get itchy feet." He chuckles and pulls a fistful of pay stubs from the pack. Diesel flips through them and whistles. This fellow has worked minimum wage at dozens of job types in a hundred places across the nation. "Look. I'm ridin' the fast freight to Fargo, N.D., to get on with the 'Temp.' It's a working town where any stiff with an SS card and picture ID willing to show up at 5:30 a.m. at the slave market gets a job. You never know the work—digging ditches to washing dishes—that can last one day or a month." We're grateful, but are riding beyond to Chicago.

FTRA is spray-painted in black on the concrete above our heads. The Freight Train Riders of America is a purported gang of men who move about the country by rail, particularly in the Northwest. The grapevine has that it was founded by homeless Vietnam Vets in a Montana bar in the 1980s, and spread. If you believe bulls—which I don't suggest—the FTRA is responsible for numerous murders of transients and freight hoppers, brutal assaults, drugs, theft, and food stamp fraud. If you have railroad tracks running through your town, the dicks avow, you already have FTRA members nearby. Yet these sordid activities have occurred in poor areas near the rails for centuries. The gang of a loose 5,000 is encountered mostly along the 1500-mile BNSF High Line from Seattle to Minneapolis where allegedly their faction color-coded bandanas are seen in RR yards, boxcars-in-transit and under bridges—the hobo realm. I personally see more bandanas in an hour on the California school outskirts where I sub-teach than I have in years on the rails. So whom do you believe? We live amid vast channels of misinformation and my resolution is to leap with common sense into the jaws with fast shoes. I think the FTRA is urban legend.

I probe the tramp about an earlier conversation with the waitress. "Be careful on the road," she warned. "This is Montana, home of wheels and guns!" The tramp looks up thoughtfully and says, "I'll leave you with a story. Once I pulled off the road into a little town to look for work. Someone sent me to the church, so I went in and pretended to pray. In came the parson with a .357 Magnum strapped to his hip. He asked what I wanted and I told him work. He got me a job. That's Montana for you: It doesn't need security or policemen."

At dusk, loco lights approach the bridge, stop, and back up. "Just like the worker told us," testifies Diesel. "Ok, troops, let's move!" I cry. Quickly we hump the packs along E. Main St. parallel with the tracks until we pass the double-header engines that clack into a car set. I lead around another sidetrack string shielded from the units, and we climb up-and-down four more strings toward the catchout train. Diesel ails from freight elbow after having climbed many ladders in a week, I gimp on the right leg, and Long-Haul negotiates with a beer in hand. We reach the target train and clamber aboard three sequential grain cars and wait, panting. Abruptly, a through freight pulls to the adjacent line sending the tramp scrambling perhaps knowing something we don't of freight chess. Our freight highballs first, and we roll at 8 mph under the bridge. A branch rail just beyond it forks south to Kansas City, and only after that do we celebrate with salutes across the facing grain cars that this rattler is bound for Fargo.

Our efficient transport is the BNSF, a single colossus born of some 400 different lines that merged in the last 150 years. I knew the parent lines as Burlington Northern and Santa Fe, and used bookstores shelve hundreds of volumes chronicling the colorful history of their ancestors. Each opened a bit of the American West over which we rattle honored. Peculiarly, BN was known for its leniency with riders while SF was full of 'hot' spots before the final merger. I'm curious to find how the extremes homogenized.

Dawn cuts the night. The wide sky of Montana I've tried to figure. The visible atmosphere holds a curvature like a high blue bowl under which the train crawls green foothills that abruptly rear to the North Dakota Badlands. Valleys, narrow and wide, snake between rock buttes and domes that were formed during cloudbursts following droughts. Then the land spreads out clean to Fargo.

After the boxcar, the grain car is the King of the Road's throne. Whereas the former is roomier—large enough for handball—the fact that it's empty signifies it may be peeled from the mainline before the goal. There are important clues in selecting a grain car: Look at the springs or kick the sides to ensure a load for a soft ride. Only half of those curved-side hoppers have solid 6 ft. x12 ft. platforms—front and back porches—at either end. Pick one with a cubbyhole within the framework, a 3-ft. steel teepee. I enjoyed the Irish tramp's company, but wished him away because his lanky frame and pack wouldn't squeeze into a cubbyhole and we'd be spotted in light.

Dawn cuts the night. The wide sky of Montana I've tried to figure. The visible atmosphere holds a curvature like a high blue bowl under which the train crawls green foothills that abruptly rear to the North Dakota Badlands.

I decide to flatten some rail coins after daybreak. The freight sides in the countryside for a priority train, so I bum pennies from Diesel to augment my own change and leap down. The wheel tread is smooth, polished steel about four inches wide—like the rail. "The art of coin squashing has nuances," I yell up. "First, ensure the engineer can't see you. Work on the side away from the empty rail. Walk, as I'm doing, to the forward set of wheels so when the train starts your ladder comes to you. Place the coins on the rail a few inches ahead of the lead wheel, but put the softer nickels ahead of the second wheel of the set. Loaded cars flatten best. Keep your head from protruding parts in case the car punches." He hollers from the back porch, "Make some 'fried eggs' from pennies on dimes!" I never thought of that, and put them on. Unexpectedly, our brakeline clicks and in seconds an Amtrak zips up the other side. "Pick a spot where your train pauses on an incline," I continue the instruction, "so the train doesn't leave without you." I move deftly now. The coins were laid on the outer rail edge to snatch without 'greasing the track.' I scoop them and climb onto the passing ladder. We examine the collection: The nickels, flat and double in size, will become fine earrings. The dimes and quarters squash less but retain the impressions for gift souvenirs. The fried eggs didn't get enough bond pressure and we decide next time a locomotive is needed.

The name 'Hobo' started before the Civil War as some men took to the rails as a way of life. Around wartime, railroads were built at a rapid rate and many veterans became hobos. By then the first transcontinental rail stretched to the Pacific. Before the century turn, a depressed economy sent numbers of men and families to the rails looking for something on the horizon. The Great Depression saw the rails blackened by train tramps, and tracks ran to all the bustling markets and industrial cities across the nation. Some commended hobos as the working backbone of the economy, and others said they were a bad lot. I think they're both, and a brand of compassion was born. A true hobo had a thing he did well: repair umbrellas, sole shoes, build, or hoe gardens. Literature says that the term hobo is a compound of hoe and boy, "Hello, boy," or of homo and bonus meaning good fellow. After WWII, the riders declined. Diesel replaced steam during the 1950s shutting the water tanks, so the trains stopped less frequently. Nonetheless, thousands ride the rails across America during the sunny months as I write these words. The types include Vietnam vets, divorcees, teen runaways, circle tramps who collect food stamps in different towns, nut-house releases, recreational tramps like us, and *bona fide* hobos in transit from job-to-job like Long-Haul Tramp.

There is a confusion of terms among the hobo ranks, but my use is: Hobo—an itinerant usually unskilled worker who is self-reliant along the rails. Tramp—whereas a hobo rides to work, a tramp is a migratory nonworker. Long-Haul tramp was an exception by name. A cute differentiation is that hobos and tramps use newspapers for insulation but a hobo reads them first. Bums—they neither ride trains nor work but are the low echelon homeguard surviving on handouts and missions. Diesel and I are just hobby hobos or weekend tramps in quest.

An individual's most vital need is freedom. Many, as we've observed on this trip, don't realize it and stagnate. With freedom comes the ability to explore one's extremes, find self-identity, and contribute freely to society. Books or travel tickle free men into the libraries, byways and, especially, railways where they touch others with an infectious spirit.

Diesel slips out his member and pees over the side as we slide into Fargo. "Piss out a boxcar once, you're hooked!"

Part 10: Bull Dance

On the other hand, there's much down time. God knows I've tried to make a life on the rails, to rove or even to live on the streets, but always was tricked back into society's nest by ennui. Fargo, North Dakota, develops into another muck night: We squat in a weed patch under the moonlight next to a small yard where our freight has terminated to resolve things. It's a quiet place with no workers and the city skyline is nowhere in view. We walk—a tramp's key gear is his boots—for hours.

Travel is a companion's hard test, and both of us feel an edge. He's conservative in the yards; I'm gung-ho. I'm safety conscious; he's impetuous. He'd starve before eating meat from a dumpster. After 5,000 rough miles in ten days, each of us is bushed and bruised. Somewhere in crossing a string in the Fargo yard, he follows too closely and I slip on a ladder. "City boys always walk a body length behind me, and country boys two body lengths!" I screech. "You've barked orders and I've followed you like a lackey for days," he screams. "Maybe it's time to split," I say. "Fine," he agrees.

Split is clear, and I make for a smoking intermodal train on a westbound line. Diesel apparently interprets split as distancing from each other while continuing eastbound. The train is about to slide away when destiny in the form of a RR bull stands arms folded and frowning in the headlight. I angle mutely from him out the yard. Diesel follows at a distance, but the bull stays put. I pause under a city street lamp and glance at my clock: Midnight.

"You were actually going to get on that westbound," he carps in the light circle. "That's right," I say. "We split." "No, we only 'split' within the yard." "Look," I continue, "my California desert is as close as your Baltimore home, and my freight stands ready. This trip has become a financial burden, but I'll continue if you provide $150 now for Amtrak fare home from the East Coast." He responds, "Will you become more conversational?" "Yes, it's back to square one." "What if I only have $100?" "Then we walk the streets of Fargo to an ATM machine." He fishes bills from the money belt and hands them over with, "I may have shorted you $10." I tuck them in my pocket without counting. A good tramp can turn on a dime, and certainly we're that. Immediately we plot the next move.

After retreating from the yard bull, we certainly erred out of exhaustion by arguing under a street lamp instead of seeking cover. A lone car cruises, stops under the streetlamp and the cop steps out and greets, "Good morning, fellows." The bull called the local police.

Police, for the most part, like to get the big picture of the 'perp' and take it apart piece by piece, jamming down the throat the ones that don't make sense. "We're on a two week tour of the North American Rockies," I say honestly, warming up. "Our bus passes ran out after Canada, so we hitchhiked I-90 here, and thought to catch a freight to Minneapolis. We just want to get out of town." Even as I deny that we got off a freight, I feel like a dolt in grubby skin with my pant cuffs tucked in white socks. The officer, a delightful typecast exception, beams, "Guys, freight hopping is illegal, but I hope you catch a train out of town." He IDs us and solicits Diesel in finding a DOB on the British Passport with South African birthplace. Second and third patrol cars arrive and he easily remarks, "Don't worry about the other squad cars unless you have warrants." A behemoth blonde in blue stands guard behind us. We're clean, so they let us go.

We wash and supply at a 24-hour store where I chew the fat with the clerk. "The girls in the parking lot just tried to get free booze. You can't sell alcohol in this state after midnight and, besides, they're underage. They said they'd pay me in the morning." Everywhere across North America—from the Yukon to the USA—we've found the youth in mass drinking and doing drugs as if life is a dress rehearsal. Illegalization of drugs clearly doesn't work. The clerk states, "Meth manufacture is popular because the ingredients are available—fertilizer is anhydrous ammonia from the farms, ephedrine from the drugstores, etc." This young man is clean-cut and determined. "The girls and drugs aren't worth losing a job. I'd be homeless."

Back in the shadows on the yard outskirts, we watch the bull van with the yellow shield patrol the yard for thirty minutes. "It's a game to him now," whispers Diesel. " He wants us."

Our first ploy is to divide to investigate opposite yard ends while keeping in radio contact. We hope the bull doesn't tune to our frequency. The radio range is 3 km and we check in every ten minutes. I hear his voice, "The bull circles and I'm nervous being with a pack. Let's..." I cut out as headlights advance and squat above a rail at an outbuilding. A peeling sign reads, 'Weigh station. Danger: Live rail.' I've never encountered a live rail and am three inches from an electric chair, though it can't be certain it was turned on. We guide each other with the walkie-talkies to a rendezvous at a closed boxcar.

A peeling sign reads, 'Weigh station. Danger: Live rail.' I've never encountered a live rail and am three inches from an electric chair, though it can't be certain it was turned on...

It sits alone with graffiti on a still sidetrack: "We are cowboys of steel riding high on boxcars looking for Mr. Quest." A hog yard engine chugs a half-mile away under the harsh yellow lights. Speedy Diesel volunteers for scout detail mentioning it could be a robot engine. Yet before he knows, bull headlights show and our cover is just the little boxcar. A tango begins behind the eight ball. We dart behind the wheels of the far side before the lights hit. The road curves around the boxcar, and we dance 360-degrees around to the start point. The dick doesn't see us.

There's a valid reason for railroad police. Nineteenth-century armed holdups and hijackings gave birth to the yard bull. Today their concerns are safety through prevention of trespassing and breaking into containers and piggy-backs. They use security cameras, motion sensors, and night vision goggles. Secondarily, they provide community education including an anti-hobo smokescreen that has dramatically cut North America freight hopping. Hobos find bulls face-to-face to be fair, outdoorsy types who give a shrug the first time and a ride to jail if caught a second. If the dick doesn't write a ticket, road wisdom directs one to reenter after his shift to try again. Earlier tonight, however, the BNSF bull indirectly cancelled our gimmie via the Fargo city police who no doubt bounced our names to him. We must stay vigilant in this yard till catchout.

Dawn tips the odds. We view a billboard at an entrance showing a yard map. It's decided to walk east along the mainline into a glen. Mosquitoes bite hundreds of times and poison ivy nips at our cuffs. The zippers on my duffle, sleeping bag, and jacket are broken and held together with string and safety pins. But the fact is an intermodal train decelerates before us, and we board the moving ladders of facing cars. Hallelujah! I'm a 'bo.

Part 11 Rails End

This is the slowest hotshot I've ever held down. In late afternoon, after multiple trips to the hole, the train enters a bewildering gridiron of rails and yards known as the Minneapolis trampdom. I want to pause to visit former road partners Iowa Blackie, once national hobo king, and Ad-Man, an advertising executive who rides the rails to national business meetings and jets home, but time is short. We ride on without food or water.

Minneapolis to Chicago is one of the prettiest runs in the USA. The rail kisses the Mississippi River and slugs through the bayous for a hundred miles. In the Wisconsin dells, the train goes in the hole in the wee hours so I hit the ballast to walk our car length fifty times for exercise. I rub my eyes on seeing auto headlights bear down along the parallel rail. It's a service truck mounted on flanged wheels using the tires for traction—the modern handcar. It speeds to the head end where there's an apparent crisis. Without warning, a retort sounds at a close farmhouse that ignites in light a chicken pen. A light also switches on top a radio tower above the woodland. The electrical problem solved, the service truck skates north and our freight lugs south.

Minneapolis to Chicago is one of the prettiest runs in the USA. The rail kisses the Mississippi River and slugs through the bayous for a hundred miles.

The sun rises yellow in our faces near Chicago. "Where's the Sears Tower?" Diesel wonders aloud, and sticks his nose into the railroad atlas. "I can't figure it, unless a new line or yard was thrown down since the book publication in '01. The compass and map have us coursing southwest around Chicago."

A giant horseshoe track appears on the industrial horizon leading into the narrowed entrance of a tremendous intermodal yard hemmed by 10-ft. hurricane fence topped by razor wire. A head-high camera floats by our car signifying a secured area. We gulp with one minute to choose before the yard swallows us. Semi-trucks pull in and out the yard at the rate of one-a-minute to drop or pick up containers, while agriculture land extends in all directions outside the fence. We can enter the gate and the let the cards fall, or bail prior. "Your call," I bawl. He drops his pack overboard without a word, descends to the bottom rung, and drops one foot to the grit. The funny thing about the first step from a 10-mph train is that the ground seems to move toward the rider for an impulse to lean backward, but then the freight's true forward momentum plants his nose in dirt. However, Diesel strides gigantically with the train inertia. I toss my pack out from the cutting wheels and likewise land. Heat beats off the dirt service road and insects buzz. "Let's get out of here!" I plead.

"Joliet Munitions Factory" an old sign reads on the road. Great humps of earth for ammo storage like dozens of loaves of bread salt the land everywhere. After forty minutes' hike, another sign informs us this is the new 2002 CenterPoint Yard, the largest intermodal facility in the world. The four-mile perimeter fence protects thousands of boxes stacked like children's blocks. A security truck pulls up that I ignore since we're on a public road, but Diesel strides to the driver's window. He rejoins me, grumbling, "I admitted we just got off the freight. The guard asked, 'Please tell me you didn't steal anything.'" I said we weren't vandals, just riders. I asked for a lift to a main road but he scoffed, "Hell no! Freight hopping is illegal." So I thank him and stalk off. I tell Diesel it was a jolly try, and we hotfoot trying to fish rides. It's a surprise fifteen minutes later when the security pickup reappears and the guard smiles, "I had a change of heart. I'll take you to a highway four miles from I-55 where you can hitch to Joliet that is 30-miles southwest of Chicago."

After that lift, we walk-thumb the busy route for an hour until a battered pickup slows, stops and out steps a bulky driver in coveralls. He applauds on the roadside to our approach. "Bravo! boys. The spirit of adventure is alive!" He offers doughnuts and warm sodas. After a life chapter as a vagabond about America, he became a bricklayer. "Now I work, even on Sundays." He cell phones a 'limo'—"Hello, Jose. Drive over to Barton Rd. near I-55. I have a gift for you." I spout, "If you got us a ride, we'll gratefully pay $5 for gas." Diesel joins, "Each!"

The bricklayer surveys us, and begins a story. "Once I picked up an old hitchhiker in the Nebraska plains. 'This is your lucky day!' the old fellow claimed. I replied that it was his lucky day, not mine. 'Why, sir, is that?' he asked. 'A few miles down the road you're going to bum me for a meal. I'm buying gas and food and getting nothing in return.' The old hitchhiker smiled, 'I am a bit hungry.'"

Jose, from the bricklayer's crew, arrives in a bashed Lincoln. "These are my cousins—except the old man. Will you give them a ride to Joliet?" Wordlessly, the Mexican unstraps the askew trunk for our packs, and drives us off with the bricklayer applauding through the rear window.

The sun sinks red on Sunday night over Joliet. Everyone we talk to gets jazzed that we just got off a freight train. "What's it like? Where'd you come from? What about the bulls?" I continue my interviews in quest of North America's heartbeat with a machinist recently thrown out of work. Highly skilled and employable, he was let go when the USA began buying steel from China. "The jobs are where the steel originates. Thousands like me are out of work. But the steel industry will bounce back—it always has," he opines. He peels from the sidewalk to a park to sleep the night. Diesel exudes, "Steel will bounce back! That's the insight." He will research it to tout in the *Bull Hunter*.

Hobos are the submerged one-millionth but the unemployed like the machinist make up the one-hundredth. It was wisely suggested that the decline of skid row flophouses is the basis for laid-off laborers being thrown into the streets. Rent is the monster paycheck eater. Diesel and I try the Joliet Plato Hotel that's full, so the clerk sends us to the Metro Hotel that's closed. A homosexual offers to put us up for 10 bucks each but we're not that desperate. We 'carry the banner' like 'bos of old hiking the main stem all night for want of shelter. We stay awake as long as we walk, having had little more than cat naps for 6,000 miles by freight, bus, and thumb in two weeks.

It was wisely suggested that the decline of skid row flophouses is the basis for laid-off laborers being thrown into the streets. Rent is the monster paycheck eater.

"Guys, you'll get jack rolled tonight if you go on!" calls a shirtless, drinking man from a porch chair to the sidewalk. "Once I thumbed tired and penniless into Hades, Texas," he states. "A man appeared out of nowhere and gave me $50, so I walked across the street and got a hotel room. I never forgot or figured out why. For that reason, you're welcome to sleep in my backyard." We spread a tarp on the 8-ft. x 8-ft. square of thin grass and mud, and fall asleep under a 4-ft. hand-carved eagle on the back steps.

In the early morning, before our host awakens into a hangover and wonders about the strange tramps in the back yard, I nudge Diesel. "Time to move on." He falls back asleep, so I stare a while at the wood eagle. The man had invited us to wash up in a kid's wading pool as the water company just shut his faucets for missing a payment. "Them that has keeps, and them that hasn't gives," Woody Guthrie preached. I've been walking on fish for days, and go into the pool first. I exit, dress, grab a disposable camera, and reawaken Diesel to tell him to dunk his head and wait for my three-beat cue on the poolside, then throw out in the sunlight for a 'Playgirl' shot. Lean and unshaven, he ducks his head and I tap the poolside twice and wait... In a minute he tosses his head back with droplets flying, and the shutter snaps.

We ride the Amtrak 'varnish' into Chicago. It's poignant that the journey ends in the hobo capital of the world. This was the rail gate between the East and West. Hobos and tramps in tens-of-thousands came to Chi-Town to layover, buy a barber college shave, blow their stake at a Madison St. saloon or bordello, take refuge in a flophouse or mission, take a job on the slave market, and attend Ben Reitman's Hobo College eighty years ago. Then those 'lost souls' struck out for something they could neither define nor chase down. Hobos were and are the highest appreciated form of the genus vagrant.

We clean and dine with Wiley Books V.P. Pam VanGiessen, Chicago pork belly king John Chikos, and legendary writer-photographer Arthur Shay. The time comes for Diesel and me to part company: he for work in Baltimore and I in California.

With enough Chicago track to equal the entire railroad mileage in one-eighth of Europe, Diesel butts his head against that for hours on the computer. He discovers a CSX railyard that sends one nightly intermodal hotshot to Baltimore. What time? He phones CSX customer service masquerading as a trucker with a container to drop, and gets the nightly express time at 9 p.m. "I'm out, partner," I bow. He takes one radio and leaves me the other. He enters that South Chicago yard alone at dusk. I get an email in hours: "Didn't get the intermodal train. Scared of the neighborhood I found myself in. Would have been chicken feed after dark, so got the Amtrak."

We're hobby hobos with a railroad fever that still has no remedy. People with the hobo heart share core beliefs on the rails or open road. Out there we're free as eagles.

A dream is lived! But it was all about the trains. How they lean and clack and shake a 'bos body.

By Bo Keeley

Before I saw the hobo way, I was a respected and productive member of society. Now I ride the rails and if you follow my story you too can be a hobo.

"How do we know which freight to hop," asks Baby Jack staring down yesterday from the Eugene Maxwell Bridge at the funnel of tracks with huffing yellow-and-gold locomotives and miles of trails of cars.

"The ones that move!" I reply.

"But Bo," he withers, "I've never broken a law in my life."

"It's time to pierce the legal skin," I retort. "Hand me your cell phone."

We dial the Union Pacific yardmaster who controls all the freight arrivals and departures beneath us, and I wink at Jack before speaking. "My wife and I are train buffs and want to take a picture of the big locos as they pull under the Maxwell Bridge. What time will that be, so my dear doesn't have to wait out in the heat?"

"Be on the bridge in one hour," accommodates the Yardmaster. "She'll get her train." We hang up.

My road partner on this outing is fresh to the rails but a gladiator of life despite never having broken a rule. Kerry Mortell is one of Hollywood's most talented and unsuccessful actors who supports bit acting by moving refrigerators. I am the veteran on this trip with hundreds of rides under my belt.

There's another beside us on this overpass who will stay behind. Our bewitching hostess Shandi sings, "Goodbye, boys!" and we heft our packs and tramp beneath the bridge into the Union Pacific yard. Every hobo takes a moniker to the rails and dear Shantdi gave us ours: Baby Jack Black and Beau Kerouac.

"Anywhere but here, Jack," I quip an hour later as our half-mile train puffs alongside and waits like a grin on a curve under the bridge.

"That's the hobo motto, mate. Now let's be quick to 'frisk the drag' for a proper car to Portland."

We scuff the grit, streamlined this morning with daypacks filled with water, books and a jacket each, walking along thousands of tons of fresh-cut lumber. Douglas Fir in full-stacks weigh heavily the springs, flatcar after car, with pitch oozing to the hot metal floors and wafting over the sides. "Here's a half-stack!"  Jack whoops at the first mountable sheaf of lumber. We clamber five feet onto the car, and another ten high up onto a hobo throne.

"We've sampled the view, Jack. Let's go back down now and hide for a good reason. This freight could start in a minute or an hour, and there's no sense risking the Bull before she pulls out." We descend the stack and wiggle into two slots, fore and aft, between lumber piles that squeeze like wood straightjackets. I count knotholes and listen to my associate's labored breathing. In thirty minutes, an electric click runs the brake line, far ahead the engineer whistles highball—one short and one long—the couplers clasp chicka-chicka BANG and our car launches. The adventure has begun.

I rise arthritically from my cubby and hobble to poor Jack wedged in the wood slot. "Get me out!" he commands, and after a long chuckle I throw a hand and pull hard. He flounders on the platform shaking his head, "No, no! That was the longest thirty minutes of my life." Then his jaw slacks on looking over the side of the rumbling freight.

The freight train is a gigantic linear machine of cars hooked tail to nose like iron elephants that pulls away. It exits the yard boundary, picks up speed, and enters the backcountry with the engineer blasting at each crossing. The rail bends north and weaves through the foothills of the Cascade Mountains where pines throw great green brushes at the lumber sides and tops. "Hobos call this the Snakey Route through Oregon," I exalt to Jack.

He has stood watching in stunned silence for an hour... They've taken the whiskers off the cornfields that lay now flat and fallow with funnels of dust devils tracing the horizon. A stream of hundreds of pulp and saw mills, noxious dairy farms, and endless fruit orchards ambles forth. Tiny old tank towns dot the way where steam engines once watered for the long pull up the coast. A startled lady in a pumpkin patch looks up and waves at us. My buddy shouts down in glee, "We're hobos, ma'am! Real hobos."

In Junction City, we zip past the Country Coach smoking plant that's signed 'Manufacturer of Luxury Diesel Motorhomes.' A jet zooms overhead prompting my partner to boogie across the deck and belt out like Gordon Lightfoot, "You can't jump a jet plane like you can a freight train." As we pull from the town limit, Baby Jack urinates over the side of the flatcar and I predict his first successful illegal train ride shall be a life pivot. The yellow stream loops back in the wind at him like a cane. "Piss off a flatcar once, you're hooked!' I cheer.

He has stood watching in stunned silence for an hour... They've taken the whiskers off the cornfields that lay now flat and fallow with funnels of dust devils tracing the horizon. A stream of hundreds of pulp and saw mills, noxious dairy farms, and endless fruit orchards ambles forth.

Our carrier through this magic is the behemoth Union Pacific RR that is the steel backbone of the timber industry with a gridiron of rails throughout the Northwest on which, today, on one track, our pitifully slow, short train sides every fifteen minutes for other lumber freights. Only Amtrak sides for us in the heart of timberland where felled trees are hotter commodities than paying passengers. We wave at them through their polished Amtrak windows and Jack gets a kick when they gape and disappear.

Inspired, he climbs a full stack high over the passing country and 'decks' it sitting on top. Now he clutches the bundle strap grinning in the bucking wind and bugs. "My god," he chimes, ducking a pine bough, "this is America through the back door."

"A hobo's got to travel, know what I mean?" I render. He yells down, "I've wanted to jump a freight train ever since I was a kid and saw a hobo framed in a boxcar door. But I got cold feet because I always did the right thing."

"That's all behind you now. Come down to hear the three rules of the rail that may save your skin today." The Irish gorilla drops lightly to the quaking porch and bores into my eyes.

- ☐ "Rule one is no loose ends." I pull a knife and cut short his pack straps as he double-knots his laces.

- ☐ "Rule two is no weapons, and carry an I.D." He taps confidently his wallet in a rear pocket.

- ☐ "Rule three, as you'll be turned upside down on this ride, is to secure your wallet." I offer him a safety pin that he declines with a guffaw.

I shrug, "Have it your way," and turn to face the vista.

He grabs my shoulder to spin me about and studies my face as a foggy mirror. Then he wheels to eye the sliding landscape as if for the first time, slapping his other pocket. He thrusts skyward a dog-eared copy of Jack Black's *You Can't Win* and balances howling into the wind, "I'm free! In honor of Jack Black and Jack Kerouac, I'm freee...!"

As the scream dies, I take the book to read aloud the first line upside down, my habit, "I am now librarian of the San Francisco call. Do I look like one?"

"It's the best inside autobiography," I tell Baby Jack, and hand it back. I open my own pack and pull *Animal Camouflage* by Powyzk, and read silently as Jack scales and beams high atop the stack. He sits there for more than an hour.

We packed no food today expecting a short ride to Portland, however the unexpected single rail with repeated sidings for other trains has extended the passage by threefold. Blackberry bushes have lined the right-of-way for a hundred miles. Duly at noon, when our freight 'goes in the hole,' I hop down for lunch. Jack languishes aboard never having caught a moving freight. "I'll bring you a handful," I call over my shoulder on the way to the first bush that is weighty with fruit.

I stuff my mug until the lips drip black and, distracted by a horn, freeze like a Norman Rockwell painting. A bright light! A freight barrels around a curve between the bushes and my own train. "I'm going to be cut off!" I shout across the right-of-way as the engine bears down. If I let it pass my own ride could leave and I'll be stranded blue-faced. Or... I peer over at Jack in a jig of despair on the flatcar when everything turns into slow motion. "I'l-l m-a-k-e i-t J-a-c-k!" I bellow, and dash before the locomotive. It rushes behind me with angry toots.

Now safe and full of myself, I kindle him from the cinders. "Let me show you how to get comfy with these metal elephants. Do you have a quarter?" He passes one down. I saunter to the rear set of three-foot wheels, stoop and put the coin on the rail an inch before the first wheel. "It'll roll any second to fashion a hobo coin for good luck. Our car is heavy enough to..." Suddenly the train heaves and squashes George Washington's long face two inches more. I snatch and clench it twixt my incisors and run for Jack's outstretched hand as the freight moves out at one mph. He snaps a photo with a digital camera and yanks me aboard.

"Don't leave me again," agitates Jack, rising above me. "I won't, Pal. Sorry about the blackberries."

Shortly, our train stops inexplicably dead on the main at a country crossing. The crossbar falls and bells clang on and on as traffic piles up on both sides. "There's no good behind this," I reason aloud. "We must keep alert."

Crunch...crunch. An advancing step jolts me. I motion with a cut of my throat to Jack. Like a big cat he scales the stack to the top unseen, and as quickly and quietly I swing around a ladder. A burly RR bull brushes between us miraculously unaware. I watch the blue uniform with gold shoulder stars, sun glasses, and bald head bob toward the freight rear. Once out of earshot, Jack and I rejoin on the flatcar where I whisper, "The cinder dick will round the tail and return, so let's hide in the lumber slits." We squeeze into them until, after fifteen feverish minutes, a wearier step trudges up the far side. The bull passes, the engineer toots, and our car pitches, but we stay low for the first mile. Finally, we extract.

"Whew! Our engineer isn't happy about the train stop, and the dick hated that fruitless trek," I inform my partner. "Normally, getting nabbed is small potatoes with a warning finger shaken in your face. But in this case, I'm sure we would have been dragged off the train to jail. How about that escape!"

"Escape you say!" roars Jack. "My stomach clenched and my underpants went brown. You broke the golden rule of not being spotted in the raspberry patch."

"You're right," I admit. "We're on a hungry ride now and must keep one eye each out for the bull and town clowns during the rest of the journey."

Somewhere in the afternoon, at the base of an unknown mountain, the track tips and veers from the afternoon sun. My throat tightens as the freight pulls aside Highway 99 East. I frown down at the shaking lumber stack and pick at the twirling tag in the wind that reads, 'Origin: Eugene, Oregon/Destination: Bar Code.' "Jack," I ask, "does it make more sense for this lumber freight to turn east to the plains or north into timber country?" He answers east. "Then can you read this bar code to tell me where we're headed?" He grins sourly.

"Sad to say," I continue, "This freight may not be our Portland Man. It could be the 'low line' clear to Montana, but I'm only a little worried since getting off-track is the hobo way too." "If you're worried," he ejects, "I'm terrified!" And he whips out a cell phone to speedily dial and yell above the wheel noise, "Cousin Jamie; meet Bo." He forks it over to me.

"Hello," I greet the mystery. "I'm guiding your cousin on a Union Pacific freight through the Pacific Northwest, but we're lost. I'll reel off the next town name and hope you can lead us to Portland." Dead silence on the far end, followed by an astonished voice, "Freight! What? Where?" I fill him in as Jack spies signs, and Jamie explains that he sits and drinks beer at the computer in a San Diego apartment '24-7-365' until he passes out, only to reawaken afresh to drink and scan the net. Abruptly Jack bawls, "I see a town limit: Ten miles to Salem." I relay it to Jamie, who snaps alertly, "Give me a moment." As quickly he's back with, "YahooMap shows the UP track courses Highway 99 East—a misnomer since it really goes north—through Salem and fifty miles beyond to Portland. You're all set, and tell me all about it later." I thank him and hang up.

Then I conjecture, "The engineer suspects tramps aboard and the train sure as hell will be searched as it pulls into the Portland yard. That city is a spider web of rails, waterways, and bridges, so we'll jump down when the freight slows 'on the fly.'"

The track threads gently north over terrain grown lumpy with verdant hills, and in two hours the freight trundles into South Portland. It enters the yard slowly enough to dismount on the roll. Jack, pack in hand, hits the grit on one boot and sprints for the right-of-way underbrush. I follow him calling, "Just walk. No sense in drawing attention."

We step over a few sets of tracks and through the underbrush to hunker under small pines and take stock. While scraping sap from the ride he feels his rear pocket and looks suddenly ill. The last thing a man wants to lose in a new town is his leather poke. Jack bolts for the train and vaults onto the flatcar, monkeys up the wood stack, kneels and reaches into the slot. He holds high the wallet, crawls down and shuffles back to me repeatedly crossing himself.

"Why, Jack. You're pale."

"Never again!" he grunts. "When I get home I'm gonna kiss my truck and never look at another freight."

I take a final peek from the brush at our steel steed stretched down the track and departing, and utter, "There she goes... don't need no ticket to ride."

So we shoulder our gear and stamp through the underbrush onto a rural road and strike a brisk pace toward the Portland skyline, he walking oddly bowlegged.

In fifteen minutes, we reach a gas station where I ask directions while he visits the men's room. After a long while he strides back and announces, "My last act of this trip was to donate my underwear to the Chevron Station!"

Thereupon we board a local bus to the downtown Amtrak terminal and 'ride the cushions' through twilight back to Eugene.

Our hostess, Shandi Sinnamon, jumps every direction at once on the receiving platform and smothers us with questions. "Don't leave out a detail, boys!" she demands. We relate what you have just read.

She laughs till she cries through the streets and then lingers in her doorway saying, "I'm going to immortalize that trip with a song."

Jack and I eye each other, and step inside where her Grammy for the 'Flashdance' song rests on the fireplace mantle. She leaves us and cloisters in the music room. Yet hours into the night, the piano, guitar, and sweet voice seep through our bedroom walls.

She bursts into the kitchen the next morning flailing a music score at Jack and me eating breakfast. "You look fresh as a haystack, Shandi," I say, studying the dreamy eyes and disheveled nightgown.

"Sorry about last night, boys," she coos. "But the great songs are written in one sitting." She picks up her guitar and gaily sings the song that gave this story a title...

> "Baby Jack Black and Beau Kerouac took off one morning down the railroad track.
>
> They hoped to hop a boxcar or a flat, promised me that they'd be comin' back..."

Well, after the song and tale are over, it dawns on me that a hobo's got to move on... Anywhere but here. Jack kisses his truck and drives it to Hollywood. I slip out the back door and jump Shandi's white picket fence for the sweeter song of the road.

Remember this story in word or tune, and decide if the hobo life is for you.

Washington is apple country and in season a northbound hobo is likely an apple knocker...

Doc Bo and Rev caught an eastbound boxcar from the biggest storm of the year in Los Angeles. We bumped the rails to Yuma... er Tucson, and there was a lot of action on this first Executive Hobo Trip since 2001.

Standing on the Pepper Street Bridge overlooking the Colton freight yard in a light drizzle, Rev's jaw tightens and bursts. "It's one thing to go into danger blind, and another to go into danger with you!" I'm thrown back to August '01 when four Executive Hobos echoed the same. I guided a NYC speculator, Silicon Valley CEO, Toronto gold trader, and a Bay Area chief of disaster response from Denver to Sacramento just in time for 9/11 (that clamped railroad security to pull the noose on the last of the money hobos).

Rev is Steven Klet, the best mind I've met since the executive hobos, and a hair faster. That's why I gave him the moniker Rev. He's the VP and computer head of family-run Vulture Medical Devices in Orange, California. I toured the factory floor beneath a 20-ft. x 40-ft. American flag where he strapped four leads of an electric device to my right arm to heal tennis elbow and invited me to crank the voltage, which I happily did, until the hand saluted. I assured his mother, the receptionist, that her only son's decision to catch a first freight was astute since, "He's bright, coordinated, and has your genes."

In August 2007 he read about the Executive Hobos in the archives of *DailySpeculations.com* and during the next three months entreated me to introduce him to hobodom, however I couldn't break from school teaching in Blythe, California, until a recent puzzling juncture.

On November 13, 2007, I was assigned to substitute Blythe Middle School Boys' Physical Education where the pupils assaulted me and each other with balls, rocks, and fists. At last bell, the vice-principal implored me to write the day's vicissitudes with suggestions, which I gladly did. The following morning, the district dismissed their ace sub, expressing concern, which they refused to put into writing about the middle school incident. I had also emailed the report to personal contacts outside the community—my parents, brother (a teacher), and other educators… that mysteriously reached the superintendent's inbox. I visited unemployment, another first, and like Jethro Bodine with floppy hat in hand called on a Palm Springs attorney who professed my case weak. I wrote letters to the editor, school board, and governor, and then hit the rails like Weary Willie for brighter horizons. The prompt to everyone was: How did the superintendent read my Hotmail?

I was thrown straight from teaching in the classroom to the boxcar!

We drove an hour in the belting rain from the medical device factory to the Union Pacific RR yard and brashly parked in the San Bernardino Hospital emergency lot kitty corner from the Pepper Street Bridge. From that wet perch we spot numerous white vans marked *Renzenberger*, the leading limousine service for locomotive crews, and salivate trusting one any minute to splash up to four huffing engines of a long train under our feet. Yet I declare, "The crew may already be aboard," and we slide down the muddy embankment to embark on a sky blue open boxcar into the secret world of hobos. "But enter carefully, Rev. The last four people I know who entered were permanently altered."

"Don't look back for two days," I urge as we inspect our packs on the metal boxcar floor.

His red suitcase holds a change of clothes, 99¢ raincoat, sleeping bag, multitool, flashlight, digital camera, cell phone, Theroux's *Riding the Iron Rooster*, snacks, and a quart of water. My black laundry satchel carries the same except a disposable camera, L'Amour western, and a sleeping bag from a chicken roost, patched and washed clean. He wears dark coveralls, and I two khaki pants with rope suspenders to stuff paper between layers against the cold. The rain batters lightly the roof, diesel wafts into the open door, and couplers clang outside and echo within our 15-ft. x 50-ft. box.

"I can't believe one can waltz into a yard and catch out," he pipes. "It hasn't left yet," I return. We hunker over the goals: First, to learn how to hobo a freight cross-country, next, to return safely with a memorable adventure. Thirty minutes of staring at the four grungy walls later, I proclaim, "I'm going to hike to the units to talk to the crew, the bull be damned."

I hop to the grit and trot eight cars ahead to the locomotives. The UP diesel-electric famous paint scheme is Armour Yellow on the bottom, a thin dividing line of red, and Harbor Mist gray on the roof. The 3-ft. red number #4714 on 'dirty face' is memorized for later use. The engines idle but the cabs are empty!

Back at the boxcar door, Rev reaches down and cheerily claps my shoulder. "We could have sat in here all night." Cold, wet, and sleepy, he believes that no problem withstands an assault of sustained thinking, and vaults down. We 'frisk the 'drag,' or walk the mile-long freight including boxcars, curved hoppers with end platforms, 'hotel rooms,' gondolas, lumber cars, flatcars, and a few piggyback and container cars.

Rev, an analytical risk taker, wishes to try to catch the moving ladder of a shuffling freight next to ours. I caution that the #1 hobo killer is to 'grease the rail' while 'flipping' a moving freight, and I persist, "Scale like a monkey with three of four appendages on the rungs." He grabs 2-mph iron, and one wet boot slips toward the 3-ft. cookie-cutter wheels. I gasp, unable to comprehend an explanation to mother why her son walks circles around Old Glory. But now he dangles safely, and shouts, "Two hands!"

He grabs 2-mph iron, and one wet boot slips toward the 3-ft. cookie-cutter wheels. I gasp, unable to comprehend an explanation to mother why her son walks circles around Old Glory. But now he dangles safely, and shouts, "Two hands!"

The yard is dangerous, more so with remote-control locomotives whisking the rails. I shout above their rumbles, "This is hell, like a toy train set." My associate has boned up on Internet UPRR history to inform me that this yard recently became the last in California to convert to unmanned locomotives. The accident rate among yard employees and hobos using automated engines is 25% higher. Also, with no sets of eyes aboard the engines, it's harder for us to glean train information.

We reach and peer around the tail of our freight for another automation called FRED (Flashing Rear End Device). This blinking red taillight is usually mounted on the last car to replace the venerable caboose and telemetrically relay the brake pressure a mile ahead to the engineer. A train is complete and ready to roll once the FRED and crew are added, but presently ours has neither. "Let's walk until we find a living soul," I yell. We search the yard for a brakie (brakeman) or switchie (switchman), while evading the bull (RR police).

Colton yard handles about 1500 cars per day and one can't miss the 10% tally of brand new cars. I haven't seen that many mint carriages in twenty years. Also miles of fresh boxcar art murals by hobos depict their faces and desert landscapes. "Union Pacific is a good investment," I tell my partner, "but hoboing is a better one." On finding no workers during the walk, we climb the Riverside Bridge over the west yard for a panorama.

The Union Pacific Colton Rail Yard has a typical configuration of two main rails entering both ends that widen into a bowl of some fifty tracks used for storing or building strings of cars. In the center lies a maintenance shed, diesel refueling dock for engines, and a five-story tower with the yardmaster who oversees traffic and sics the bull on tramps. Colton is the primary train-building yard in southern California, so it's more likely that we'll catch a constructed freight here instead of a 'through,' one changing crews. The tracks are numbered starting with the two mains on the north side. We squint down the overpass for infrared cameras, see none, and are studying the paved service roads stretching a mile to the Pepper Bridge when Rev exclaims, "I see three FREDs!"

"Memorize the vista!" I answer. "We must know the three track numbers and car types." Seconds later, we clamber down the bank to pursue the standstill trains. We reach the first FRED on the tail of a parked freight of unrideable oil tankers and sealed boxcars. One track over, we see another FRED blinking on a second freight of hoppers with mountable platforms. "I prefer a dry boxcar on a stormy night," objects Rev, so we press forward to the third FRED on the original #4714 train that sports plenty of empties as well as our original sky blue boxcar.

Three freights champing at the bit after five hours wait!

We stand like statues on the ballast between our blue boxcar train and the curved hopper freight, packs shouldered and on tiptoes to catch the first that moves. The hopper jerks and we scale the ladder, but it halts in fifty yards. The boxcar heaves and we belly flop 5 ft. onto the floor. Four locos roar like T-Rexes, belch smoke through our door, and the couplers drumbeat to our boxcar that pitches knocking us to the floor. We stand again as it rattles under the Pepper Bridge, and slides along Interstate-10 east for twenty minutes before entering a green tunnel of Salt Cedars for ten minutes to emerge into a colony of giant 'Naked People.'

The Naked People of Palm Springs inhabit a wind farm of 4000 white windmills on the Gorgonio Pass of the San Bernardino Mountains. Each stands 150 ft. tall with blades half the length of a football field to turn turbine generators that power the Coachella Valley into which the freight plunges at 55 mph. The boxcar, with a light load of two tramps, picks up a harmonic that rock and rolls us into the 70s. I observe Rev's face bounce in jubilation during the acceleration. One hand grasps the boxcar door and the other a Marlboro. "Smoke out a boxcar once, you're hooked!" I scream. This is Norman Rockwell's America through a side-door Pullman, and there is no better history.

Jumping as if he's touched a ghost, Rev yells, "Doc Bo! We forgot to stake the door." Yes, in the rush to choose trains I had discarded a two-by-four wood and he a RR spike to jam open our single sliding door. He reflects with the lit cigarette along the door hinge and gleefully reports it welded open. The boxcar is now sacred, the bread-and-butter hobo ride. It provides moving shelter from weather and bulls, or if you please to stand or sit at the 10-ft. x 20-ft. 'window' on nature. We forage cardboard from previous riders to fashion two bird nests a safe distance from the door on which to plop the sleeping bags to buffet the bounce. High on springs and nests, we sashay down the track with the added comfort that not a thing in the world can get us—telephone, tax collector or spouse.

I breathe easier that we're sliding along the rails. The skies open to stars on the eastern flank of the Coastal Range as we glide down, down to the desert within thirty miles of my digs in Sand Valley, and then across the

Colorado River into Arizona. The engine whistles through night burgs for hours and Rev still refuses to leave his post by the window.

A train tramp has much time on his hands. We read by headlamp, sightsee out our bucking screen, chat very little, and every so often sit at opposite ends of the car reciting hobo poetry (flatulence). He seems preoccupied with the novelty of the trip. Sometimes I think like Voltaire and other times I am like Descartes, but when I ain't I sleep. I awaken throughout the night to see him still at the door 'getting into the world quick,' an old expression describing a young man bitten by wanderlust who takes the first opportunity to jump a freight out of town.

Our focus is the next division point along the high iron where the crew changes and we will have options. The points are spaced about ten hours apart within big yards where the units pause for a minute to an hour to change the engineer and conductor in the lead unit. Before sunrise, our train brakes and stops at the Yuma Amtrak bench, a tempting minute's walk from the city skyline. We grab our gear to detrain but hear voices outside, and peek out the boxcar. The crew changes in a record thirty seconds, and abruptly the freight highballs. Should we leap to the concrete ramp at 3 mph, try to ride like gentlemen a mile away to a mission to debark for free breakfast, or stay aboard? In five  seconds, the 8-mph freight is too fleet to jump with switches hidden in the morning shadows, so the train pulls away with its hobo cargo. "Sometimes you think and sometime you run out of time," I offer at the door, and Rev shrugs as the train accelerates, "I've never seen Tucson."

He sits and wraps his boots in plastic sacks for warmth and watches the rolling tract. Miles later, a strange thing happens: the freight 'goes in the hole' for the first time, stopping. Rev looks up with a pinched face from zero sleep and multiple business texts on his cell. "What's the scoop?" he asks. A rumble on the blind side of our car shakes our feet on the floor, and I peek through a rust hole in the closed door where a westbound 'unit container train' races for the Long Beach container yard. It clears, but fifteen minutes later our freight goes 'on the farm' again for another priority train. Rev glumly surmises, "The other track disappeared." I echo in alarm, "We're on a single rail. This freight just became a dog."

The effect is halving the number of lanes on an Interstate route with laws that the slowest vehicles must stop for others to pass from fore or aft. Our mixed freight is the lowest priority that will pull onto side rails at thirty mile or so intervals across the Arizona desert. My cohort vows to buy a police scanner for the next trip and preprogram it with each RR and yard frequency to listen in to passing engineers and within the yards. We side 22 times in the stretch from Yuma to Tucson.

It's Christmas time. Freight is on the move in America, with lots of toys for little girls and boys. Some container trains from overseas or intra-country are double-stacked, and all whiz by at 70 mph. It's the hobo season of disaffiliation.

Does everyone have to wear society's tight shoes? In the town where I live the citizens fear thought like nothing on earth, more than death, so they squeeze into noisy blocks without an inkling of the city limit. One in ten-thousand steps outside the limit and becomes a philosopher. The trouble with most people is they think with their clichés rather than options and fail to see the switches in life. Not Rev, and other executives I've met. There are sundry reasons for taking to the rails: Irrelevancy of modern society to a thinking man, seeking alternative explanations of an unorthodox lifestyle, quick discovery of self into the unknown, on the lam from John Law, a jilted lover, failed business, or doomed job like mine. I'm free, unchained, debtless, got an itch to travel and the boxcars roll in all directions.

I'm also Rev's exit counselor to ease him from a lifelong program of socialization and thrashing for the buck. Once he becomes aware

Does everyone have to wear society's tight shoes?

of the obvious flaws in the place he's from, and the benefits of another lifestyle, he may step out often as other executives have voiced, 'to taste other realities.' His affiliation to family and business is fierce–I want to steal him to the hobo experience for two days, for balance.

"Well, I used to ride this same steel road home throughout the '90s for Christmas with my family in Dallas. Back then the line was called

Southern Pacific. You never saw such surprised looks on faces, or willing ears to listen to stories of perspective on how I reached them."

Rev dials the cell from the door of the dancing boxcar and looks west. "We're ok, Mom. Eastbound…You too!" He texts his dad, "We're on a freight to Yuma, er… Tucson," who instantly answers, "You've done a great thing that few do!"

Later, the freight trundles to a stop at the Tucson terminus. I look regrettably down the UPRR overland route toward Dallas, and back to Rev, who gently says, "I haven't slept a wink. I didn't want to miss anything, but I have a business to run tomorrow." Yet the train jumps! I must order to stay or bail, so heft my pack, glance from the jiggling floor down at the light scattering ballast and then at Rev framed in moonlight leaping through the boxcar door, and chuckle at how the superintendent got the damning email. The district hung itself in public and I got out just in time for Christmas!

CHICKEN KETCHIN'

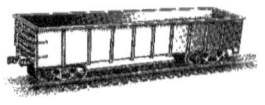

After Easter with the folks in Ft. Worth in the 80s, I boarded an eastbound boxcar and napped, woke up in a mystery town that read Texarkana...

I climbed a little hill away from the yard and hitched a ride along the highway. A U-Haul rental truck picked me up for one of the strangest experiences of my life, and that's saying something.

The lady driver, a fat bitch to this day that owes me for a day's work, opened the roll-down back to the rental truck and said, "Hop in." It was dim in there with scratchy light filtering through the tiny cross-hatch window into the cab, but my eyes adjusted to discern six young people lolling about the floor and on crates. They stared at me with better adjusted eyes, but I could see something the matter in the way their faces twisted and unkempt hair.

'Howaryamorn, mister?' garbled one. A couple others jerked chins in agreement, and one girl giggled. I was in a locked dark van with a half-dozen retards. It wasn't that bad, and I don't intend the term derogatorily, but they crowded the King of the Road stinking of the rails to dig his story.

I did some magic tricks like swallowing my thumb, and pulled a paper wad from the girl's ear– that gave me room to ask, "Where're we goin?"

"Chicken ketchin'!" one cried, and the others nodded eagerly.

We took the smooth road for an hour, then rutted dirt lanes for two more, until the truck bumped to a halt and the door slid up with a bang. What followed was the longest, hardest workday of my life, and that's saying something again.

The teens, girl, and I herded no less than 1000 chickens from one end of a huge red barn to the other, the lady kept them at bay with a flapping sheet, and the rest of us dipped knees and grabbed chicken legs—two in one hand and three in the other per the quota. We carried them twenty flapping yards through the barn door outside to a semi-truck parked with wire chicken crates where one guy perched as each grabber shouted "Birds! Three and two!" and hefted his five up to this cager to stuff into rows and stacks of little crates for the trip to KFC.

Imagine dipping, catching, clutching, lifting and yelling "Birds!" a hundred times for 10 hours with one 30-minute break for salami sandwiches and water. It got hot at noon, freezing after sunset, I was dizzy, covered with feathers, and when the last chicken was scooped and stuffed the old bird herded us into the back of the truck.

"Where do u want off?" she demanded, and I wearily replied, "Freight yard." There's nothing like sitting with peers after a long day in reminisce; they explained the whole way that nobody but a dummy would shout "three and two" and actually hand over that many birds!

The lady turned into the RR yard, I gave her my address for the paycheck, pulled my thumb out my mouth for the crew, and went down the hill to the next adventure.

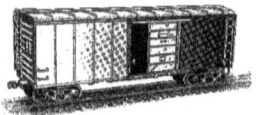

Washington is apple country and in season a northbound hobo is likely an apple knocker...

I'm on a southbound boxcar and there's a clomp, clomp, clomp, outside the moving door. It doesn't make sense and maybe I've gone soft in the head pursuing the American Dream.

Clomp!!... Clomp!!... Clomp!! The steps are further spaced as the train accelerates. A burlap sack sails through the door and bangs the far wall. Suddenly there is a scrape on the wooden floor next to me and a foot disappears out the door. Again a shoed foot enters the door, scuffs the deck and exits. A hobo is trying to catch at 20 mph!!

I peek out the door and there hangs a 'bo on the latch. He's graying, strong, and in tattered clothes, no doubt an apple knocker in trouble. The metal latch of a boxcar hangs like a two-foot stem and 'bos in days of old would grab it on steam trains and swing aboard. It required sharp timing and I've never seen the technique used on modern faster-moving diesel freights.

A pace is reached at which it becomes perilous to let go of the latch and face the ballast, and that's the fate of my peer. His strides are fifty feet long, his lungs heaving and his foot thrusts into the door shortening. In seconds he could grease the rail. He doesn't realize my presence and to pop my mug out the door might frighten him, so I make a decision.

From his perspective, a hand descends from the sky. The skin is tanned, fingers willowy and it beckons. I feel a meaty grasp as his takes mine in a death-lock. The train picks up speed.

I've traveled most the gridiron west of the Mississippi, camped the jungles. Been around the world in a boxcar, I tell folks, since that's the estimated rail mileage in some 300 rides. Though I'm just a boxcar tourist out for summer scenery and adventure, it's ironed the body.

From his perspective, a hand descends from the sky. The skin is tanned, fingers willowy and it beckons. I feel a meaty grasp as his takes mine in a death-lock. The train picks up speed.

Now a King of the Road dangles like a scarecrow from the side of a fast freight, attached only by my hand. He's my size and I pull hard, but it's a tug-of-war as the rail joints click by. Seated, I skid along the floor toward the edge and waiting space. Then my trouser seat catches an oil spill and I scoot to the door.

BAM. My foot hits the door frame and braces for the final pull. Tenaciously I lift. He has blue eyes, like mine. With a heave he's in the boxcar and safe.

There are a number of unwritten rules of the steel road:

- ☐ First, don't steal anyone's boots.
- ☐ Second, look after yourself first.
- ☐ Third, if you're okay then give a hand to peers.
- ☐ Fourth, no need to speak of the obvious.
- ☐ Fifth, partings come easily.

The fellow crawls panting to a far corner, dragging the burlap, then sits on it in silence. We jiggle along for miles without a word. The sun sinks and still nothing, as the train passes from Washington to Oregon. Somewhere in California the freight stops and he slides out the door, shaking my hand.

I've never picked an apple, but I've picked a hobo.

I was with Terry Terrific in a borrowed VW van that had 10% brakes. In the early evening in Lansing, Michigan, in '78 we approached RR tracks...

...where the lights were flashing and no swing-down gate was present. I looked left and right twice, then proceeded *slowly*... BAM!

The train emerged from behind a building obscured in the darkness. The VW bent in half and slid 10 ft. off the ground on the cowcatcher. I hung onto the steering wheel to keep from falling out the driver's window onto the rail before the oncoming locomotive wheels. Both thumbs

sprained, I watched the world slide by, as the girl hit her head against the window and passed out. The freight stopped within a few-hundred meters and the engineer helped us down. The next morning was golden—my gal still had a pretty face that could stop a freight train, and I had survived my first hobo ride.

Painting courtesy Linda Mears

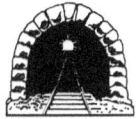

"A hobo is plumb loco to go into that mountain on Dirty Face. Bulls drag out guys long past lookin' blue."

That's what yard workers and old 'bos caution on the transcontinental route west of the Rockies because engine smoke snuffs life. Nevertheless, a few hours ago in Nevada I was obligated to board an eastbounder just behind six big engines that rumble like beasts.

Now the flatcar rolls under my buttocks and the Colorado breeze and sunshine smack full on the face, until I look up and see the tunnel mouth approach at 30 mph. There're many ways to skin a cat, and I tick each off:

> *"A hobo is plumb loco to go into that mountain on Dirty Face. Bulls drag out guys long past lookin' blue."*

- ☐ the ballast's a blur and too sharp to jump onto

- ☐ the engineer's mirror shows him rapt or I'd wave to slow

- ☐ the brake hose dangles nearby for an emergency stop, but the bulls would have my ears at the next yard

The last option is to count the green pines marching like a gauntlet to the opening in the mountain.

The car I hold down is a piggyback—semi-truck trailer mounted on a flatcar. This pig has a history: It may have begun at a San Francisco port loaded with Oriental windup dolls, then hauled by truck to the freight yard. There the trailer was placed on a flatcar for the sweep by iron road to New York, where it'll roll off and be pulled by truck to a store for unloading. The pig is always part of an express train that cannonballs across the nation faster than a Greyhound bus, and with more comforts. I can recline beneath the belly, or lean against one of the fat tires as I do now for a 360-degree view. It's a throne for a king of the road, ordinarily.

Photo by Josh the Wanderer

Now the bore engulfs the six locomotives and the tail of smoke touches the throne, then my world turns black. I feel in the rucksack for a bandana to snug around nose and mouth, and a sweater to wrap the jaw and neck. I've passed through hundreds of tunnels in America without incident, but never the Moffat, the longest at six miles.

"If ya gotta ride through Moffat, don't sit near the engines or yer last breath will be a hot, stinky one." I can't heed the warning today.

One mile into the tunnel _____

Noise ricochets along the shaft. Air burns. Dizziness arrives. Deep in reflection

Two miles into the tunnel _____

A road partner, Iron Horse, and I once rode into St. Louis. Let's jump before the yard—big city bulls are nonsense, I say. Lead the way, he replies warmly. But a white Bronco with a CB antenna pulls aside the moving freight before we vault. A pistol points at my heart, and a bull behind it. "If you have a weapon I will shoot you."

The freight jerk-stops and the Bronco brakes. "We have no weapons. Shall we disembark here? I do three things in the initial minute with a bull: Show my hands even if he doesn't bring up weapons; acknowledge his authority by asking permission to move; and toss a two-bit word to tip I'm not an unintelligent drunk. It surprises how high a bull's eyebrows raise with the mention of a three-syllable word.

Get off. Iron Horse and I hop to the ground looking like we just rode from the Pacific, which we did, and the dick separates us from our gear before putting the gun away. I place him as a Viet Nam vet by age, demeanor, and an earlier cheekbone hollow now filled by easy living. There are lots of war veterans on the rail carrying a bindle or wearing a badge.

Iron Horse is a Minneapolis stand-up comic, and veteran dumpster diver. Right off, he butters the bull. "Officer, what's the most feared animal in the freight yard?" "Not sure," I answer for the cop who glares at Iron's dirty beard, tattered overalls, and rats nest hair. "The weasel, officer. Whoo hoo, look out for the train weasel."

I shrink, and don't blame the bull if he shoots Iron. Instead, he guffaws. "I'm giving you guys a break, and a ride out of the yard. Come back and be arrested." Iron takes the cue and launches an advanced repertoire. The bull flees shaking his head like he's been in the funnies, with my partner yelling as we board the freight, "Officer, this train leaves in five minutes. Be under it!"

*Three miles into the tunnel*_____

I slip deeper under the piggy-back for cooler breaths but find only rank gas. Noise deafens. It's pitch black and another memory takes hold:

Once, I wish to catch a freight from Salt Lake's Rio Grande yard, tarrying all morning by the main line in the woods. I enter the yard to solicit information. The ploy is to hide the pack and stroll boldly through the employee gate wearing a washed face from a nearby brook and clean overalls to pass for a worker. I get the dope from a brakeman, then exit without the bull knowing better. Later, the intelligence proves false as no train arrives, so I case the area for a telephone. If one's found the ruse is to phone the yardmaster who monitors arrivals and departures. The conversation typically goes: "Hello, this is Mr. Jones calling from Farm Lane outside the city. The wife wants to snap a photo of the engines passing our barn. What time's the next train leave?" The usual response is, "Two p.m., Mr. Jones. Say hi to the missus." Sadly, today the nearest phone is at too far a march, so I search for a novel stratagem as the day's light fades.

Although too greasy now to reenter the yard as a worker, fallen tree limbs litter the field between the woods and the workers hut next to the security tower. I devise to rascal in as a tree. I hold a branch my height and having thick foliage at arms length and edge toward the hut. Ten slow steps—pause—ten more. I'm inside the yard in five minutes where a different brakeman provides the correct departure time, and I retrace the same way. Sure enough, here she comes on schedule fresh full of diesel. I slide into a gondola and ride out.

*Four miles into the tunnel*_____

Beside myself with suffocation, I must remember or pass out.

Years after my debut as a tree in the Rio Grande yard, a bull tangle leads to a court date. This time it's at Salt Lake's sprawling Union Pacific yard with two partners—Gizmo Kid, a computer wizard at IBM, and Colorado Casey, a best-selling business author and consultant. We ride atop a portable parking lot (automobile carrier) into the Mormon city.

Three specific freight cars the tramp must turn to with caution:

☐ the locomotive, though I've ridden them through snowstorms to be near the heater

☐ the piggyback with its valuable cargo under lock and key

☐ and the car carrier where radios and tape decks can be heisted

Why does an honest man board the latter? Sometimes a car door key is taped under the bumper, and that extra set of springs is comfy, especially with a hoboette. There's music, and a plaque on the window with the car's destination.

In fact, I point out a previously broken car window to the two men that leads to discussion on what to do if the bull spots us getting off. He'll surely inspect us and the automobiles. In any other scenario, the cop's first nab is a courtesy let-go, the second is a ticket, and the third is a ride to the cross-bars hotel. But today, there's a vandalizing that could finger us.

The train stops with the quandary still hanging. The hobo code says to keep quiet and let others, except road partners, fend for themselves. However, another urges to protect the good hobo name. Squeezed by the thoughts, I decide to tattle if the bull nabs us, but if not that's that. The bull spins up in a white Scout. "Sir, there's a window we didn't break." He doesn't swallow it and writes three summons to appear in Salt Lake court within three days. We go the next morning.

The judge, with a graying top and leftover smile from decades of pounding the mallet, sees us instantly. I propose to take the rap since I ratted to the bull, plus the other two have business meetings later this week. His honor asks us each about ourselves, and even so the Gizmo Kid eyes the elderly man's Freemason ring. The Kid, having once caught a set of encyclopedias in his head, flashes the judge the secret fraternal sign.

Dismissed without prejudice! I gawk at the Kid who whispers it means we go free. I start to mumble thanks, but the judge cuts me short, "Men, it's all part of the adventure."

*Five miles into the tunnel*_____

I'm a poisoned bug on a mechanical worm. Smoke balls the stomach and limbs twitch until, with one mile to go, I faint.

At the opening there's a sharp sweetness of fresh air and sunlight. I made it!

On the downhill miles, I philosophize. I didn't go into that tunnel reckless and didn't come out brave, only scrambled inside. It ain't disgraceful to dance a dying jig to the grim reaper's fiddle, and this just was one of those days. I'll hold down a different pig another day, but not through six miles of smoke.

"Yer plumb loco to enter Moffat twice."

[What happened to them? Colorado Doug Casey is a noteworthy financial author/advisor who moved to Argentina, Arthur 'Gizmo Kid' Tyde III created the two billion dollar LinuxCare and flies a private plane. Iron Horse Iowa Blackie was elected National Hobo King on a platform of stamina rather than humor on the sixteenth try at Britt, Iowa. Doc Bo Keeley is still seen in a laptop glow behind Dirty Face, the locomotive.]

October 19, 2006

It was Fall of 1985 in Lansing, Michigan, sixty years after the last hobo class had been taught in America...

Dusting my clothes after a rough and tumble summer in boxcars, jungles, and skid rows around the country, it dawned on me as the first snowflakes fell on my nose that those who can hobo do, and those who won't any more teach.

There is no more fertile ground to plant a romantic theme than a campus. I walked cold into the Sociology Department at Lansing (Michigan) Community College and shook hands with Dr. Dean Heater. "My name is Doc Bo, and I want to teach a class about hobo life in America." He turned white behind that red tie but his blue eyes twinkled and he surprisingly replied, "Tell me more."

"This is the season," I explained, "when hobos beat a path to winter quarters, and I haven't picked mine." I enumerated that I was a jack-of-all-trades including veterinarian, author and publisher, pro jock, landlord, speculator, and world traveler. I had been a boxcar tourist for ten summers in riding all the high irons west of the Mississippi, plus many of the mains to the East. I had attended five National Hobo Conventions in Britt, Iowa, collected maybe the world's only and largest hobo library and, smiling quickly, added, "I need to make a stake for the spring."

"Okay," said Dr. Heater slapping his thigh. "Sign up the minimum eight students and you have a hobo class." I pumped his hand optimistically and blurt, "I'll call it 'Hobo Life in America.'"

Promotion was the first step. I tacked green posters on every building and telephone pole within tramping distance of the college. These portrayed a Weary Willie with a beer in one hand and text in the other under the banner, "Hobo Class—I Want You!" I also notified local barbers, waitresses, and college teachers to spread the word. The responders were eclectic but with three strange commonalities: They were sober, stable, and eager.

The first two, a deaf mute and an attorney, trailed the sparkling hallway to the sociology office and paid for the course. Three more, an anthropologist, electrician, and historian signed to threaten the class minimum... and then, as Dr. Heater announced, "All hell broke loose!" as thirty-six enrolled. They included a deejay, accountant, computer programmer, two secretaries, three housewives, waitresses, many local students, and a couple of in-house professors.

The next step was to fulfill Dr. Heater's sudden order to produce a syllabus and class text. Most of the students I had previewed sought the course for fun, a little bite of the hobo life, and four easy credits, but they hadn't reckoned how leather-tough their prof had turned from those tens of thousands of rail miles.

I rented a basement for $100 per month and bought a $50 coffin from the college woodshop teacher who was desperate for cash. It was a simple pine coffin that I lined with electric blankets against the blast of icy Michigan winds through the window cracks, and each night prior to the first class a week away, I lowered the lid with growing distress. I hadn't been in front of a crowd in years.

Next to the coffin lay an unused door that I put on blocks as a desk and piled it high with old hobo books. I had perceived that teaching hobo life at a college was original and novel, but reading late one night I'd found an amazing precedent. Sixty years earlier, Dr. Ben Reitman started a Hobo College in Chicago. Dr. Reitman was an oddball hybrid of physician and hobo king during an era when syphilis and steam trains were very hot stuff about the nation. The iron roads across America crawled with itinerant workers, families adrift, travelers with dream-filled knapsacks, and boxcar vacationers looking at the scenery.

Thus, each fall as chilly winds sniffed up their cuffs in the Windy City, hundreds of enrollees poured into the heated Hobo College. They were a fascinating stew of the road including educated home guards, apple knockers, harvest hands, gandy dancers, and nobody knew who else that tumbled from a freight and rambled along back streets and into the Hobo College. They initially entered a warm, spacious room to swap soup line and slave market addresses, exchange bull tales, sing out bawdy tramping songs, and bury their noses deep in the hobo library. One and all awaited the arrival of Doc Reitman.

I read, as if there, that he strode into the hall with an easy, confident purpose as befits a traveled man. He spoke from the hip with animation on topics ranging from self-image as the first rung in the ladder in life, to the tramp in the American work ethic, to practical advice on pocketing urinal soap against gray soldiers (lice). The throng sat enthralled. Group courses followed Reitman's introductory remarks on English composition, philosophy, public speaking, and law. In the evening, the Doc invited in noteworthy speakers such as E.W. Burgess (sociology), Herman Adler (psychology), and Jim Tully (literature) to round the education.

However, the main thrust daily was clean and simple: Identify the void in a person and fill it. Predictably, a week after entering the College, a down-at-the-heels walk-on could 'graduate' with a job, flop, clean clothes, extended vocabulary, and the association of peers. How often anywhere at any time in the United States have the masses received these options in rounding a bend toward prosperity?

School doors swung open each fall and closed every spring for two decades through smoky criticism, so that by the end of the 1920s thousands of men roaming the countryside had been educated at the first Hobo College in Chicago. I sat on the edge of my bed and determined that my course would run as parallel to Reitman's as a set of old rails.

Inspired by his muse, I bore down and in two all-nighters in the basement wrote the 100-page combined syllabus/text called 'The Hobo Training Manual.' The next day, just hours before the term's opening bell, I placed it in Dr. Heater's hand. The Dean thoughtfully paged for ten minutes, nodded and proclaimed, "It's a go, Doc Bo!"

Predictably, a week after entering the [Ben Reitman's Hobo] College, a down-at-the-heels walk-on could 'graduate' with a job, flop, clean clothes, extended vocabulary, and the association of peers. How often anywhere at any time in the United States have the masses received these options in rounding a bend toward prosperity?!

That night the wide-eyed arrivals to the first class entered not a classroom but a hoboemia of RR maps, steam engine photos, company flags, early Salvation Army posters, and on one corner table a hundred-book hobo library. The rolling lyrics of the 'Wabash Cannonball' echoed from wall to wall, and the math teacher in the next room took one peek in and shut my door. However, I saw it all from outside my room window, and then down at the lavatory with the backwards trots. I drew purpose there from the memory of Reitman, rose tall as I could, and strode down the hard hallway and into my door.

I turned down the music and began, "I've traveled the world, and hopped about 300 freights in this country. Dined in some of the finest restaurants in the land, and eaten on Exec Hobos floors. Been surrounded by hostile lawyers on movie deals, and circled with grim men the last ounce in a community wine bottle. Crossed international borders with sleight of hand, and worked out of skid row jams by telling an anecdote from across the tracks... And found room in other tight spots by relating tales from the real hobo world to a group like you. This perspective, I believe, qualifies me as your instructor to talk the rest of this term about Hobo Life in America." I shut my mouth, shrank into my overalls, and stared out a buttonhole awaiting the class reaction.

They thundered applause!

Thereafter the victory, I loped into the room with a ready grin in overalls and a different suit coat from the Goodwill... a tweed one night, a woolen the next, for variety. I climbed atop my desk at the front blackboard covered with RR maps, and instructed a bandana-blinded student to stick a pin with a ribbon into the country map behind me. I was challenged to produce a chestnut from my past within an inch of the tack. Thus my teaching method evolved to stoke them and then push home the lesson.

Each class presented a fresh sliver of the hobo life without ever stepping into a rail yard! Each topic had a new expert speaker:

- ☐ Michigan Supreme Court Justice Mike Cavanaugh explained 'Law and the Hobo'

- ☐ MSU economics professor emeritus Charles Larrowe detailed 'Bo-economics'

- ☐ Reverend Moncrief pounded tramp religion at my class

- ☐ English professor Mike Steinberg contrasted Huckleberry Finn to the modern tramp

- ☐ an anthropologist traced hobo history back to the hoe-boys of the Civil War

- ☐ a venerable steam train tramp named Ole Gravy reminisced his early rides

☐ Peter Carrington taught wild edibles, professional dumpster diver Tom brought watermelon from his digs

☐ psychiatrist Andrew Homa clarified the breakout of mental patients onto the rails in the 1970s

☐ and Boogie Bob Baldori of the Chuck Berry Band ground out good old hobo blues on a mouth harp

The class reaction? Lots of hand clampin' and foot stompin' every night. The deaf girl even brought a signer. I watched everyone hurrah and file out the room after each session, sometimes amused or shaken, but always eager to return.

Until one night a big RR bull came to class. This is the railroad cop, the cinder dick, the hobo nightmare. He hulked in the frame of the class door with hardly a prior notice—as a good bull should—as the period opened. I stood up front as we checked each other out in a classical bull vs. 'bo standoff. He was out of uniform in an impeccable coat-and- tie with a tiny gold lapel star, while I wore the flawless tramp attire of bib overalls and a Pendleton shirt. He eyed me even as I looked up and back. From the crow's feet at his graying temples, I imagined he had 'made' a thousand stiffs like me, much as I had sized a hundred bulls like him.

In a flash, we struck a warm accord. He walked in and introduced himself as the supervisor of security for Southern Pacific RR. "I've just driven ninety miles from Detroit to investigate this hobo course," he said simply. He squeezed into a front row desk. I took a deep breath myself, thought of what Ben Reitman would do, and started the lecture on bulls. Things proceeded normally for twenty minutes until he suddenly rose from the desk and announced to all, "There is nothing wrong with this class. I am enjoying myself and want to make sure I'm not obstructing routine." I replied at once, "Please come to the podium," which he did. "The job of the railroad policeman..." he spoke and held spellbound the class to hear the other side of the coin.

Maybe his concern about the course was justified. Over the weeks, word of the hobo experience spread from Lansing throughout Michigan and into neighboring states. The original glimmers appeared in a couple of local underground newspapers. Then the Lansing College newspaper burst a front-page banner, 'Doc Bo teaches Hobo Life in America.' Two state university papers picked up the story, followed by public newspapers throughout Michigan. Letters to the editor surged with responses that were never tepid.

Meanwhile, my course chugged forward as more speakers rallied to the podium. Radio stations thrust mikes before my mug, and many television interviews followed. A movie crew showed in class to document a special, 'Hobo Life in America.' I brought our house dog, Tramp, to throw the limelight off me but my blood pressure climbed and sleep became difficult.

One day out of the blue, Dr. Heater summoned me to lower a boom like a clanging traffic crossbar. "There's bad news, Doc Bo," he cried plucking a letter from a stack on his desk. "What's the bum doing teaching our young citizens to be street people?" he read. "Get rid of that hobo or drop me from the Alumni Association," he quoted another, and then tapped one more note to the Governor of Michigan that he wouldn't let me view. The exasperated Dr. Heater then looked up kindly and clarified, "You aren't teaching that but it's the public perception. This meeting is just to prepare for your future, Doc Bo." I left the Dean's office feeling suffocated as if having passed through a tunnel of smoke in the Rockies.

A week later on graduation day, I pulled from my mailbox a notice bearing the Lansing College presidential seal. It was a 'cease and desist' order for the hobo class. The prez being untouchable, I stalked to Dr. Heater and asked, "What gives?"

A week later on graduation day, I pulled from my mailbox a notice bearing the Lansing College presidential seal. It was a 'cease and desist' order for the hobo class. The prez being untouchable, I stalked to Dr. Heater and asked, "What gives?"

"Just as easily as your class door was opened by public interest, it was shut by public pressure. Your course, though successful in terms of pupil numbers and financial gain for the college, made life miserable in the sociology and president's offices. Today an order for its termination came down from the highest." He shook my hand and bid, "I'm sorry. It was a grand class!"

Before the final bell toll, I returned the final exams to the students-everyone passed- and handed each a hobo diploma at the door. A few hats lofted through the air. I turned, locked the door, and slipped the key under the crack.

I saw the triumphant hobo class as just another curve in life. I'd made a spring stake, sold the coffin for a little on the side, and hit the road.

Any beggary tips I proffer are from observations on a hundred skid rows across America and in a hundred countries, with one exception.

Hobos call it 'throwing your feet' with so much walking and standing. It stares you in the face that the more panhandlers, the worse the times, and the higher the takes the bigger the boom.

Quick on the heels of a begging market comes the calamity of a region being bummed out. One year, I hopped out a boxcar along the Milk and Honey Route because of the easy alms in Salt Lake City, the Mecca. Tightened mouths under drawn hats greeted me on every corner in tramp heaven until I asked, "Why?"

"The city's bummed out!" one, and then the next cried stretching palms.

"But why?" I wondered.

"The Bishop's givin' eats." I followed a string of pointed fingers to the Bishop's front porch and a queue of thirty willing workers to sweep, wash dishes, or run errands for one hour for a big sack of groceries. The news had spread like fleas up and down the rails to bring a great flux, until supply-demand had forced the immigrants to throw their feet like common beggars.

Salt Lake was bummed out. The missions jammed with not a tree remaining to sleep under, and it took a month to recover. However, I

was set like Aesop's grasshopper with twenties in my boots.

Panhandling is the world's second oldest profession, whatever the times, so reach out to a beggar with austerity. Fully 80% of the men leaning on stop signs at intersections with upraised hands are on a government dole. The single women there have a man hiding behind a bush or building to periodically pop out to bank the cash before she's looted by another panhandler. They are nearly all welfare moonlighters.

A Las Vegas Viet Nam veteran asserted—at least he wore a veteran's baseball cap—"I clear $50 daily in the casino parking lots, and on busy days $100." He migrated casino to casino judging people to tap by their gesticulations after leaving the one-armed bandits. He sauntered off chewing a hash brownie. I estimate that 50% of the millions panhandled in the US alone go for drugs and steaks rather than the "Please give for food," "Baby needs milk," and so on that is covered by Food Stamps.

Panhandling is the world's second oldest profession, whatever the times, so reach out to a beggar with austerity.

Bear times and holidays throw open hearts to win jackpots everywhere. Easter and Christmas bring the best pickin's and I can't say the number of times I've hidden behind a park bench or dumpster to keep a holiday do-gooder from forcing a turkey dinner on me.

Internationally, I recently tailed in a busy Saigon market a blind panhandler with a white cane strapped to his back and an outstretched tin cup in one hand, bullhorn in the other, bellowing pleas. I know he was blind because he walked into a truck mirror, yet when I followed him beyond to a coffee shop he pulled a thick wad for coffee and donuts as others clustered around the table. Legitimate beggars have bankrolls to share with less fortunate friends.

The beggar stakes his busy territory and guards it jealously. If a region is bummed out the fix is to move into trafficked lanes. In many countries such as El Salvador they board buses and hum a tune, pass out 'I am deaf' fliers or sing a psalm before staggering the aisle for payment. It is simply a job to rise to each morning. One Guatemalan beggar was a smiling legless, armless basket case who boarded my bus on the shoulder of his amigo and ambled the aisles at great profit. At the next stop he was chucked to another man who boarded a selected full bus, and little doubt each porter took his fee.

In India a crippled or scarred beggar is the golden goose, with a protective owner because beggary runs the low life economy and in a hungry recession he or she becomes the mark. Here in Lake Toba, Sumatra, the coming rains have decreased tourism and turned Batak villagers to cultivate the fields where drunks live hand-to-mouth knocking on fence posts to pull weeds for small change. There is no tinkle in the cup because a dine is a paper bill.

In Egypt, in a miserable sandstorm, a man dashed from an alley, pleaded for alms, and when I shook my head emphatically no he jumped on my striding thigh and humped it like the affectionate dogs up and down the kennel arteries of veterinary school. It is no shame that when people get hungry they will resort to anything to feed themselves and families.

Music moochers are everywhere. In a NYC subway once a roughly dressed young man closed in singing patriotic songs so pathetically that when I put on earmuffs to block the din he drummed on my shoulder with a dollar bill until I shouted, "I don't come that cheap!"

Virtuoso panhandling is a joy. How does it differ from the chamber music you pay a ticket to hear? My Sand Valley neighbor Sweet Pie altered New England statutes for burlesque music and has a standing invitation from Jay Leno to appear clad in the scantiest frill jockstrap to play the piano with a left hand signature Liberace said was the best he'd ever seen. His CD melodies confirm, and a scrapbook of *Playboy*, *Penthouse*, and other risqué rags arm-in-arm with Dolly Parton and other musicians. He rejected Carnegie Hall until the contract allows after a performance to 'pull the purse' strolling the audience with a saddlebag hanging from his scrotum to hold up to 30lbs. of tips like the good old days.

Then there are the egghead beggars. The best I recall was a San Francisco adept on Pier 39 shouting mathematical solutions to columns of numbers and long divisions from passers-by to win change for each correct answer. But who could check him?

Are you surprised that a pro makes more per hour than you or I?

The single exception to never having less than a hundred dollars worth of twenties in each boot was in the mid-1990s in Minneapolis where the boots were stolen. It was the projects section and so simple to borrow a quarter for the phone. On learning penniless at midnight that support would not arrive for three days, I walked into the police station and asked for a cell to overnight. Instead, the manager ran me in a squad car to the psych ward for a three-day hold pending the mental state. I was released on being able to memorize the serial numbers of a few bills in the head shrinks wallet as we played liar's poker.

I could make the beggar venture anywhere because of an early mentor. Beggary, after all, is business or sport where the path is paved by an early teacher.

In Los Angeles in the late 1980s the classic Midnight Mission catered to down-and-out stew bums, car tramps, and hobos alike. You walk in the peeling paint arch, sign an alias, put your gear in a locker, and take a towel, bar of soap and hot shower. Then you read donated dog-eared *Women's Days* for an hour until the supper bell beckons 'feed the spirit before the stomach' and you stuff into church pews among the lot of demon tattooed cursing jailbirds, and good tramps, too, to listen to an 'ear pounding' from the 'sky pilot,' which is to say a sermon. The meal follows, and a winding stair into the building bowels to drop your pants for the Wood Lamp lice check whom are not the only creatures glowing in the dark. Then back up the stairs to the bunkhouse to sleep with your wallet between your legs. I heard gunshots outside all night in a crescendo of snores and flatulence.

The next morning I exited the Mission and was instantly accosted by a man with a tin leg that he banged with a long .45 revolver alternately pointed at my forehead, and wouldn't stop bragging about his nitroglycerin bank heists in the old days... until a tall shadow overtook him. I looked up and a large bewhiskered old man blocked the sun.

"Put the guy away you fool!" The tin legged man simpered off with a resounding ping, and I turned to face my benefactor.

Now I understand it was a likely set-up for my donation; however all I could offer was, "Thank you. How can I possibly repay..."

He held high a huge black palm, brought it down square in front of my nose and smiled with seven teeth, "A tip will do."

Instead, I bought a begging lesson from the beggar.

That my mentor had persuaded the American metropolises became obvious as he removed his hat, stringy hair drifted onto his chest, and he pushed it aside to assault each five-minute passer-by with, "I'll bet you're from so-and-so." When he was right he got a bill, when he was close he got their attention, and when he missed the people walked on.

He instructed to always have a tale to stop a Santa Claus in his tracks, and punch it with a reason for a bit of change—$0.83 to be exact that would fetch a dollar. I had a bank of stories and stood at his elbow competing for alms, beseeching while listening, and imitating each trick with my next mark. The key lesson like any sales pitch from Walmart to Macy's is know your customer, break the ice, and appeal to his logic, emotion, or intellect... to get into his wallet.

He won hands down as I could not volunteer tears to my eyes to close the big deals. My few dollars went into his hat that I saw as a free begging lesson.

The tips I picked up are:

Advanced Beggary: 10 Steps if You Please

"Who should I give to?" at the fingertips of a beggar. A ten-step resolution to the quandary:

1. When I receive something of value then I give back in same whether it's to a beggar or otherwise.

2. If the beggar is a hard case cripple then I give unless he's in a pool of givers, which is usually the case.

3. Don't cave into children because they're usually sent by parents or older siblings,

4. I've never met a down-and-out female.

5. You may know anyone not as a beggar but an honest person by his condition: bright eyed but thin from lack of nutrition is in need.

6. You may know a needy person by his acceptance of a meal instead of money for the story of his life.

7. Never give to anyone with alcohol on his breath.

8. Never give to the mother of many children.

9. Don't make favorites; a panhandler with one favorite has many.

10. Don't yield to an animal act such as the mouse riding the cat riding the dog.

by Emilie Dannenberg
April 6, 2011

London born Emilie Dannenberg came to USA to study computers and as Boxcar Dolly follows Boxcar Bertha in this book's dedication for telling breathtaking yarns. This is her version of our Hobo Halloween.

Nevada is dark and cold. We prowl the outskirts of the freight yard and scan the fence for holes. We dart furtively in and out of shrubs. Then the quiet gives way to chaos. Horns bellow. Pistons hiss. Metal jars, catches on metal. Hard, blunt drums puncture the ringing of steel. The wheels arc. The rhythms renew. An anguished screech rips from under the wheels, and the train grinds to a stop.

"Now we are peering into the yard," Bo says. "We memorize the cars and take a mental note of the rideables."

I met Bo a year and a half ago at a shamanism conference in Peru. He promised me a freight trip but had to cancel when hepatitis intervened. This is the makeup trip. I've ridden freights a few times, but I welcome the opportunity to learn the ropes proper. Bo has been riding freights for decades. He is more than 30 years my senior. He has taught a sociology course on hobos and has made a hobby of taking high-flying executives on the rails. It seems I could have no better guide.

We walk briskly around the perimeter of the yard. Bo is hypersensitive to every possibility and exudes paranoia. He rambles in a thick, continuous flow. Every hundred yards he conjures a new story to tell police in the event that we are stopped.

"Our story is that we hitchhiked in from the Bay with a trucker," he says as we walk by the highway.

"Our story is that we are catching a freight," he says as we approach the yard.

He continues to monologue. I lag behind and try to plug my ears with my fingers. We head down an alleyway that is dark, infested with weeds and disused fragments of track. We enter the yard into a gritty orange light that barely dilutes the darkness. A car rolls up the service road toward us. Its headlights glower at us, searing and clinical.

"Hide, hide behind the bush!" Bo yells.

We press our backs to the wall of a building. The car bears down on us. The headlights sweep over our stiffened bodies, and we are illuminated by lights from above, lights from the side. We are blatant, luminous fugitives. But the car swerves past us out to the road. Maybe the rail police don't trouble themselves with such inept attempts at stealth.

We walk briskly to a grain car with a platform. We spend the next hours cowering from cars and yard workers in sleep-deprived paranoia. Bo constricts his hood around his face and retreats inside so that only a white moon of nose and mouth are visible. Our train spasms down the track in frustrated increments. The cold sun rises over the mountain. My senses are warped from exhaustion. Bo climbs into the cubbyhole of the

grain car and falls asleep.

Finally, the train moves forward, and our grain car jolts in a steady rhythm.

I stir out of a heavy sleep. I watch the desert roll by. What a strange color Nevada is, I think. Pastel pink and green, the sweeping, pointed mountains.

In Elko, Nevada, Bo tries to crush coins under the train wheels. "A classic hobo pastime," he tells me. The train jerks unpredictably and the coins have to be abandoned.

Our car is afflicted by a nervous tick. Often, it falls out of sync with the car behind, and the couplers slam together, the impact creating a mini-explosion. Our car spasms and I am thrown forward. My nerves are shaken.

"Next stop: Salt Lake City," Bo says.

Snowcapped mountains rear up in the distance. The light thins into darkness.

I fall asleep, but throughout the night our car convulses, and I'm sucked back out into rattling metal, the biting air and the land reeling around me.

A fresh turn of the earth. The land has become craggier. Sediment rock stacks up into jutting towers and sheers off into canyons. The color of the land is harder.

The sun crests toward the horizon.

There is no Salt Lake City in sight.

"Slow f***ing train," Bo says.

Darkness blankets us again. We pass through a town. This must be Salt Lake City, I think. But we shudder straight through.

Bo pries his upper body from the floor, still wrapped in his sleeping bag.

"We're lost," he says. "Loose adrift across America."

He glances behind him. When he turns back to me, there's an incredulous look on his face.

"Look where we are."

I peer behind him. A large, illuminated sign pulses in a dull yellow light.

Welcome to Cheyenne, Wyoming.

The sign sweeps behind the train.

The train slows and the racket dims, only to be replaced by Bo's curt, bossy voice. "Memorize the last three restaurants we pass. Every time you see a new one, drop the last on the list," he says, just one of many orders I tune out. This man is obsessive, but it is a strange pathology. He exhausts himself exerting whatever small control he can in activities that defy control. "Neurotic hobo:" an uncomfortable oxymoron.

The train comes to a stop, and I cast my rucksack from the train with a feeble throw. I have not eaten in 36 hours. My legs are rickety. We step briskly across a wide dark road, toward the big neon sign of the gas station, and a cold wind nips at our faces. In the gas station, we deliberate how to return California-ward. Bo takes charge and grumbles his demands.

"Call the information line," he says. "Call Greyhound."

"Ask for the next three buses," he says. "Ask for the fare." He is gruff and impatient.

I end the call and he says, "Did you ask if the route was direct? Did you ask for schedules from Salt Lake City?"

His voice has an edge of exasperation. For a moment, I feel like a subpar secretary; then irritation springs up inside me.

"You ask," I say.

"No."

"Why?"

Does he think I like riding freight trains because I enjoy taking orders?

"I'll tell you why," he says, "because it's a wilderness out here, and you don't know what to do."

This does not bend me into submission.

"Go on, walk out the f***ing door right now," I say.

"Let's compromise," he says, not missing a beat, and I hand over the phone. It turns out our best chance is a bus from Salt Lake City that leaves the next day at midday. We will catch a freight back to Salt Lake City tonight.

Back outside we march along the tracks in the darkness. Bo pulls far ahead, a solitary, sulking silhouette. I realize Bo offers no security. He is no longer a leader; I must fend for myself.

It is not long before a train winds up the track. We jog between stack cars and climb ladders, searching for a crevice. We jam ourselves into a trough. It is too small for two long-legged people.

"You take the other platform; there isn't space for two," Bo says.

He has a smirk on his face because my trough is on the front side of the car. If the train makes an emergency stop, I'll be the one crushed by the load.

"Good call," I say, and cross over.

We pass back through western Wyoming. The crusted, gritty landscape yawns out on either side. Grey clouds pile up into storm clouds, then the cloud loosens and disperses, and the sun pries a gap through the clouds and anoints the land in great rectangles of light. I watch the stretched, golden land. I watch the trailers and creaky farm buildings reel by. The sun grazes the horizon. I have forgotten about the bus.

Dark green vegetation spreads over the coarse desert and takes charge. A crystal river winds amongst the trees. White mountain peaks tower into the sky. The train stops. I ask Bo, seasoned hobo, if he has any idea where we are.

"Looks like Idaho," he says.

"What?" I say.

This is not the state we were aiming for, but I stare out in wonder as the day fragments into final bursts of white light. The light flashes out from behind black, angry storm clouds. The metal angles of our car grow more severe, as if solidifying or bracing themselves against a sky in turmoil. The wheels spin madly as if trying to flee the vast, apocalyptic beauty of the land. We twist by hillsides cast in dark shadow. I cower from the searing, gaping sky. I can barely look at the mountains because they frighten me.

The wheels spin madly as if trying to flee the vast, apocalyptic beauty of the land. We twist by hillsides cast in dark shadow. I cower from the searing, gaping sky. I can barely look at the mountains because they frighten me.

I feel like we are careening toward the edge of the world. But the darkness draws in, and inside my sleeping bag, cradled by the noise and rhythm, I feel strangely content.

The next day we get off in La Grande, Oregon, to stock up on food and drink before continuing west. Back in the yard, a string of refrigerator cars pulls in, and the engineer tells us that they are heading for Portland. We climb up a ladder, onto the high, jutting platform. We pick up speed through pine trees stacked up slopes, past rivers edging into banks, more trees. The noise is deafening. The freight churns deep, pulsing drumbeats and frantic snare drums. The sound works open the cracks in my head and sweeps the fragments up into sound. Choir voices align from the wheels and friction. They overlay ricocheting drums and sing out into the night in harmony. My senses are inundated by sound and I am left with my thoughts. They merge leisurely into one another.

I lie down and hook one end of a bungee cord through the platform, the other around my wrist so that the train doesn't buck me off. There is no way I'll sleep, I think. But then the noise fades out and a serene silence veils the chaos. There is no more sound. My vision contracts, and though I can still see the car shuddering about me, it is diluted, almost washed out, and the hard steel angles are pushed farther into my periphery. Then a rich golden glitter carpets my vision like magical, white noise. It envelops me and expands into the silence, and my girlfriend materializes from the gold and is running naked toward me in slow motion, her mouth crinkled in a smile. The scene consumes me. Then I am asleep.

When I wake, our train is backing into a warehouse. The warehouse of alien experimentation or toxic chemical spray draws closer. Meanwhile, Bo is strewn across the platform fast asleep, an inert lump.

"Bo," I point at the luminous mouth of the warehouse entrance gaping wider.

"What?" Bo shakes his limbs from his sleeping bag in a flurry. "What?"

We throw our belongings from the platform. Luckily the freight slows enough for us to jump down. Bewildered, we watch car after car roll past only to be consumed by the warehouse. Then they stop. There is no hint of movement or pulse or steady drumbeat, just cold severe metal and wind scratching up inside steel hollows.

"I don't understand," Bo says, his eyes squinting at the night. "I don't understand," he says over and over. The unexpected has won.

We stumble through an overgrown field to the highway. We hitchhike downtown, and our ride tells us we are in Pasco, Washington, a few hundred miles off course. We sit on a bench outside a gas station. It is 2:00 AM; the streets are barren and windswept. We snipe insultingly at each other. It is time to bail. The Amtrak at 5:00 a.m. is our salvation. We navigate the dark streets to the train station.

"Should we catch another freight? Go to Canada?" I say. I laugh maniacally.

Outside the Amtrak station, I lie on the lawn by the car park and sink into a deep sleep. At five, I stagger like a zombie into the heated, cushion-clad passenger train. I sleep the best sleep of my life. Bo and I part ways at the Sacramento Greyhound station. I see him queuing sternly for the bus; then he is gone.

Finally, I walk down Escondido Road. My grime-caked clothes begin to thaw under the warmth of the sun. There is more dirt crusted on my skin than on the pavement beneath my feet. Bikes whirr softly by, too polite to raise their voices, content to disperse their whisper amongst the beige buildings. I walk

into the lecture hall. I sit down in the aisle, a disheveled pile. The professor's words resonate importantly. I try to summon my focus but I cannot hold it. Soon I lie down on the clean-swept floor. I close my eyes. Echoes of steel shudder in my ear.

Adrift in America appeared in *Claw Magazine* April 6, 2011.

Bo 3/24/11

I met all the celebrity Kings of the Road, and many executives among the 10,000 crush to view them at the Britt, Iowa, Hobo Convention (since 1900)...

It seems the grass is always greener on the other side of the track in America, with the hobos dreaming of being executives and the executives wishing to become Kings, but few over history made the transition.

Two men leap to mind. At the turn of the 20th century physician-hobo Ben Reitman practiced boxcar medicine and taught the first Hobo College in Chicago before my veterinary attempts around campfires and a community college sociology hobo class, Then, at the turn of the 21st century, Minneapolis advertising magnate Tod 'Adman' Waters kept one foot on each side of the tracks by flying to nationwide appointments and riding the freight home. Adman told the other Britt celebrity hobos that I was the only one who could walk into a jungle with a $5 bill on my forehead, that proved a proper introduction.

Steam Train Maury drove a cheery Cadillac to Britt, taught me to forage wild edibles, gave me an autographed postcard bearing his likeness, and asserted, "That's a get-out-of-jail-free card for any railroad bull that nabs you west of the Mississippi!"

Steam Train spoke highly of Fry Pan Jack who gave me the moniker High Pockets after one night in the big celebrity hobo tent on the Britt jungle ground. A lost child was being eaten alive by mosquitoes, so he crawled between my legs and slept the night. I was too naive to think it queer. Fry Pan took note, and the next morning seemed proud to give me the name.

Another *bona fide* 'bo was Cardboard. He slept across the tracks out in the weeds away from everybody, a fascinating, stalwart antisocial whom I kept at arms length for one, two, maybe the fifth convention when he finally glanced at me. I had researched his approximate birth date, and the look afforded an opening to offer him a lucky railroad nail with his birth year on it. I had all the years in my pocket clustering around his guessed birthday, dated on the head from the year the ties were laid. He was pleased to accept, and cut off the sharp point, drilled a hole, shined it up and wore as a necklace charm to keep from greasing the rails.

I knew all the celebrity 'bos who ran for Hobo King, and they knew me from not wearing shoes or for one thing or another: Harmonica Mike (wrote a tune about me), Hobo Hafe (visited his extensive basement train set in Flint, Michigan), North Bank Fred (some of my stories are still up at his website a couple of years after he caught the last 'westbound'), Arkansas Traveler (challenged me to a wrestling match on the jungle floor he thought was for fun), Virginia Slim with the sweetest voice that side of the Appalachians ...

But the one real 'bo at the convention (besides Iowa Blacky whom I rattled the rails with for a few thousand miles) was Hobo Herb of Denver. He was a Catman-nine-lives come and gone and still smiling-just from riding trains. There were alligator stories, bull horrors, knife fights, a beer train that derailed... He lived on the fringe of Mile High's skid row with Dirty Face Josie (dirty face is a freight train's nose, and his wife's name) whom he bragged could sleep in boxcar excrement, but he nonetheless slipped out the bathroom window every spring to ride the rails alone, or once took a pup in his pocket that he swore thought the ground was moving along the boxcar. Every Tuesday at home, he fed anyone who wanted food from his front door, behind which leaned a Louisville Slugger. Those were some fine 'bos, and still good company in my mind.

"I need it!" Dolly gushes astride the Reno Rail as I keep an eye out for the bull.

For Halloween, I'm taking Boxcar Dolly, a six-foot svelte Stanford hobo symbols expert and a fraction my age, trick-or-treating around the USA. She contacted me a year ago at Bo Keeley Executive Tours while studying hobo pictographs for a computer class—get a sit down meal, beware of dog, and others.

A wild-and-wooly ride trailed fifty Central Americans through Mexico to the USA Promised Land. She jumped down that Mexican freight lusting more, but had to go to Berkeley.

The ABCs of how to hobo freight are direct and illegal. Walk into a RR yard. At one side, find two shiny mainlines for west-east (or north-south) and vice versa traffic. Ask a yard worker when the next freight leaves for your destination. 'Frisk the drag' he points to by walking on the shadow side close to the cars to select a ride- boxcar, gondola, flatcar, cement hopper, van or container car—and, if there's time, check the tail end for a blinking red FRED (Freaking Rear End Device) that replaces the caboose. Climb on, sit back, and when she cannonballs, hang on for the ride of your life!

Midnight, October 28, Reno, Nevada in the Sparks RR yard

The full moon dances on the rail, as Dolly pulls a stocking cap over her curls and crouches next to me in the bush between the Nugget Casino, where the car is parked, and the mainline. Slot machines chime in one ear and freight cars crash the other, as diesel smoke intoxicates us gamblers.

Our 'Man' spins back and forth along the track, adding gondolas, flatcars, hoppers, and boxcars... until the power engines clang on, and we grab iron to swing aboard the back porch of a cement car. "This is your Salt Lake City Ma'am," calls a friendly brakeman.

The electric-diesel engines belch two stories black smoke, tug mightily, couplers drum a mile front to rear, our tail car lurches, and we're swept under the McCarran Bridge and spit into the Great Basin with the loco headlight bobbing like a National Geographic camera.

Elko, Wendover… and other desert burgs with clanging crossbars, until she asks, "Are we in Utah yet?"

"I don't know," I admit.

Opened for traffic in 1869, with the driving of the last Gold Spike at Promontory Point, Utah, this transcontinental iron road first connected the Atlantic to Pacific that built the American empire west, bringing many Civil War veteran 'hoe boys,' our predecessors. I tell a bedtime story on the shaking platform of the Irish, my lineage, and Chinese immigrants, as Dolly is half-Chinese from Britain, laborers competing from east and west to pound that final spike… "Stop me when you want to hear who won," I sustain.

But something goes wrong in the Great Basin.

"Medicine Bow," she coos in an ear, God knows how many hours later. Dolly has the most honest eyes in the world under pressure, but is pathologically Shakespeare in her speech replete with puns, layered meanings, and fuzzy purpose. I pop my head from the sleeping bag to gaze upon snow capped peaks, and inform her that we've bypassed Salt Lake and are adrift on America. "Don't worry; you can never be lost in a boxcar."

Green River, Laramie… the rail climbs, ponds ice, and snow confettis our hair.

The freight finally slows, and stops, in a sprawling unidentified yard—it doesn't matter where. This is a crew change town, one of a string posted every 300 miles—eight hours freight drive—across the nation. The tired engineer and conductor descend their heated cab, as a frisky crew climbs aboard in a matter of 5-15 minutes. Cold and hungry, we clamber to the frozen ballast. Having memorized a mile sequence of gas stations during the last arrival mile, we wheel and scuff 30-minutes to the nearest.

Cheyenne, Wyoming, 6000', 10pm at the Essex gas station

The old-time cashier's change shift at the register counting, "$900..." as I drop my black duffle with a thunk. "She has to get to Berkeley—is there Greyhound?" Dolly, my height with the dark cap insistently pulled down to feign a boy, despite the curves below, looks like a thug. The seniors blanch, blind with fright.

"Closed," avows one, as the other moves a finger for the alarm. But she has a cell phone.

A shaky stage arises to introduce a feminist to the hard hobo ethic that 'the fish gets the information.' The fish, a newcomer hobo or hoboette, is responsible for gathering intelligence to smooth the trip. Our voices rise- "I didn't say you're a life support system for a vagina; just a fish-call Greyhound."

"Wink off!" she storms.

We compromise—she dials and I chat to discover that no 'dog' (Greyhound) nor 'cush' (Amtrak) run the highly trafficked I-80 east-west corridor. So we default to the chilly RR yard where an orange-helmeted worker advises us to lie low due to heightened tension surrounding a recent derail.

The present target is the Pacific to get her to class on time, and already she hunches against a hurricane fence under the harsh yard light nosing through Milton Friedman's *Capitalism and Freedom* (Friedman) for a justice course, and citing cases. The yard is busy with working engines banging cars, but our hope rests on the mainline. In thirty minutes, two long through freights head up at our feet. We slip unseen aboard a container train just behind the huffing engines as the crew changes, and I lecture on the sea-land commerce between America and the Orient for one minute before the example pulls out.

Our link rolls about eighty containers drawn by three locos and pushed by another 'helper,' so it rarely sidetracks in hot pursuit of the West Coast. Cranes offload the US merchandise to Pacific Rim ships. Emptied on the other end in, say, China, the containers refill with merchandise for the USA, sail and port, reload onto trains, some onto semi-trucks, and drive to the East Coast. Back and forth, the link is ongoing.

Our perches are alike, but adjoining, 2-ft. x 8-ft. steel platforms– hers at the front end of the trailing flatcar on which the box is securely inserted, and his on the leading car notably out of the wind since my Therm-A-Rest flattened last night on the bucking cold steel. We nestle in blankets communicating with Praying Mantis signs across the 10-ft. expanse of gliding couplers, alert but long enough to see great icy mountains rear.

Rawlings, Rock Springs, Boise… I awaken with Polaris hanging above the locomotive smoke.

The freight slides through a sprinkle in Lava Hot Springs, Idaho, punched against a mountainside, and other bucolic towns warmed by placebo TVs and nonsense newspapers in woodstoves. We hold down that container freight all night and through the next day, and on into the night until sunrise when at last it ceases. Boxcar Dolly eats and drinks nothing in the cold draft for 36 hours, punishing that machine for just cause, and hops off to whoop, "That was freakin' wonderful!"

Sunrise over the water tower in La Grande, Oregon

"Is it normal for you to get lost on three straight freights, Doc Bo?" I add it up, and smile, "The value of the journey isn't as much the country as the conditions under which the country is observed."

It's Halloween and we look it, sliding dirty faced in crumpled overalls onto the hard bench of a Mexican café to order in Spanish hot burritos. A spider drops from my hair to the table, and another crawls on Dolly's greasy pack. Two men in coveralls at an adjacent table grin appreciatively, and spotting them as RR men, I admit we just detrained and want to ask key questions.

"We-hell," drawls the portly one. "Ya asked the right guys. We're UP mechanics. "Yep," abets the other. "Yer stuck on the rails. Greyhound don't go west, Amtrak don't stop, but the yard's a-flurry with northbounds." "Ahem," instills the other. "What we mean is there's a train every hour, but up the road at Hermiston forks—one in 10 freights bends east to Spokane, and the rest turn west to Portland. From Portland you can catch a bus or passenger train home."

"Great odds!" I thank them. Nonetheless, we're a bit wigged from three straight days on metal platforms, so after one snaps our photo, we amble out the café for a mile to I-84, and fail in an hour to thumb a ride. A stop at the library Internet confirms the helpful yokels' report that there is no way home except by rail.

Back at the La Grande freight yard, just past the comfy sofa beneath the underpass, a baseball diamond outfield fence offers a stiff backrest and scoreboard to hang last night's game clothes, and to gaze up and down the mile-long yard tracks. It's 45 degrees F, sunny, but the birds have beaten us south. In minutes a northbound freight glides up, halts, the crew changes next to the pitcher's mound, and I cuss the monster before us.

"What's Armn?" she gasps at the black, block print on one side each of forty silver boxes with refrigerators tacked on like cold noses.

"Never heard of it, nor seen the likes of these reefers (refrigerator cars)." Each boasts a thin 2-ft. x 10-ft. steel lip raised 15 ft. over the track, with a flimsy guardrail. Surely it's going to the coast, to Portland, we concur, but she trots to the engineer to confirm, "Portland Man." We scale the ladder and, in seconds, the reefer team chugs out.

At dusk, the freight arrives, and pauses, at the Hermiston fork, a three-mile long classification yard on the Oregon high desert where freights are built for points west to Portland, our direction, or east toward Minneapolis. The train steers obliquely NE that is worrisome, and accelerates. Dolly groans, "I gotta be in class in twelve hours," blinks, and phones classmates to hand in work and explain, however, to the professors her absence. We tie to the catwalk, and sleep end-to-end assuaged that we can't get off.

Some hours later, "Bo, wake up!... What do you reckon we're backing into?" I whirl. The rolling stock is entering an elongated spaceship on a dark runway, a quarter-mile shed bursting white light from inside. Our car is seconds from consumption. "Loco!" I screech at the moon.

"I'm too young to be processed!" shouts Dolly, tossing her pack, jacket and hat off and away from the 5-mph wheels. I unchain from the grate, jetsam gear in a high arc to the ballast, and follow Dolly down. Stepping off a moving freight is like striding off an escalator with a dandy giant step... and then the world is stable.

The train disappears into the french-fry shed. We circle it on cats' feet by a red RAILEX sign, and past forty blue lights of loading ramps for semi-trucks. This isn't a sprayer, processor, or UFO, but a gigantic transfer plant for refrigerated food in a rail-truck link.

Railex, we will discover, is the first ever perishable unit train from Wallula, Washington, to Albany, New York, in 5-day transit weekly, 52 weeks per year. It's our luck to catch this week's train. We were fortunate to have avoided being stuffed and turning up on your dinner plate.

Trick or treat!

Silence on the right-of-way

We hunker in a musty cornfield by the vacant track next to the plant, until I mutter, "This is a hobo survival test." We are at point X (unknown); the goal is point Y: Portland; and the means to get there must be analyzed before moving an inch. It's a starry night, 40 degrees F, no crickets, but owls and trains hoot in the distance. The north star displays if the track courses NE, the wrong direction; a compass confirms our wish to bear west toward town lights at ten miles; and my *USA Road Mini-atlas*, Rand McNally *Handy RR Atlas*, and the *Crew Change Bible* are useless since we don't know X.

"Surprise is the pulse of the rail, Dolly. We're lost again on America."

"I was starting to have too much fun, anyhow."

We strike afoot over hill and dale. I warn her to watch for streams under the moonlight, and not to stumble into a barbed wire fence. We untangle and circumvent a lake, to finally edge onto a dark country lane. Minutes later, she steps in front of an oncoming car with the cell blue light under her chin, and two bewildered Mexicans stop, jabbering Spanish that we all speak.

They just left the Railex graveyard shift, and are headed for the Pasco, Washington, lights.

Pasco, Washington, midnight at Amtrak

Pasco is a railroad town and the farthest point up the Columbia River a seagoing ship may reach. We sleep in the weeds until the Amtrak station opens at 4 a.m., are whisked 'on the cushions' to Portland, and then board a Greyhound to California.

Greyhound along the Pacific

Finally, there's time to talk without the rail clatter.

We made a string of correct logistical decisions on the trip, I tell Dolly, but statistically it's scary to be lost in seven states in as many days. Yet who's confused? We knocked on the back doors of Northwest USA—industry, skid rows, playgrounds, farms, outhouses, and gardens—and you can't convince me there's an on ongoing recession with double the freight traffic in twenty years, and not one other hobo seen trick-or-treating adventures along 2000 of Union Pacific's 32,000 miles of track.

The hobo grab bag triggers a change in thought and lifestyle.

Your peers say it's OK to screw up, emote, follow the herd, and be less than what one may. People don't have to be smart, they just have to follow the rules. That isn't the hobo way. The rails are an underworld selection technique where drunken, nonanalytical tramps are cast to bum the streets and named Stubby and Two-Finger Charlie after 3-ft. cookie-cutter wheels size them down.

We take off the gloves and shake hands at the Sacramento bus terminal. Dolly lands late for show-and-tell at Berkeley, with frostbite and ghoulish bruises, and a faint glow that brightens each second like an oncoming locomotive.

The American Dream has no border, especially along Texas, New Mexico, Arizona, and California. The Latin hobo ethos is the ability to arrive in USA and participate in the society and economy to prosper as they may not south of the artificial border. Their Dream includes the opportunity to work, marry, and for their children to grow up and receive a good education and career without barriers.

With the USA wrapped in a nightmare of Latino immigrants and issues, South African CPA Diesel Dyson—recently landed in US to pursue the financial version of American Dream—and I sashayed under sombreros and dressed like Mexicans with fair Spanish into the Mexico Junction Sufractia hornet's nest of Mexican and Central American trampas waiting to catch out to the Promised Land.

Part 1: Central American Express

El Sufractia is the hobo Grand Central Station of the Pacific for freights south-north between Mexico City and Mexicali at the USA border, and for ones east-west through the Copper Canyon toward Texas and the Florida Gulf.

There is no town, just a 15-track wide yard...pressed against the flat fields with a small *tienda* at its edge selling sodas and cigarettes to the types that frequent rail yards. Expecting a tidy 11 p.m. departure, we got there just after dark. Diesel called the spot a hornet's nest. He made the mistake of jiggling loose change in his pocket and was speedily hemmed by two men in front and one behind. I raised my pack to look bigger at the outside and called him safely out the lock.

We angled from the *tienda* across the yard tracks under harsh, yellow lamps. Two soldiers in camouflage intercepted us walking toward the Chihuahua freight. I dubbed them Thick, with a shotgun, and Thin, with an assault rifle, as Diesel spoke in quiet tones.

"We are Americans riding freights for adventure. We want to see your beautiful country without the windows of a passenger train, to feel the air, hear the town noises, and look directly at the people." They scrutinized our passports and cross-examined our intent for fifteen minutes. Thin injected, "Señor, you tremble. What do you hide?" Diesel responded softly, "I don t-tremble a bit. And I hide as little." "Hold out a steady hand then." My partner's accountant paw was a rock in the light. "And, senor, now yours." I thrust it and observed, "His shakes more than mine." They drew and lit cigarettes. "Your hands tremble, señores," I said, and added, "and the other hands hold weapons." They pushed their hands aside ours and Thin said as steadily, "Your train leaves in an hour. Have a safe journey." I snapped their picture against a boxcar.

A nighttime yard is a sliver of Halloween. Our train, a headless string without attached units and nevertheless identifiable by the track number, slept on a rail. Bats flew in and out yard lamps grazing insects as many as the stars. A rat the size of a guinea pig scuttled a tie. Frogs croaked in a stinking drainage ditch. Smart hobos always walk a drag to memorize the potential rides before the engines hook on. Twenty minutes later, we rounded the string with a complete mental picture of two grain cars at the head, a gondola in the center, and some lumber cars at the tail. Freights south and north of the border display a FRED or Flashing Rear End Device in lieu of the venerable caboose, an electronic box mounted on the last car coupler that relays the brake line pressure to the engineer in the locomotive. Hobos call it the F***ing Rear End Device because you can't ride it like a caboose.

The Chihuahua string on our right would depart in an hour at 11 p.m., and the Mexicali train on the left stood ready to roll with units agrowl. A shadow loomed between them and we screeched in the gravel at seeing a two-foot sharp poker. I blinked twice to remove its long gleam from my retinas. "Halt!" commanded a voice, and it was a comfort as already we were shocked still. The shadow advanced, became a uniform, and I followed the poker point up to the hand and discerned the rawhide face of a soldier. He ordered us to lead him out of the dim between the cars. As we sashayed the Mexicali train, it became apparent that the soldier was on a hobo Easter egg hunt. He talked to dozens of *trampas*, including one *chica* (girl), hanging along car platforms or to the roofs. The Mexicans he let stay on but the Central Americans he pulled off to build a walking clutch of eight Latins plus us two *gringos*. I thought, this hunter with the poker is both brave and stupid.

The brakes hissed and departure was imminent. The soldier whirled and looked up between two boxcars, then shrugged and turned to us. He spun again and caught two faces, Hondurans, whom he motioned with the rod from the deck. He told all the Central Americans they weren't permitted to ride, and that we two *Americanos* should walk ahead to wait for our 11 p.m. Chihuahua train. As Diesel and I crunched onward, I jerked a thumb back and muttered, "It's *mordida* time."

We leaned against a wall to view the open of the night's main event. The yard still held dozens of immigrants as the Mexicali freight pitched forward. Many were Central Americans boarding at the last second to avoid the sharp poker. Ten pairs of legs pumped rapidly for the moving wagons and loped easily on. The load would make Mexicali in 24-hours and some would cross into USA the following day. If a Mexican wants to sneak into the US he takes the bus to the border and then crosses illegally. But if you are from Guatemala, for example, you have to enter Mexico illegally first. Once inside, you can't ride the bus without documents or the checkpoint police will catch, fine, and deport you. So the Mexican freights are jammed with OTMs (other than Mexicans). This Mexicali freight had the most OTMs and Mexican trampas of them all.

"The scum has cleared the yard," joked Diesel, So I guess we're safe. The cleansing freight, long and heavy with living cargo, snailed only ten steps from our feet but we wanted the Chihuahua train. An auburn teen carrying nothing came up to divulge a thirty-second history. Life is tough in Honduras. Forty days ago he started with the clothes on his back and is heading north, like the rest, for the American vision. He will step down from this train tomorrow in Mexicali but is uncertain how he'll cross the border. He doesn't know much about the USA but is passionate beyond worry. He glanced casually at the moving freight and bowed goodbye. He sprinted and vaulted aboard like a gazelle. The FRED shrank to nothing in the north.

Diesel stood and howled. "Think of it! A kid leaves home with nothing and illegally travels a country he knows nothing about to one where he knows no one!" Tom Dyson was the managing editor of *The Daily Reckoning* until two weeks ago when he eloped with the boss's ex-gal.

It's a weekly wrap-up of contrarian investment analysis. Before that he worked as a CPA at London's Salomon Smith Barney calculating the traders' daily profits and managing their books. His passions still are finance and freights. He looked in a London office window three years ago and reflected where his life path headed. He quit, emptied his pockets and caught a flight to Mexico City. Penniless and without plastic, he begged twelve little liquor bottles from the flight attendant before disembarking.

He walked straight to the freight yard a hobo virgin and in the next two weeks bartered the alcohol for meals in riding the rails through Mexico and the USA. A year ago, based on the *Dyson Diaries* of those adventures, he was hired by the Baltimore-based *Daily Reckoning*. Six months ago, he emailed me to freight the Canadian Rockies that was told in "Hunting and Hunted on the Rails." Our road names on this Mexico trip are Dennis the Menace and Mr. Wilson, and we are a team. But long ago they called me Doc Bo. I've grabbed 300 freights and taught a college sociology class "Hobo Life in America."

Life is tough in Honduras. Forty days ago he started with the clothes on his back and is heading north, like the rest, for the American vision.

Three soldiers came up on cat's feet. "*Buenas noches*," spoke the corpulent sergeant with a dancing mustache and .45 pistol. Two skinny privates deferred to his every move. "Your passports please," he asked in Spanish. We produced them and I backed up to witness my partner finesse the soldiers. Sarge examined the documents as the other two searched the bags. "Ah, a South African citizen!" cried out the rotund man. "Yes!" returned Diesel, "so rare to meet someone who knows the passport." He whispered aside to me, "The everyday Mexican sees Americans as invasive wealthy snobs who care little for their country and less for them. So they're astonished when you compliment their land or people."

The private with the poker raced up and leered to the group, "I tried my best to keep the Central Americans off, but they got on the Mexicali train!" Everyone knew he had levered a bribe. The Sarge covered us with a hasty scowl, "Do you shoot doves? Some Americans shoot doves, you know!" "No," cautioned Diesel, "I hate killing." He scratched the gravel with a boot and the other three their chins. We chitchatted until the Sarge ultimately assured us, "It makes sense you are here, señores, because *gringos* are nuts." They scuffed away and he bellowed, "You know where to find us if there is trouble." Diesel opened his arms wide to the night, "But we have very little."

While the departing train held the yard's attention, we snaked inside to board our best ride on the Chihuahua freight. The pick of the string was a bizarre, oversized boxcar with an atypical platform. We left a large stone there in a corner as a weapon and sat thinking about the recent activities and discussing contingencies. I grew sleepy and Diesel fussed about the lack of activity on our track and left to investigate. We had working radios now and buzzed each other every ten minutes. There was a lapse and he returned breathing hard, "There is terrible as well as tremendous news! Our train has been canceled for the night due to lack of Chihuahua-bound cars. However, a half-mile ahead is a private *gringo* train that's touring the Copper Canyon and leaving tomorrow morning. The crew is spitting and polishing as we speak. Maybe we can hitch a ride." We hiked to four sleek, silver cars with Mexicans spilling elbow grease in the interior. Unfortunately, the Americans whom we hoped to talk to were sleeping in a distant motel and wouldn't arrive until the morning takeoff.

We plowed slowly the ballast feeling oddly relaxed for the first time in days. Each failure on the rail of life brings another turn. So we checked into an abandoned motel next to the tiny store on the yard edge. Six adobe rooms, mostly without doors or windows, lined either side of an open-air hall. Eight Central Americans occupied them all but spilled out to greet us as a serious novelty. They had never seen *gringos* on the rail! We conversed in the hall for an hour.

They had bused from their home countries to the Mexico border. Then they hoboed the northbounds picking up as they went intelligence about direction and border crossing. All were married males who had left with the family sanction to illegally enter and work in the USA for about two years, and then to transfer their wives and children. A week ago, some witnessed in dismay one of their fellow countrymen slip from a ladder trying to board a moving train and get cut in half at the waist by the rolling wheels. They could do nothing for him except continue. The Mexican people were kind to them, but the soldiers and guards brutal.

"They have extorted $1000!" a swarthy man roared. That collective bank had dwindled from the bribes and, yesterday in Las Moches, they had bought a Mexican *coyote* with the last $1500 to meet them in Mexicali to cross by foot into the US to a waiting mini-van. Mexicali, tangible now on the brink of the USA, was a 24-hour freight ride away. Today they rested. Tomorrow they would board the freight. The following day they could be in Los Angeles, and the next stooping in the fields for hard cash!

One OTM insisted that the sleeping hotel owner could be aroused at 3 a.m. I found myself tapping on the window of a nearby house and repeating softly, "Nellie," and wondering if I was a fool. At no answer, the friendly Central Americans invited us to sleep on their floors for a dollar. We showered instead for fifty cents under a trickle that could be turned neither on nor off, and exited into the night.

We found our bed, a skinny platform 100-yards long between tracks in the yard center, for a short and restless sleep. The concrete platform was littered with sleeping *trampas*. Each man lay in the shadow of his personal roof pillar as a spacer from the next body. Diesel and I chose adjoining posts and before turning in reflected on the first seed of this whole Mexico journey last spring. We'd read *Black Like Me* on the Canadian trip and designed, in the spirit of John Griffin, to dye our skin and hair brown, don floppy hats, and pass as Mexicans with me acting dumb. That plan adjusted to floppy hats only that we now buried our heads into, rolled down shirt sleeves to gloves, and stuck legs under blankets to hide every bit of lily skin. No tough rising in the night to pee might identify us as marks. Before losing awareness, I glimpsed my wrapped colleague, twice Mexican size and snoring, and wondered if he looked 'Latin like me' and we would awaken in the morning bleeding. Freight cars smashed just feet from our ears.

In safe daybreak, we rose with the other *trampas* to greet an extended freight arriving along the Pacific coast from Mexicali in the north. A dozen men leaped down alone or in clots and greeted some of the in-yard *trampas* with back slapping. Diesel and I padded to a secluded corner to discuss whether to await tonight's supposed Chihuahua freight through the Copper Canyon. "We must!" he insisted sweeping me.

Rather than fritter the day in the Surfractia yard, we bused twenty minutes to the nearby town of San Blas to stroll the day and use the Internet café. San Blas is a representative wedge of what we'd seen in the Mexico pie throughout the week. Lively faces bobbed the sidewalks on anxious feet toward future goals. This, I told my partner, was a far cry from days-of-yore siestas under dead saguaros. The country is ripe for capitalism, he agreed, though it was not quite in place.

The low-life indicators in Mexico are propitious. The winds of economic times start in the gutters and alleys and blow into the financial district. We found long cigarette butts on the sidewalks indicating coming affluence and, moreover, fewer people smoking them than previously. A high ratio of new cars, taxis, and buses plied the clean streets, didn't honk, and obeyed traffic signals. The policemen sported snappy uniforms and pedaled bicycles in dispensing few tickets. Two prostitutes threw themselves at me and commanded proud fees of $40 and then stalked away without second offers as I shook my head in disbelief. The freight trains are long and frequent. Our conclusion was that we we're hoboing an upward bound country.

A farmer with two hired hands strolled up to the downtown stand to order long tacos. He mainly wanted to fracture English and explained there were 100 cows on his rancho and only two bulls. He handed them tacos as the sisters tittered. Four leaning chairs about the counter created a hump on the side of the busy town strip where pickups spilling vaqueros honked and hooted. It was also small-town America. *Chingar*! the sisters merrily cursed them. To fornicate! To work hard! The farmer quaffed a beer and offered to hire me to teach his children English, perhaps to grow to curse bilingually. I declined but wrote the beautiful sisters a poem conjured from high school Spanish in mirror image on a napkin: *.sedetsu ed sojo soL :natsug em sam oreP .et al atsug eM .ehcel al atsug eM* "I like milk," read the farmer with great labor… "I like tea. But most of all, I like your eyes." He passed the note to the sisters, paid for my meal, and I walked from the uproar down the street to find the Internet.

Wherever there's electricity in Mexico, there is a cyber-café with computers to rent at $1 per hour. I kicked aside a dead scorpion from the sidewalk and walked into one in the pueblo of San Blas, a quick bus ride from the Surfractia rail yard. I was followed in the door by a man in black, stocky and used to getting things his way by wit or force. He sat at the computer facing me and struck up a conversation in rare English.

He offered to be a *coyote* for anyone I wanted to get across the border. I wasn't interested but he described anyway the route via Juarez and fee at $1500 per head. Then he rose to leave without using the computer. He wrote his name and phone first, saying, "If you need anything in this town just ask for Rocky." A few minutes later, Diesel walked in.

We decided that the thing started last night in the nearby rail yard where we were confronted by the soldiers, guards, and friendly workers—who no doubt lived and reported here in town—that for the first time two *gringos* were freight hopping with thirty illegal Mexicans and Central Americans toward the border. Maybe the *Americanos* are *coyotes*. "Rumors spread like wildfire in *purblos*," Diesel surmised, "and Rocky wants to extort or bust us. We should bail." I agreed, and we bused to the yard to catch the 11 p.m. freight through the Copper Canyon once and for all.

Part 2: Village Idiot

We were in Surfractia for the second evening try, and initially scampered behind the hotel to avoid the mill of *trampas*, rail workers, and guards at the *tienda* (store). There we found a brown whip of a man and his fawning brother planting trees at sunset. They glistened with the day's work. "Hello," chirped the older whom I tagged the Elder.

He stood under the new trees with the crickets singing and described the Central American Express in strong English. It's been forty days of hard, steady travel since Honduras. They bused through Central America to the Guatemala-Mexico border where the Express starts. Thousands of illegals were camped at the border that leaks like a sieve. We paid ten pesos ($1) each for a boat ride across the *rio* and went to the Mexican freight yard. The train left about three times a week as the cars stacked up. He once saw 1000 *trampas* on a freight nearly two-miles long. Most of them, like the Elder and his brother, carried no gear whatsoever in order to deceive the soldiers, guards, and police. A man who appears to own nothing isn't worth extorting and, besides, he runs away fast. They had paid zero bribes but, of course, had secreted money.

The freight lines branch within the Mexican interior so the thousands of *vagabondos* spread like funneled liquid on the approach to the USA border. At the major Surfractia Junction on the Pacific, the line forks north to Mexicali that most illegals ride, or east over the hump to Chihuahua and on north to the Juarez crossing at Texas. The Elder and his friends had selected Juarez where an amigo would put them through a hole in the border fence, and beyond it was a short bus ride to Colorado.

Besides, local muggers robbed the OTMs in coastal pueblos along the Mexicali rail. The Central Americans differ from the Mexican *trampas* by their lighter skin and gentler lingo. Mexicans with any money at all ride buses to the US border, but Central Americans lacking documents for the bus take freights. This is why in Surfractia the majority of hobos were skimpily clothed OTMs with a preponderance of Hondurans when times are especially tough.

"Maybe we shall meet again," said the Elder wistfully. He held two brown hands to form a steeple. Quickly the fingers intertwined. "Little groups join for protection." The fingers separated and built again the steeple. "We separate until the next time."

Diesel and I moved to the hotel front yard dust to keep an eye on the yard and ponder the general consensus that there'd be no Copper Canyon train for the second straight night. Diesel likened us to sitting on the center

Mexicans with any money at all ride buses to the US border, but Central Americans lacking documents for the bus take freights.

of a clock that read ten minutes to two. Mexicali would be at the end of the minute hand and Chihuahua would be at the end of the hour hand. Mexicali was completely in the wrong direction but we should consider the train because we were tired of that place. Units revved and rolled fifty-yards away on the main line. In a split-second decision we dashed for the Mexicali freight and caught the rear platform of a sausage-shaped grain car.

The click of wheel over rail is significant. When rails were split every dozen paces during my boxcar heyday in the 1980s, those expansion joints slow-clicked under the turning wheels as a freight decelerated into towns. The modern rails north of the border are continuous rail, welded at the joints for strength and silence, but the old clicking ones still slow coming into *pueblos.* I awake in the dark in a start as a strange man leaps onto the moving ladder of our platform. He looks down hard under the moonlight. His hand moves slowly to a pocket and withdraws a metallic object that flicks open. A faint glow envelopes it that I think is a florescent jackknife. "*Trampas!*" he shouts at the knife. I believe him deranged.

Diesel snored like a hound and seemed not to hear anything in the engine noise. The Mexican signaled with one arm around the car side and a slim man climbed onto the ladder next to him. They stared as the train jiggled and then two more heads peeked over the top grate and the men dropped. The four were not shabbily dressed, with trimmed hair over fleshy faces flashing in-and-out of the town lamps. The first monkey and I threw eye daggers at each other for some time and one of mine must have hit. He suddenly motioned the others to vamoose and they silently slid off on my partner's side. I think they were local thugs with cell phones, rather than citizens crossing the track, who were caught off-guard by our large white skins. The freight rolled on in the early morning and I went to sleep myself.

The morning train sliced the coast through cactus prairies and dirt-poor farms and pueblos of homes with leaky tin roofs where nothing changes but the weather. Diesel and I reveled the rails at each whistle blast.

It stopped in Guaymas on the Pacific about 10 a.m. The engines dynamited, releasing pent air from the brakes with a WHOOSH that signaled a protracted wait. Central Americans up and down the train stepped ashore and kicked along to knot at mid-train. Then they moved *en masse* to the head passing the other side of a boxcar where Diesel and I ducked behind three-foot wheels to observe in astonishment under the car belly. Forty sturdy legs marched by and fanned the neighborhood to beg at doors and back yards, often successfully. "It's like the American Great Depression!" I informed my colleague. "It is a depression," he replied. They were hungry, smart. and on the road.

A brakie told us the train wouldn't continue for eight hours, so we ambled two blocks out the yard to a store for breakfast. We crossed paths with a friendly Guatemalan with gorilla shoulders from picking bananas who was now so drawn from hunger that I broke a personal rule and gave him five pesos in order to eat. We may expect company now, chided my partner. "I can't deny a hungry man," I answered. Then we sat on the dirt and sewed our large peso bills into the seams of our walking shorts.

We talked to some who had been on the road for a month or more with few or no possessions. They wore rail-greasy clothes without jackets or packs and with little food or water, but all wore smiles. Men with nothing but that are small targets and run faster after trains and from thugs. The Promised Land was close. Most planned to walk through the autumn desert for two days to patient friends or *coyotes*. They would mushroom across the nation, mostly the Southwest, for cash work at agricultural labor, construction, or dishwashing for a while. They would buy false documents on the streets and improve their lives. Money would be sent home to families or to stake new illegal journeys.

"99% of these riders are not thieves," observed Diesel with a wink. "I realize that they're preyed upon by local dirt bags when the trains roll slowly through towns. That's why they clump together in yards." He ate vegetables while I downed chocolate milk for breakfast, and between swallows we agreed not to wait on this pokey northbound but instead regress by bus to Surfractia for the Copper Canyon quest. Third time a charm?

Everything was the same as the previous two nights at the yard. Two dozen new *trampas* lounged on the concrete platform at sunset, yard workers swung lanterns between cars, soldiers checked their safeties, and the tiny store next to the abandoned hotel burst into light for the evening traffic at Surfractia Junction. Characters in their uniforms walked woodenly in and out with iced sodas and smoking cigarettes as though life is a set. More so, it seemed to Diesel and me, because we were beat to our souls and stuck out. We retreated to the hotel backyard for a peaceful dirt pile.

The Elder was there beside his brother and a small fresh squad of Hondurans. "But I saw you get on the Mexicali train last night!" he blurted. We explained the turnaround to chase our dream ride. They seem friendlier at having seen us off and now returned on a freight. The Elder surveyed all with warm, grey eyes that missed nothing, and began in perfect English, "I lived and worked in Colorado Springs, Colorado, for seven years..."

He kept a low profile at all times with a bogus driver's license and Green Card. "The real immigration problem," he kidded, "is that a large illegal population creates an active market for illegal documents." He operated heavy construction equipment for $17/hour, had a girlfriend, two kids, a bank account, car, and cell phone. Rudely, two months ago, his apartment was raided by a SWAT team to arrest a boarder, a small-time drug dealer. The cops found ten vials of cocaine in the dealer's room but also charged the clean and clueless Elder with possession. He was sent to jail for three months and deported by jet to Honduras where, after a month, he turned around with his eighteen-year old brother in tow. They had also hooked up with two friends who got lost south of Surfractia but whom they hoped to rejoin before Chihuahua.

Diesel stayed with the main group as I peeled off toward a broken picket fence. "You speakee Eenglish?" squeaked a voice low and behind my back. I twirled to see deep-set eyes boring mine. The dwarf giggled and said he was Harry the Honduran. "You want something, you ask Harry." Then he tumbled off. I instantly recalled the voice on our arrival two nights ago suggesting that I tap on Nellie's window, the sleeping hotel matron, and later to make ourselves at home on the hotel hall floor. I raced after him tonight to be checked by a little girl who twirled her finger at a temple to say he was one sandwich short of a picnic. I brushed her aside to engage him. He lived in one of the windowless hotel rooms and slept on a bare mattress. He knew all the train times and, for the past year, had abetted thousands of *trampas* who paused at this major juncture in their lives on the Central American Express to the USA. He evaporated into the night.

"He's the underground railroad middleman," I reported to Diesel. "He's the village idiot!" Diesel exploded. "Don't be so sure!" I snapped. The dwarf pulled the major purse to the local storekeeper and hotel owner, Nellie, who treated him kindly and traded chores for room and board. All the Central Americans knew the simpleton who provided a continual flow of information to twenty new faces a night. I bet my partner that Harry was renowned throughout Central America as the Surfractia Connection.

We propped against the fence bewildered by the mixed information we'd received on whether or not there'd be a Copper Canyon train this night, the third in Surfractia. Diesel yoked a yard worker and asked if the freight had been called. This means that the crew is alerted at home or hotel an hour or so before a departure to allow time to drive and man the locomotives. Once a train is called the hobo walks the line, picks a car, and may sleep guaranteed of its departure. "It hasn't been called yet," answered the man, "but if you buy me a soda I'll go to the tower and see if I can discover what's going on." The contracted worker never returned.

All the Central Americans knew the simpleton who provided a continual flow of information to twenty new faces a night. I bet my partner that Harry was renowned throughout Central America as the Surfractia Connection.

However, the village idiot did approach to say that two soldiers resting against a truck under a lamp wanted to speak to us. Diesel sauntered over for a short, vigorous exchange that propelled him back with a vegan smile. The simpleton told the soldiers that the *gringos* wanted to talk to them. He told us the same of them. Nobody wanted to talk, but somehow we know now that the Chihuahua train departs on time at 11 p.m. Having waited three days, we burst, "Let's go!"

Three units blew thunder on the main line. That was our cue to board. I nearly lost my shoes in Diesel's footsteps chasing the eastbound that tugged, being long. The Elder, brother, *chica* and sundry *trampas* piled on. All the comfy rides along the moving line were occupied so we ran faster to the first car behind the engines. That rear platform was clogged with apparatus but the front was open and we puffed until we took it. "The smoke will keep us warm up here," asserted the romantic. "We may exit the other side cold," answered the realist, but his ears were sealed shut.

Part 3: Copper Canyon

Mexican diesel locomotives operate seemingly without safety standards such as emissions controls. Diesel states, "If they run, they hook 'em up!" I thought the rust should have been painted over.

The Copper Canyon route is a mountainous ascent from sea level to 10,000 ft. in 200 miles. That, or to claim engineering wizardry after 90 construction years, is why they bored 88 tunnels, built more than a hundred trestles, and put in a corkscrew loop between Surfractia and

Chihuahua. Most of the tunnels occur on the sharp climb out of Surfractia to the Continental Divide. Some are ten sooty minutes long, and we knew the descript engines would spew exhaust like a smokers' marathon. This may be the most scenic and hazardous hobo ride in the world, and that's why we wanted it.

It got cold in the altitude. Tiny feet on the back of my hand took it to the moon. A seven-inch lizard clung for warmth and wouldn't let go. The reptile, born on the car or dropped from a branch, had more frequent rider mileage than all the *trampas* combined. I shook him to the ground as the train slowed on an uphill curve.

Diesel and I sat on opposite sides of the metal platform just one coupler-length from the three engines where I provided no preinstruction because he's bright. The first tunnel took us in the dark. We sickened in every one.

A routine of echolocation hatched instead of seeing tunnels approach in the black. With each, I listened, ducked into my child's sleeping bag, and grasped close the end for seconds or minutes. The smoke bounced up the smokestacks and reflected off the ceiling directly onto us. My god, I thought, he has just a blanket, and nearly passed out. The echolocation practice was: Sound... Hold Breath... Heat... Pass Out... Quiet... Breathe! My sleeping bag nearly caught fire 88 times in eight hours. His back blistered. We got knocked closer together.

The morning was better because the tunnels could be seen coming and going. At long last, the holes stopped. Diesel crawled out of the blanket with a black face and light glinting off his lenses, and asked drunkenly, "Didn't that affect you?" I shook my head stupidly.

The next morning the freight dropped a string of cars in Creel in the heart of the Copper Canyon. We descended the ballast and, fearing for the welfare of the T-shirted *trampas* who rode the rim all night, walked back. Each beamed this morn from a new sooty face and made no mention of the previous cold or heat. Diesel said they were noble beings, but it's true that a good quest is also heartwarming.

He is a vegan every minute of the year except in Mexico where he wolfs *carne asada* every meal doused with the hottest sauces. I warned him to cut back or suffer a personality change. "I'm sorry," he burped this morning squatting on a rail. "I've lost everything in my pockets." His pen, light, coins, safety pins, and wedding gift had blown overboard. "I lost my visa too," he shrugged, "but it doesn't matter since we're illegal."

He saved a detailed bathroom kit that daily he set out between his legs on a rail or car. He pulled it out today on a Creel park bench with the most primitive aboriginal culture left in North America watching like a documentary special. We saw him trim his nails and brush his teeth twice and swab his ears like a good London lad. He smiled sweetly at them, I'm also getting used to his filthy flannel shirt. There was a fungus infection on the right big toe for which I had prescribed Iodine that he alternated the brush from the toe to a tongue canker. He paraded about town with a bare purple toe and Chow's tongue searching for *carne asada*. A white tether dangled from a loaned cap to the backs of his calves, and he'll be told in mountain legend for generations as the famous Mr. Kite

Daily, I tried to break his innate, dangerous verve by adding more weight to our regular misery. He entered Mexico kicking heels at the sky. I sat him on two-by-fours that replace the passenger seat in my sedan and cranked the heater with the windows closed to prepare for the hot ride. I ate and drank minimally in the initial days on the rail as an example of what a hardy hobo can accomplish, and he followed suit. He endured tedious transplantations despite my passable Spanish. There were constant safety drills that he hated. A year of planning; a second of perfect execution! When he boarded the car behind the smoking units and rode through 88 scorching tunnels, I didn't argue. These were nothing I wouldn't do myself, and for his own good. To date, he's gotten worse and I felt outlasted. Today the alpha hobo wore a primal grin about town and felt more daring than ever.

The freight cast off with a goodbye toot to the Creel aborigines. It flew east shorter by some cars. We dropped anchor hours later at the Continental Divide, El Cielo, and all stole glances through the pines to puzzle why. From the west a silver streak gained and slid alongside our rust bucket freight on the side track, and stopped. It was a fancy private

train like the one Diesel and I had tried to hobo two nights ago in Surfractia. Dirty faces atop the grain cars stared across a narrow space into the second-story tinted windows at jolly people looking back who paid a grand each for the tour. We sat on grates in the sunshine; they sat at tables with white cloths and glassed roses within the dining car. The sun shifted over time until we saw only our hungry reflections.

We waited an hour until the priority train raced off, and lumbered after it on a single eastbound rail through the Sierra Madres. The passenger and freight trains run the same scenic rail rim of the Copper Canyon into which four Grand Canyons could be dropped! Sunshine brought everyone up onto the car decks for the vista. The locomotive exhaust tossed thick pine branches ten-feet above the smokestacks and then the branches pounded on us on the first car. The train dove into tunnels that would scrape a haircut but we flattened, and Diesel whooped and shook his fist after each exit.

Freights are decked more often south of the border because the prevalent ancient grain car roofs have a steel grate—a two-ft.-wide walkway—lengthwise over the grain hatches. This is the Mexi-hobo bench with a 360-degree view while punching wind with

When he boarded the car behind the smoking units and rode through 88 scorching tunnels, I didn't argue. These were nothing I wouldn't do myself, and for his own good.

faces. Our car carried corn from the coast to the interior, judging by the spring weight and spilled kernels on the platform ends. Ladders there lead to the top.

The grate overhangs the car ends by a couple of feet so that with leap frogs one may travel from car-to-car the length of a train. I leaped once to be able to say I could, and now leave it to acrobats. A hobo painter with a brush mustache and speckled shirt bounded the gaps from the rear train to join us. He remarked that at the next pueblo he would disembark for a month-long job, but first he wanted to meet the oddball *gringos* to tell his coworkers about. He had been deported about forty times over the years from the US and the last time was inserted into the dread computer. Caught again it was straight to jail for four years. So he had retired to paint in Mexico at one-third pay.

A Guatemalan also grew bolder and crossed cars to sit beside us on the deck of the 35-mph freight. He pulled a wrinkled baggie from his pocket and carefully extracted a 4-in. x 4-in. worn, thin booklet that I clutched like the original Genesis atop the devil's tornado. The title was *Help for Central American Immigrants through Mexico*. Seeing I wouldn't crack it in the whipping wind, he summarized into my ear, "It says that an immigrant, legal or not, shall never be harassed or pay bribes to any authority while passing through Mexico. It was printed by the Mexican government and distributed along the Central American border, and he claimed it had great power when shown to Mexican police and soldiers."

I adhere to three strict rules atop a moving freight: face forward, keep one handhold, and sleep with feet forward. Most of the *trampas*, who had spent a wakeful, cold night in thin shirts on bare metal along the rim, flopped like pups in the deck sunshine to catch forty winks. My partner swung his head up there to announce, "I want to be able to say I didn't sleep in a bed for two weeks," and reclined on the sunny grate with his head beating wind. I didn't like the smell of his feet mixed with the smoke and peril, so kicked hard after he almost got decapitated by a branch. "Hey!" he jerked, and I admonished, "Look back at the other sleeping *trampas*!" They swayed and snored smoke with the train, feet first. He sheepishly turned about and slept.

What's it like to ride a Mexican freight? Each day's minute and every night's hour the train shakes a ribbon to your goal. You hold the bucking floor with a pack between your legs and watch a thousand scenes scramble by. The mind relaxes and the past peeks in. You scrawl a diary, chat and the wind rustles the clothes and hair. You may visit other trampas along the upper grate and hop between cars. There's plenty of room out here! The two missing Hondurans reboarded once as the freight huffed impatiently for the engineer to grab a taco at a mountain stand. The trampas decked all the cars to dance and ripple laughter across the townsfolk heads like a Fourth of July parade.

Suddenly, there came a disturbing WHOOSH as the train rumbled through a pueblo. "That wasn't a mechanical release!" Diesel spouted. "Somebody broke the brake line!" I added in a tick. We were atop the steel grate of a car with six other riders who all peered over the side at the ballast that stopped. The town had turned out for the train in waves.

The lovely smudged *chica* jumped down and ran through the right-of-way to fall into the waiting arms of her clean townsman Latin lover. It was a wedding! Citizens applauded from the sidewalks. The engineer touched the brake hoses and the freight jerked to Chihuahua.

The train was short now, only fourteen cars glancing down the country. It passed an enormous red-white-and-green Mexican flag the size of four boxcar sides. The trampas grew lively in spirit with each decreasing mile. How they waltzed on the freight decks! Almost to the USA!

The trampas grew lively in spirit with each decreasing mile. How they waltzed on the freight decks! Almost to the USA!

Chihuahua City, nestled in foothills, livened as street lights ignited at dusk when the train rolled in. The Hondurans asked for twenty minutes at each bridge if this was the one to jump down into the yard. Diesel good-naturedly abided, "*Mas.* A little farther." Four illegal Hondurans and two illegal *gringos* coiled side-by-side on the thin rear bumper until "*El puente!*" shouted Diesel, as the locomotives nosed under the correct bridge.

The train hissed and squealed decelerating to 20 and soon 15 mph. First, the Elder leaped and one foot hit gravel followed by the other. He sprinted alongside for a hundred yards to check the three youngsters didn't slip under the cookie-cutter wheels. We disembarked on their heels.

The party assembled under the bridge as a comfortable darkness settled over the city. Diesel and I conferred and then told them that since they now were four instead of two we wouldn't encumber to enlarge the group by hiring them as *coyotes*. So, the hands—white American and brown would-be American—clasped and unclasped beneath the overpass. We pitched in different directions into the darkness.

"We are the first to hobo North America's three most scenic freights!" I cried out. "The USA Royal Gorge, the Canadian Rockies, and Mexico's Copper Canyon!"

Part 4: Nabbed in the Rio Grande

We became illegals in Mexico almost as we hit grit in Chihuahua because of a week-old Mexico Immigration foul-up that issued us 7-day permits for a 14-day stay. Diesel shrugged at that Cinderella hour, "Head for the border!" So we beat a way north to Ojinaga, Mexico, on the bank of the Rio Grande.

Atop the only hill in the pueblo at dawn, we beheld the Rio Grande valley and its infamous liquid border with Presidio, Texas, on the far side. I lingered at the vista. "Look, partner," instructed Diesel, "I know you're a careful fellow. But it doesn't matter if we get caught on the Mexican side because we'll bribe out; and it doesn't matter if we're captured on the American side since we'll say we're day hikers. The great improbability is to get nabbed exactly in the middle of the river, so relax."

We descended dirt steps dug into the hill and melted into the tall sawgrass on the valley floor. It was simple to trace the illegals winding trail of fast food wrappers and water jugs. We remembered to pick up a Doritos Chips wrapper and jug to later ferry the Rio.

Diesel halted before six snarling mongrels. "This is the end!" he backpedaled. I stepped up, "These are Mexican dogs. Watch!" I feigned picking up a stone and the pack scattered. Shortly, the way was blocked by a fence so we took turns parting the barbwire. On the other side, Diesel straightened at seeing a half-dozen foraging cattle. "Those cows have horns!" And he backed into the fence. I followed the startled cows through scrub along their easiest path for the river, and he trailed. Later Diesel, alert for rattlers, vigilantes, and burrs, marched into a Live Oak copse with a dozen beehives for fertilization. I hummed a warning in time and we swung around the hives.

The pueblo was thirty minutes behind when the region dipped to a brush-skirted river that we presumed was the Rio Grande. We hawed on the bank of the 5-mph current of unknown depth and 25-yards width. "You're a fine swimmer," I urged. He stripped to shorts, tiptoed to the edge, and probed it with a five-foot stick that disappeared from sight. The worst drummer I ever heard beat a tattoo starting a pueblo parade far behind us. Diesel muttered, "I'm going to sit on the bank to acclimate."

"Are there snakes in there?" he soon grimaced. "No," I replied. "Are there crocodiles or anything else I should know about?" I soothed, "There's only your fear of the unknown." He slipped into the dark water. He then kicked expertly to the middle, returned and hollered up, "Hand me the load!"

The Fox, Chicken, and Grain dilemma faced in crossing the river was that we had cameras, penlights, money belts and passports that couldn't get wet. Yet we had scavenged only a Doritos Chips bag and one-gallon jug to float it all. "How did the farmer solve the riddle?" I questioned. "He took the fox, chicken and grain across in the correct combinations and sequence so nothing got eaten," Diesel responded. His accountant mind clicked. Likewise, we ferry a few valuables while you watch the ones left on shore that they aren't stolen.

I loaded the jug with half the stash and handed it down the edge. After a five-minute labored crossing using one arm and legs, and back, he flopped before me gulping like a banked fish. "You swim the next load!" Surely he joked. But pride prevailed. I exhausted at mid-river and swallowed water clear to the far side. The return to Diesel with the empty canoe was easier and, following a breather, we swam the Rio together.

Welcome to the USA! We gasped to each other at land's touch. The sun dried our clothes quickly as we hiked on. I insisted on walking backwards over soft dirt to throw off the Border Patrol. "I tell you," he griped, "There's no provable misdeed if we're caught." But he clumsily followed my lead. Later, we brushed our tracks out with branches. Then we encountered a narrow canal that he assured could be taken with a leap, and did majestically, as I waded. Soon we were thrown bolt upright at a Spanish sign *Rancho Pobre* in the corner of a pasture of scrawny, staring cows. My ally moaned, We're still in Mexico!

The reasonable course was a compass bearing north over cow puckies and around creosote bushes. We halted before sunset at a wide stream bubbling over rocks. "THIS is the Rio Grande!" he exclaimed. "I'll go first," and I entered the shallow water in boots. At midstream, a US Border Patrol wagon pulled alongside the far shore.

I was nabbed in the Rio Grande with one foot in Mexico and the other in the USA!

I waved at mid-river in false glee and hollered to a jolly giant Patrolman, "I have no weapons!" He inquired, "Citizen of the US?" The officer questioned me on shore while awaiting a report from the paddy wagon computer on my California license. Where did we start hiking? On the USA side. What time? Three hours ago. Did I know this was the Rio Grande River? No! My voice cracked; it is hard to lie to an honest man. Abruptly, a hunter in camouflage with a red vest materialized from the riverweeds and the riddle of our capture was answered. He grinned and introduced himself as an off-duty patrolman hunting doves. Likely he spotted us birds and radioed the giant.

Meanwhile, Diesel posed on the Mexican side of the river with glasses balanced on nose tip gazing at the sky. The big officer finally waved him over. By slyly freezing, Diesel had committed no crime. Now he was summoned to illegally enter the USA by the Border Patrol. We watched him from thirty yards bend slowly to remove shoes and socks, then toe the water. "He's a city boy," I advised the officers. They grunted. I added, "Probably never waded a stream before."

He held up his shorts like a sissy to reveal a bold tan stripe while blinking upstream. "Doesn't want to wet his pants, I tendered," and the two men guffawed. He faltered on the rocks barefoot in knee-deep water. "The slicker needs help!" I yelped and waded in. I grasped his pack and murmured, "We began hiking in the USA three hours ago and got lost." He showed his teeth.

Part 5: Back in the USA

Diesel's problem on the other side of the Rio Grande was his birthplace. South Africa is one of a handful "red list" nations that is scrutinized by the US Border Patrol. Their nose is the NCIC. The National Crime Information Center is a computerized index of criminal justice information (criminal records, fugitives, stolen properties, missing and suspicious persons) available to federal, state, and local law enforcement, and other justice agencies. It operates 24 hours, 365 days to provide a database for ready access and prompt disclosure to an inquiry.

"Gentlemen," began the tall Patrolman, "There's nothing wrong with getting lost on a hike. However, you entered the US at a non-port so I must take you to Immigration." I took a photo of the officer with Diesel against the paddy wagon before he locked us in the back. We sat on a steel bench in pools of water staring through a peephole at dust settling over ten miles of twisting roads. "Chin up, mate," consoled my partner. "The man claims there's no wrongdoing." However, I knew the scenario would blow apart if they separated us at Immigration. "Stick to the story if they split and grill us!" I burst. He cocked his head. I, in turn, discerned a wall speaker and pinhole camera in the back of the truck, and withered. I exhaled and changed into a pair of dry, black slippers and took off my cap.

The Immigration and Customs building in the center of the bridge over the Rio Grande between Ojinaga, Mexico, and Presidio, Texas, intercepts most travelers to check documents and baggage. A forewarned US Immigration officer bounced out to greet us as the wagon door swung. "The bad news is I can fine you $5000." He guided us two steps to the building. "The good news is I'm not going to." The Border Patrolmen parked the truck and followed.

The US Border Patrol operates outdoors and draws patient trackers while the US Immigration officers sit for hours in borderline phone-boxes like statues with moving eyes. One gestured for us to sit with a knot of presumable illegal Latins inside a polished room guarded by tight-faced officers. In a minute he ordered, "Mr. Smith, please enter the room ahead and sit on the bench." Already the toying began when the agent called my middle name. Separated—Doomed.

I sat hard before a tiny camera and the officer in blue who opened, "What happened?" I offered the lost hikers story. "So, you didn't know you were in Mexico?" "No," I lied, for there was no way out. He placed my index fingers onto a film linked to the FBI computer in Washington D.C. "The last time I got printed was to become a California sub-teacher," I bid. "It took one month to get the results so I could earn my first paycheck. How long does it take here?" Two minutes," he snapped. Content, he ordered me from the room and summoned Mr. Dyson. Diesel popped out in a minute, so I feared that we'd said something apart in contradiction.

"I don't understand why my Green Card isn't in the computer!" he ejaculated in the polished room. "Everything else is fine. (Winking at me.) I've had it for twenty-five years!" Immigration turned a cold shoulder, so I cast a look of entreaty at the Border Patrolman who shrugged. A new patrolman, an old, wise Mexican who was the supervisor, ambled in to confer with the other.

TV rumor is that three powers turn the world: brute force, wealth, and information. There must be something else, I thought, yet all I had was what I call my CIA slippers. They point straight ahead as to be interchangeable. I stood up and crossed my feet placing the left to the right of the right. After deliberating a few seconds, I changed the slippers to opposite feet, stared, and sat down. The big patrolman groaned with stifled giggles. Then I engaged the wiser, older man in green as Diesel argued with the blue immigration. We spoke rapidly of tarantulas, scorpions, rattlesnakes, and illegals for which he warmed with anecdotes. "Once I chased an illegal that was bitten by a rattlesnake and performed the first aid myself," he told. I asked, "Then did you help the wetback?" Humor brings out humanitarianism, the instinct that Jesus was human only and not divine. A smile separated his ears, and if only we could leave the room with that edge. Finally, the Immigration officer snorted, "I release you to the Border Patrol with its bigger data base."

Humor brings out humanitarianism, the instinct that Jesus was human only and not divine.

We were locked in the wagon and transported two miles to Presidio, Texas, and into a fenced compound with parked off-road vehicles bearing the green Border Patrol logo. They ushered us into an airy building lined on one side with desks stacked with rows of computers and along the other lay three empty holding cells. I was no concern, they said, and free to leave, but I wouldn't go. They took Diesel's ten prints instead of just the index fingers for "absolute identification," plus his picture. They delved into his personal history because of the birthplace and British passport. We were held for two hours and never attended a more instructive seminar.

An officer pivoted the monitor for us to watch the computer "think" about Dyson's life. The top line displayed standard bad-guy arrests and felonies and was immaculate. The second line of more profound data blinked continually, so an officer sat down with pen and paper and asked Diesel to dictate his autobiography. "I was born in South Africa but moved to London at age four... I was raised by Mum after they divorced... I attained a Green Card at an early age because papa worked in the USA... I graduated university with a CPA and Spanish minor... I became a London accountant for three years... Two years ago I took a job with the Baltimore-based Agora Publisher writing a financial column... The elopement caused an office scandal... I've known Mr. Keeley a year, and here we are."

Doubt punched holes in the truth with each new question. He got fired from his job a month ago for eloping with the boss's ex-gal... His bio and photo were deleted from the Agora website a week ago... No driver's license because he didn't like cars... No home address since his newlywed was house hunting in Florida near a new Agora job... His cell phone was stolen a week ago. "NCIC wants more information!" lamented the green giant. "They say there's nothing on you in the system." The second line winked continuously. Another officer tersely hung up on NCIC after their half-hour harangue for more. Privacy occupies a shocking, low rung in America. Now Diesel's life is on record.

The patrolmen ultimately dropped their pens to ask for financial advice. Diesel pranced the white tiles looking each officer in the eye. "Agora is a contrarian publication. I love America and the opportunity to work and live and travel here, but there are some little things the government screens from the public. We cover President Bush with a dirty blanket of facts that even a Texan can't pull off!" Mr. Wilson was never prouder of Dennis the Menace. The three men blinked under fluorescent lights. "Buy anything you can hold in your hands—the earth, gold, and houses—because the bottom soon will drop out of this paper world!" They took investment notes and he detained them into the night.

Meanwhile, I got the US immigration problem and solution straight from the Patrol. It seems clear-cut. Word of the 2000-mile wide open door between Mexico and the US spreads like free fire through Mexico to Central America. Daily, tens of thousands flood the border of which 15% are Central Americans. In Texas and New Mexico, apprehended illegals are given three tries and then thrown in jail on the fourth. "I put one at the Mexican bridge yesterday and warned, "If you get caught again, it's to jail for six months. He won't return... to Texas. He'll go west where the opposite rep keeps the California border busy day and night. The illegals in California are put in jail only after forty or fifty deportations."

The Mexicans who originate from the interior are sitting ducks—or doves—not having heard of infrared vision, seen a helicopter, or understanding seismic detectors. "The majority of illegals hire *coyotes* for $1500 to guarantee safe passage. The Border Patrol routinely assumes that every illegal alien caught and returned home subsequently tries again and succeeds. Typically, a Mexican *coyote* escorts an illegal group via assorted routes across the border where they're hooked with an American *coyote* who shuttles them to various USA destinations. "It's big business. A month ago we caught 100 illegals hiking the desert with the same brand backpacks containing the same articles."

The patrolmen were interested in the small things that I study which persuade the grand overview such as what's in an illegal's pocket rather than large facts and numbers. Illegal immigration opens a forged document market that endangers national security. What about terrorists? "True documents have watermarks and other secret features that are classified," one officer explained. "I was given the classified sheet and told to memorize and then destroy it." I suggested to the patrol that a shadow law undermines the rule of a country. "I'm no angel, but as a schoolteacher when a keystone law is disregarded the classroom becomes a mockery."

I asked the old supervisor if there are Border Patrol undercover agents and he reddened. "They would murder someone like that in Mexico! This is because the illegals are mixed in with drug smuggling. This is how the drug smuggling works: each border town has a boss who controls a plaza, a large sector of the city. A drug trafficker pays *mordida*, a percentage, to pass through the boss's turf. The boss in turn pays the generals and politicians. The money trickles up as the protection trickles down." He studied me from toe to head and maybe thought us undercover, as I envisioned he once was. "It is a mean business," he closed.

There are cheap, legal ways for Mexicans to become US citizens but it takes time and know-how. "The border could be leafleted with instructions," I suggested. Lacking that, a smart Mexican can buy for the price of a *coyote* an air ticket to welcoming arms in Canada. "Don't think the illegals contribute to the American economy," the patrol insisted. "A little Mexican community pools its money to hire a *coyote* for one selected male. He enters the US to work and send money back so that other males follow. It's gallant of the Mexicans but it's a geometrically sad affair over here when we really can beat the illegals."

Lacking that [knowledge of the many cheap, easy ways for Mexicans to become US citizens], a smart Mexican can buy—for the price of a coyote—an air ticket to welcoming arms in Canada.

If you want to sneak into the USA, try it in California or Arizona and persevere. In the last two weeks, we had talked with Mexicans who'd been deported up to 40 times and were going back. But not in Texas! The Patrol succeeds in Texas and fails in California and Arizona for a single reason: "The West Coast judges release illegals saying their jails are full. In Texas the judges jail 'em. Likewise, *coyotes* caught in California are slapped on the wrist the first time, but in Texas they go to jail for two years. So, Texas isn't a popular cross for large groups. It's a short step in logic to figure that the allowance of illegals into other states gives them leverage to hire an army. Presidio is considered a hardship post for new officers because of the remoteness and its quiet."

Free in the night streets of Presidio, Texas, on the Rio Grande, I couldn't wedge Diesel off the phone with his newly wed. I left him in my clothes after ample warning with a blanket, not the first bold adventurer to be crucified on the cross of a young wife. His mind will clear and he'll welcome the chance to strive with nothing but a brilliant faculty like the other illegals. According to the Border Patrol, 20,000 a day try to take the USA border and 60% succeed. The failures try again and again. I decided to dive deeper south to Central America and work my way from the start along the underground railway.

The afternoon after leaving Diesel, I sat in a Sonora canyon in a dry streambed next to a golden eagle. I started thirty feet away, and gradually decreased the distance until we sat ten feet apart. It had a dark brown body with lighter brown head that was wetted from fishing a nearby pool. He stood about 18 inches but was slouched, probably digesting, and didn't rustle a feather of a likely six-foot wingspan. There was a long down-curved beak and one-inch black talons. Nictitating membranes blinked at me every minute, and maybe he mused he was the only golden in the world to sit ten feet from a wingless biped in slippers.

Final Siding

I have just shared from the boxcars, jungles, yards, and rails my most remarkable adventures with so many memorable Executives and Kings of the Road.

From my first ride on the cowcatcher of a locomotive through the apprentice years peeping over back fences, teaching hobo sociology, recruiting the first executives and starting the tour company, and on deck of freights with Latin Americans, riding the rails makes me feel alive and connected to the universe.

I only wish everyone might thrill to his first ride. The road is still out there, even after 9/11, and you can still find me riding the American Dream... looking for you.

The venerable **boxcar** or 'empty' is the standard hobo ride. It's out-of-sight yet there's a 'window' or open door, the equivalent of a wide-screen TV. Bulls don't much care if tramps hold down boxcars, gondolas, and covered hoppers, but regularly kick them off piggybacks, container cars, double-stacks, and definitely the units. You can string a hammock across a boxcar, or once I played handball since it's the right length until the ball flew out the door. The floor is five feet above the ballast making getting on or off on 'the fly' dangerous.

Coal cars are open-top gondolas with V-bottoms that unlatch to release coal. It's a dirty ride and everyone talks about the bottoms releasing but It would be rare and I sit on top on a tarp and tie myself to the side. Coal cars are usually strung in a mile-long 'unit' train going from or to the mines.

Container cars are similar to piggybacks except without wheels on top. They haul overseas or intracountry merchandise. There's usually a well in which to sit at the end of the container on the flat car, and it's advisable to take the rear one to avoid a shifting load in an emergency stop.

Double-stacks are containers mounted two-high on a flatcar.

Flat cars are emergency choices off which I've lost gear and also been nabbed by railroad security. Always tie everything down including yourself.

Gondolas are rolling shoeboxes without lids that haul pipe, scrap and hobos. Of all the cars, this is the most touch-and-go for 'shifting load'—the third most frequent killer of tramps (after boarding on the fly and 'silent rollers'). Tramps ride is at the rear of any car with a sliding load that could crush them during an emergency stop. The gondola sides vary from waist to above-head high and have the advantages of an out-of-sight and windless ride, but they can turn the box into an oven on a sunny day.

Lumber cars are flat with a vertical lengthwise center piece to which lumber is secured. At either end is a phone booth size area that can be ridden for short hops.

Oil tankers and some others have only a ladder and two-foot bumper to ride, so they're inadvisable.

The portable parking lot or **automobile carrier**, nowadays, has two tiers with impenetrable mesh all around. The older unenclosed carriers were favorites for 'bos to sit in the pickup beds or car seats and listen to the radio or stereo with the heater on during winter. The automobile ignition keys are often taped where tramps know where to look. Sometimes autos are vandalized so if the bull nabs you on one it's usually straight to jail. There's a window sticker with the vehicle destination, a big help if you know where you're going.

The **piggyback** (pig) is a flatcar that carries semi-truck trailers. One leans against the big tires and views 360-degrees of rolling scenery under the trailer belly. The piggyback doors are sealed and bulls frown on pig riders, so hobos secret between the rear wheels. I've also ridden side-saddle shielded outside the tires through hot yards. Things blow around and away on pigs, so rope everything down.

The **caboose** hasn't been ridden since the 1990s when it was replaced by FRED, the Flashing (Fu****g) Rear End Device, that transmits electrical signals the length of the train to update the engineer on everything but how many hobos are aboard.

Dirty Face or a locomotive is the best ride going if you talk to the train crew first. There's a captain's chair, heater, fridge with water, toilet, whistle, and an instrument panel that can electrocute you. The engines are called units and the crew drives in the first unit leaving the trailing units vacant.

For 19th Century Hobos and 21st Century Executives
By Bo Keeley

An ethical code was created by Tourist Union #63 at its 1889 National Hobo Convention in St. Louis, Missouri. One century later at the Britt, Iowa, National Hobo Convention a hobo in paint-spattered overalls sided me and said I might like to join Tourist Union #63.

The story goes that in the mid-1800s several hobos found themselves in a jungle next to a mainline with something in common. They all had been repeatedly kicked out of RR yards, off trains, and out of towns because they had no visible means of support. It did no good to explain they were migratory hobos, and they had all seen the insides of the cross-bar hotel.

A nationwide organization was needed to protect the hobo migrant workers' passage, and the grassroots Tourist Union #63 was formed on the spot. The articles stated that every hobo would not be prosecuted for vagrancy while riding to or in any town attempting to gain even a few hours of employment.

Sixty-three founding hobos were present that afternoon; hence the union name. It was registered in Cincinnati, Ohio, and in August of each year—in Britt starting from 1900—the Tourist Union #63 held a National Hobo Convention to renew friendships, collect annual dues, and sign up new members.

I gave him $5 and he handed me a booklet to sign after I'd studied and agreed to the Hobo Code of Ethics, and then turned on his heels and walked away.

The code reads this way and I show it to my executives for their amusement and edification:

1. Decide your own life, don't let another person run or rule you.

2. When in town, always respect the local law and officials, and try to be a gentleman at all times.

3. Don't take advantage of someone who is in a vulnerable situation—locals or other hobos.

4. Always try to find work, even if temporary, and always seek out jobs nobody wants. By doing so you not only help a business along, but ensure employment should you return to that town again.

5. When no employment is available, make your own work by using your added talents at crafts.

6. Do not allow yourself to become a stupid drunk and set a bad example for locals' treatment of other hobos.

7. When jungling in town, respect handouts, do not wear them out, another hobo will be coming along who will need them as bad, if not worse than you.

8. Always respect nature, do not leave garbage where you are jungling.

9. If in a community jungle, always pitch in and help.

10. Try to stay clean, and boil up wherever possible.

11. When traveling, ride your train respectfully, take no personal chances, cause no problems with the operating crew or host railroad, act like an extra crew member.

12. Do not cause problems in a train yard, another hobo will be coming along who will need passage through that yard.

13. Do not allow other hobos to molest children; expose all molesters to authorities, they are the worst garbage to infest any society.

14. Help all runaway children and encourage them to return home.

15. Help your fellow hobos whenever and wherever needed, you may need their help someday.

16. If present at a hobo court and you have testimony, give it. Whether for or against the accused, your voice counts!

The following list, aside from the executive items, is reasonably comprehensive and has stood the test of time.

Bandana
Boots
Camera
Cell phone
Clip-on tie
Compass
Condoms
Credit cards
Dark sweatshirt
Day's food supply
Earplugs
Flashlight
GPS
Gallon water jug
Hand-held computer for email
Hats with straps
ID
Infra-red goggles
Journal & pen
Lighter
No weapon
Overalls
Paperback book
RR atlas
Rope
Scanner and frequency list
Sleeping bag
Soft pack
Tarp or tube tent
Toilet kit
2-way radios
Train timetables
Wallet tethered to clothes

From the *Education of a Speculator* by Victor Niederfhoffer

Victor Niederhoffer's blockbuster autobiography Education of a Speculator *(1996), and two prior reports from Bo Keeley to Niederhoffer called 'Rail Indicators' (1994) and 'The Hobo Network' (1996) originated a system to predict stock and commodities movements that attracted the attention of Wall Street investors and were picked up by Barron's, the Wall Street Journal, and The New Yorker.*

Throughout the late 80s and early 90s I kept one foot on each side of the railroad tracks, drawing from the world of hobos to abet business and from the latter I applied principles to survive on the rails. Victor Niederhoffer, the #1 speculator for four years running, believed and often requested RR Indicators.

The tide of business is high or low, always moving. Currents affect the whole from within. Everywhere, fish flick their fins and flip their tails. Can the tide be predicted by observing enough fish? We thought so with RR and low-life indicators.

I rummaged them from the rails and around the globe... Niederhoffer's computers and staff gauged their efficacies and lead times in predicting market movements. Investments in millions of dollars were made based on the length of cigarette butts, red light district activity, and numbers of freight cars rolling across American soil.

Here, for the first time, I will reveal the key indicators we have developed.

Railroad car loading in the early 20th century was once a key harbinger. Market players focused on the statistic with the same simple-minded attention they devote today to such ephemeral numbers as the money supply and unemployment claims. But railroad figures fell into disuse as other forms of transportation—trucks, cars, and planes—rose in popularity. Doc Bo and I, however, have improved on the early statistics.

First the difference between a hobo who hops freights to travel from job to job and a tramp who doesn't work, is that the hobo reads the Wall Street Journal before using it as insulation and the tramp simply uses it for insulation.

The hobo:tramp ratio is a good indicator of the employment situation because it rises directly with the number of available jobs. Hobos are inveterate readers because they have so much time to fill waiting for freight cars to arrive, so a good first indicator of the employment situation is the number of issues of the Wall Street Journal found underneath the bridges where hobos congregate. The number of freight cars passing by fixed points is a direct indicator of economic activity.

As recently as February 15, 1996, speculator Vic received a bulletin from Dr. Bo that freight cars were going through key locations in Jacksonville, Denver, and Salt Lake City at twice their normal rate. The number of freight cars was also increasing. The employment situation was obviously good, so I stayed short the bond. Sure enough, the February employment statistics showed an 800,000 increase, one of the largest ever, and bonds dropped three points.

After hopping freight, Dr. Bo likes to take in a movie at one of the 24-hour cinemas on Skid Row. The amount of popcorn being sold in the movies, indicated by litter on the floor, as well as other unmentionable activities in the aisle, is a good representation of the economic tides for the lowlifes who attend. When he leaves the movies, Bo likes to count the smiles:growls ratio. Those with thin wallets are generally happy when the income distribution becomes more equalized. If they're not doing a lot of smiling, relative to the fat cats, it usually means bad times for employment.

The next stops for Dr. Bo are veterinarian clinics. Dr. Bo is a veterinarian by training but gave up the practice to play racquetball. Still, he likes to stay in touch with his fellow vets. We turn the contingency into profits. Unlike human medical care, vet bills must be paid for out-of-pockets. Dental work on dogs is a highly sensitive leading indicator of consumer expectations and well-being. When owners anticipate good times, they feed their dogs richer food, which causes cavities and gum problems. If the disposable income is available, a visit to the vet is scheduled. In the Spring of 1996, Bo reported that business at vets was quite brisk. I shorted bonds on this intelligence.

After visiting the vets, Dr. Bo likes to follow the bums into the Sally. The Sally here is not the venerable government bond dealer. Its the Salvation Army. By calculating the beef:potato ratio in the meals they serve the bums, or the number of suits and shirts on the apparel racks, Dr. Bo gets a good indication of available disposable goods in the working sector of the economy.

The missions are a hotbed of information in this regard. They collect food from fast-food establishments. If there are six donuts per hobo for dessert, look out, business at the ubiquitous donut diners is down.

Another good indicator, incidentally, is the length of the lines at soup kitchens. Long lines mean bad times.

After a good night of worship, food, and sleep at a mission, Dr. Bo takes in the fast-food establishments. The amount of food left in the dumpsters is a two-pronged indicator. On one hand, it varies with economic activity. But on the other hand, the harder the times, the less that's eaten. I will not reveal the adjustment Bo and I have developed, except to point to the amount of sodas left in the Coke and Big Gulp cups in the dumpsters.

Bo and I pay particular attention to the kinds of boxcars traversing the rails. A disproportionate mix of coal cars, with its augury of cold weather, has a pervasive effect on all speculations. A shift to oil cars tells that energy is on a roll.

Automobile carrier trainsportable parking lots in 'bo language are a key indicator. Not only do they tell where auto stocks are going much before the weekly sales figures are reported by Wards, but examining the sticker prices on the vehicles gives a leg up on the inflation numbers. Along with employment numbers, the PI sisters are the two keys that move markets the most month to month.

Not all indicators are as easily interpreted. As I return to the red-areas conveniently located near the freight yards, says Dr. Bo, I find the same sidewalk princesses plying their wares year after year. It doesn't take a lot of smarts for a 'bo with a small wallet to establish a correlation between economic conditions and the cost of the cookie. The fluctuations are wild and evident. I have never been able, however, to figure the lead time of the indicator.

The Bo and I like to get a grasp on the government sector by monitoring the movements of circle tramps. These tramps ride the rails to collect food stamps in three to five locations in a circle of cities around the country. Each has a few social security numbers and a verifiable address (generally under a bridge), and stays one hop and two steps ahead of pursuing social workers. The standard exchange rate for food stamps is 50 cents off the face value. When the circle tramps find government handouts less plentiful, it's a good indicator of the lean hog type of operation our politicians like to run with taxpayer's money.

The fundamental hobo indicator may now be revealed. The size of cigarette butts on the ground is directly proportional to the health of the economy. The hobo is always on the lookout for a discarded butt. And when he has to smoke one very short snipe after another, then hard times are here. The original smokers are so strapped they are smoking right to the ends as not to waste a penny. To be fair, Rose Wilder Lane, in the *Discovery of Freedom*, was the first to note international differences between the size of discarded butts. But I believe that Bo and I are the first to track changes systematically within a country over time.

I recently made millions by applying this theory in Brazil. My agents there noted an increasing prevalence of long butts on the ground, and I rushed in to buy Brazilian stocks.

Hobo argot is lavish, and one hears it up and down the rails and around the jungle campfires.

Airedale: Someone who travels alone rather than in the company of others. Lone wolf.

Alki: Alcoholic.

angel food: Mission sermon.

back (or front) **porch**: Metal platform at either end of a grain hopper. These have curved sides and are a favored ride with a viewing area and shelter via a portal into the car bulwark.

bad order: A car or track in need of repair.

Beggardom: The world of a full-time beggar. The area they panhandle.

bindle stiff: The 'roll,' 'bindle,' or 'balloon' was popular in olden days, rarer now with modern backpacks, when tramps picked up their bed and walked or rode.

Big Rock Candy Mountains: Hobo paradise as described in song by Harry McClintock.

blowed-in-the-glass 'bo: Born to be a hobo.

boxcar: See Appendix A: Hobo Rides. Also side-door Pullman.

boxcar art: Inscriptions, monikers or hobo graffiti on trains and in yards. Different from 'tramp art' below.

brake test: The engineer tests the brakes just before starting to ensure the brakeline is pressurized. There is an accompanying electronic click along the train that's the standard cue to be ready to pull out.

Britt, Iowa: Home of the annual August National Hobo Convention for the last century.

build a train: To assemble or 'make up' a train by piecing together sets of cars bound for a general destination.

bull: A railroad policeman. Also special agent, cinder dick.

bull horrors: A pathological fear of bulls seeded by stories along the grapevine (and Hollywood) of bull mistreatment of hobos.

bum: A low-status 'homeguard,' or 'local,' who may have let himself go, dressed in inside-out shirts and mismatched shoes padding the streets smelling like a brewery.

bumper: The small platform at the ends of boxcars, oilers and others, a two-foot wide steel mesh that's used to climb across cars or ridden in a crisis.

cabbage head: Someone who's used so many drugs in a lifetime that recovery is improbable.

California blanket: Rolled newspapers under the clothes.

cannonball: A fast freight, hotshot.

carry the banner: Walk the streets all night.

catchout: To jump a freight. The catch-out yard is usually a division town.

call: (the train). A new crew is phoned at their homes or motel when a freight's arrival into the RR yard, or completion of the train being built, is anticipated by about one hour. A tramp asks for the "call time" to know when he should come back to board in time before it moves out. One asks for the call time rather than ETD.

catwalk: Walkway atop boxcars and others sometimes used to "deck" a car and jump from one to another.

croaker: Doctor.

container: See "Cars the Executives Rode."

control tower: The highest building in the yard occupied by the overseeing yardmaster.

crew: The operators of the train including the engineer, conductor and perhaps brakeman, who ride in the lead unit. The conductor used to travel in the caboose until FRED came of age.

cross-bar hotel: Same as jail, calaboose, hoosegow, or the "can."

crumbs: Lice, or gray soldiers. 'Crummy' is to be lousy that requires 'boiling up' or cooking the clothes in a pot, a common sight in jungle yesteryear. Many hobos refuse to stay in missions where crumbs abound.

crummy: An unoccupied caboose in transit in the middle of a train that hobos sometimes ride.

cushions: Amtrak, a passenger train.

cut-out. To drop or "cut loose" cars at a RR yard or siding. Will mine be cut out? is the hobo concern. To "break a train" or "shuffle the deck" is to rearrange the cars.

dead-end siding: One that leaves the mainline and doesn't come back to meet it at the other end. Here the rider may find his car and self cut from the train, and afoot.

dead soldier: Empty booze bottle lying beside the road or jungle.

deck: To ride atop a car looking forward to bridges.

dirty face: The head locomotive, also used to name a train, *e.g.* the Salt Lake dirty face.

ditched: To be thrown off the train.

division point: The major yard or city where a crew changes. These points form a cross-country string of knots about ten hours apart where hobos may detrain alongside the crew to eat and freshen, knowing another freight will stop within hours. Division towns are replete with transients and amenities such as the Mission, Goody, and Sally.

dog: Slow freight train. Slang for the Greyhound bus.

doughnut philosopher: A satisfied fellow with the price of a coffee and feed in a bread line. He doesn't object to a doughnut hole getting larger because it will take more dough to go around it.

DPU: Distributed power unit, a locomotive set added to the middle or rear of heavy trains for a boost up steep grades. It is remote-controlled from the lead engines. Also called a 'helper.'

drag: A train of mixed freights that makes a 'milk-run' stopping at many local yards and sidings. Also, a work train or 'turnaround.' This lowest priority train is eschewed by riders.

dynamite: When the engines uncouple from the rest of the train with a resounding blast from the air brake being released at that point and heard to the last car.

ear pounding: The sermon before the meal at a mission.

engine: See Appendix A: Hobo Rides. Also called 'power,' units, or locomotives.

executive hobo: Boxcar tourists with a regular well-paid managerial or administrative job, usually millionaires.

fish: Newcomer rider, greenhorn.

flat car: See Appendix A: Hobo Rides.

Flintstone Kid: The latest generation of hobby hobos who use credit cards and may dress the part.

flip: To board or flip a moving freight. 'On the fly.'

flop: To sleep, or a place to sleep. I coined the 'bum flop' after years of watching with envy tramps stretch out on a park bench or boxcar and fall fast asleep in seconds. A flophouse is a cheap lodging place used by transients where the normal setup is a large room with many bunk beds.

fly catch: To board or dismount a moving freight.

FRED: Flashing Red End Device. The blinking red taillight on the last car of a freight train that replaced cabooses with the shortening of crews during the 1980s. Hobos call it the Fu****ng Rear End Device when they miss the train.

freight: A train made up of non-human cargo, often plus illegal riders. This book uses 'train' synonymously with freight but most hobos wouldn't.

FTRA: Freight Train Riders of America, a loose collection of riders originating from a small core in the early 80's who display colors of their geographic set via bandanas. Spin-off gangs have been convicted of violent crimes, giving the whole lot a poor name.

500-mile paper: Cardboard used for padding and warmth on freight cars.

frisk the train: To walk a freight before it pulls out in search of a ride. Sometimes you board at once or, if it's exposed like a piggyback, you hop on with the brake test.

gandy dancer: Laborer for the railroad.

gentlemen of the road: Hobos who display mannerisms, speech or dress of having once been white-collar workers. 'Executive Hobos' have the potential to become these.

get into the world quick: An old expression embracing a young man bitten of wanderlust who takes the first opportunity to jump a freight train.

gondola: See Appendix A: Hobo Rides.

Goody: Goodwill, source of used clothes and other items.

gooseberry picking: Stealing clothes off a clothesline.

grainer: Grain car, a curved-side hopper.

grease the rails: To get run over by a train.

grey soldier: Body lice.

head up: The spot in the yard on the mainline where the locomotives pause for a crew change. This key information allows hobos to board before the freight moves out.

helper (or pusher) **engine**: Extra units added to a train in the mountains to provide power uphill, then removed at the other side for trains climbing the opposite direction. Also DPU.

highball: Equivalent of putting the pedal to the metal on a railway.

high iron: The mainline.

hobby hobo: One who rides as an avocation instead of a vocation. Also, boxcar tourist or weekend hobo.

hobo: A person who rides freights from job to job. Used comparably with 'tramp' in this book, however history splits hairs in a triarchy: At the bottom are street people, bums and 'homeguard' none of whom travel. In the middle are tramps who rides freights and may take occasional jobs from town-to-town. At the top, hobos ride freights from job to job. My favorite distinction is that tramps and hobos both stuff newspapers under their clothes for insulation, but hobos read them first. Also, Knight of the Rail, King of the Road.

hobo code or rules: The unspoken rules that govern Exec Hobos and gatherings. For example, leave kitchenware for the next user, don't steal from the camp, share chores, and submit to the 'kangaroo court' of peers if a rule is broken.

hobo colleges: A man named Eads How organized the first string of hobo colleges in major cities in the 1910s, followed by the most successful, Ben Reitman's Chicago Hobo College. These were not formal teaching institutions but lecture halls where anyone could drift through to debate popular issues with speakers, and find assistance, work and brotherhood. The modern version was Doc Bo Keeley's 1985 sociology class "Hobo Life in America" at Lansing (Michigan) Community College with guest speakers including a state supreme court judge and where honorary degrees were awarded at graduation.

hobo culture: Hobo life on the rails, jungles, and at work. The history of American expansion within the continent is seeped in the culture. The fraternity of the rail had early beginnings in the 1890s and matched pace with track building. They had a lingo, written symbols, codes, colleges, and a philosophy that creeps up today along the rails.

hoboette: A female hobo. Sister of the road. Likewise, a 'moll' pals with hobos. About 1-in-20 train hoppers is female.

hobohemia: The area of the town inhabited by transients.

hobo nickel: Originally, hobos carved nickels of wood for barter, then later used minted Buffalo Head nickels to file ornate designs on the face. Today they are collectors' items.

hobo poetry: Tramp flatulence, especially around a campfire.

hobo sign: Tramp pictographs rarely seen now but necessarily popular in depression era hoboing. Examples are: a comb with teeth (cruel dog), a stick figure in triangle dress (kind woman). See Appendix G: Hobo History and Pictos.

hogger: The engineer or 'hoghead.' The 'hog' is an in-yard locomotive.

hopper: A covered grain car, also called a 'grainer.' The curved-sided hoppers have front and back 'porches' used by 'bos to stay out of sight or bad weather during a journey.

home guard: Local street people who don't hop freights.

hotshot: A high priority, fast train that others side for. Its status is due to cargo such as mail, containers and piggybacks.

hot yard: One busy with bulls chasing hobos.

hump. The raised ground in a 'hump yard' used to classify and build trains by gravity. Strings of cars are pushed up the hump, uncoupled in sets, and roll downhill to a widening funnel of destination tracks where switches are remote controlled.

in-the-hole: A train on a siding. Also 'sided' or 'on the farm.' It occurs with two trains bound in opposite direction or when one overtakes another in the same direction on one mainline—the lower priority train must wait on a sidetrack until the other passes.

jack-roll: Rob a drunk.

joint: The seam in a track where two rails meet and are bolted together. Joints cause the railroad's clickity-clack and provide an indicator of speed, so are the tramp 'alarm clock' if the train slows down to get off. Most modern main rail is continuous or smoothly welded at the joints, so the wheels glide over them silently. Also, slang for prison.

jungle: Hobo camp site.

King of the Road: The well-placed hobo. Anyone who feels the freedom of flipping a freight. The title of Roger Miller's hit song. Also, the perennial title bestowed at hobo conventions to the most experienced, best representative of the open road. The most popular event is the Britt, Iowa, National Hobo Convention, since 1910, where the King is crowned with tin cans, but always it's a solemn event.

Knight of the Rail: Respectful term for a hobo.

library bird: Those who roost in libraries to pass time, poor weather, or educate themselves in soft chairs.

mainline: The major rails between cities that form the American railroad gridiron. Most follow original right-of-ways established in the nineteenth century. There are regularly two mainlines—one in each direction so trains needn't side often—except in the mountains where it is often single.

Man: The freight train, e.g. the Denver Man bound for same city.

manifest: The goods a freight carries. Also the list kept by the conductor showing each car contents, origin and destination. A hobo may ask him to check for an 'empty' going to a particular destination.

mission: A place, usually sponsored by a church, for free food, short-term lodging, and spiritual counseling.

mission stiff: A tramp who lives in a mission or shelter most the year. Some volunteer to get 'saved' by the sponsor for the free flop and food. Missions are also the elephant graveyard for the elderly and retired 'bos, or the first step of a new road kid to cleaning up, getting a job, and leaving the road for straight society.

moniker: A hobo's nickname or handle. The road name provides privacy and often tells a bit about the person.

Mulligan stew: Hobo stew.

open road: The system of railroads that can take you anywhere you like, as in the 'call of the open road.'

piggyback: See "Cars the executives rode." Also pig, or pig train.

pie in the sky: The reward in the hereafter after one catches the last 'westbound.' A culminating phrase of a mission sermon is often "There ain't no pie in the sky."

pound the ear: Sleep in a bed.

priority train: Based on importance of cargo hence speed of travel, the highest priority train is Amtrak, next the mail trains, followed by container cars and piggybacks, then mixed freights, and, finally, drags.

portable parking lot: Refer to Appendix A: Hobo Rides.

profesh: Experienced hobo.

punk: Young tramp, fish, tenderfoot, road kid.

reefer: Refrigerated boxcar.

rubber tramp: Migrant workers traveling by car began to put a dent in the hobo population with the rise of the automobile in the 1920s.

Sally: The Salvation Army helps million of Americans yearly. Most familiar at Christmas time as bell-ringers with alms kettles, this is the small evangelical church of 125,000 members called soldiers. Officers are ordained ministers who work long hours for scanty wages. The Army raised $88 million following 9/11. Donations are distributed to soup kitchens, shelters, toys for kids, and thrift stores that many tramps shop.

shack: Brakeman.

shuffle the deck: To change the order of cars in a train. This occurs within a yard or en route when a string is added or cut off.

shooting snipes: Tramps too poor to afford 'tailor-made' (store bought) cigarettes collect butts from the ground until enough accumulate to roll their own.

sky pilot: Mission preacher.

side: To pull off on a parallel side rail to allow a priority train to pass.

silent roller: A car or string that glides engineless, without light and quietly—and dangerously—along a yard rail especially in the hump yard.

slave market: Employment agency.

slow-order track: One that's in bad order or under repair so engineers are required to slow. It's an opportunity for a 'bo to get on or off at a slow roll.

snipe shooting: To hunt for snipes or cigarette butts in the gutter.

snowbird: Tramps who use trains instead of RVs to follow warm weather to the south, especially California, in the wintertime where they camp out or stay in missions.

stack train: One made up of flat cars or well cars that are loaded with shipping containers, sometimes double-stacked. Also called an intermodal or container unit freight.

staging trains: Trains holding for release on a mainline due to a backup of traffic at a point on line, for example, to allow room within the next yard to build trains on the receiving track. 'Trains held out' is the number stacked to enter the yard.

stake the door: To block the door of a boxcar preventing it from sliding shut on an inclined track.

stamp tramp: One who rides town-to-town, often in a grand loop of the country, to collect food stamps or other assistance using different identities. New food stamp restrictions have greatly reduced their numbers. Also called stamp collector, circuit tramp.

standard gauge: The usual track gauge of 4 feet 8 ½ inches, one giant step, used in the United States and many other industrialized countries. The other less common is narrow gauge.

stem: Street.

stiff: A tramp. There are working stiffs, mission stiffs, etc.

streamline: To travel without or with only a light pack for the purpose of disguise and agility from freight yard to yard.

surf: The top of most cars has a metal walkway along which a tramp may go with peril and hop from car to car. To 'deck' or ride the top of a freight car.

switch: To move a car or train from one track to another at a junction in the rail that is controlled by the 'switchman' who throws a switch.

switchman: Employee in a yard who throws switches at track junctures. Modern switching may be via remote control.

the road: The open road, traveling freely, living the life of a hobo.

through train: Or a 'run through,' this freight usually doesn't take on or drop cars at yards, and sides only for higher priority trains and stops only for crew changes.

tied down: A train waiting on line for a relief crew or other reason with the power still on.

touching hearts: Begging. panhandling, or putting the 'touch' on someone for money.

tramp: Used synonymously in this book with hobo, a tramp is traditionally thought of as a non-working hobo.

tramp art: Artwork by hobos and itinerants often made of wood and carved using a simple tool such as a pocketknife. Hobos used to fashion ornate furniture and carve 'hobo nickels' in exchange for a meal, room, or money.

unit: An engine, the 'power' or locomotive. The engineer and conductor ride in the 'head' or lead unit, while the 'trailing units' are normally unoccupied. It's a great offense for a hobo to be caught aboard any unit unless by rare invitation of the crew. Most hotshot freights boast two to four units.

Photo courtesy Josh the Wanderer.

unit train: One made up of a single commodity, e.g. coal, piggybacks, or containers.

varnish: A passenger train such as Amtrak. Also called 'riding the cushions.'

westbound: A train a hobo dies on. To catch the westbound, die, or find the 'big hole of the sky.'

Willy: Good Will Industries of the Methodists.

yard: The location where freight trains are made up and crews change. Generally, two main lines funnel from either end into a yard of some dozens of parallel rails used for storage and shunting cars. There's usually a maintenance section, and a "hump" area where yard engines back cars to the apex, the couplers are released, and car strings roll by gravity to a switch point and onto one of a number of tracks in building a train.

yardmaster: The railroad man in charge of a yard stationed in the main tower.

yard worker: The 'brakies' (brakemen) and switchmen who work a rail yard from whom hobos solicit train information.

I own probably the largest hobo library in the world that seeded as the instructor of a 1985 college sociology hobo class and has filled out over the years with contributions and hand-picked selections during flurries of publications following each economic recession.

Work	Author
Autobiography of a Super Tramp	Williams Davies
Beggars of Life	Jim Tully
Bound for Glory	Woody Guthrie
Citizen Hobo: How a Century of Homelessness Shaped America	Todd DePastino
Damndest Radical	Roger Bruns
Deep Enough: A Working Stiff	Frank Crampton
Diary of a Hobo	Bill Driscoll
Done and Been: Steel Rail Chronicles of American Hobos	Gypsy Moon
Executive Hobo: Riding the American Dream	Steven 'Bo' Keeley
Evasion	Crimethinc
Fishbones: Hoboing in the 1930s	Fishbones
Freighthopper's Manual for North America	Daniel Leen
Good Company	Douglas Harper
Hard Times	Studs Terkel
Hard Travellin'	Ken Allsop
Hobo	Eddy Joe Cotton
Hobo	Richard Dillof
Hobo Camp Fire Tales	A-#1 the Rambler
Hobo Life in America: Training Manual	Steven 'Bo' Keeley (Lansing Community College, 1986)
Hobo	Roger Gassiott
Hobo: A Depression Odyssey	Richard O'Malley
Hobo: A Young Man's Thoughts	Eddy Joe Cotton
Hobo on the Way to Heaven	Art Linkletter

Work	Author
Hoboes: Bindlestiffs, Fruit Tramps, and the Harvesting of the West	Mark Wyman
"Hobos"	Peter Spielmann, Penthouse pp. 138-45, May 1979
Hobo Sapien: Freight Train Hopping Tao and Zen	Wayne Iverson
Hobo's Odyssey	Sam Hobrecker
Indispensable Outcasts: Hobo Worker 1880-1930	Frank Higbie
Knights of the Road	Roger Bruns
Life for the American Hobo	Jo Ann Gurule
One More Train to Ride: The Underground World of Modern American Hoboes	Clifford Williams
Once A Hobo : The Autobiography of Monte Holm	Dennis Clay and Monte Holm
On Hobos and Homelessness	Nels Anderson
No Pie In The Sky: The Hobo As American Cultural Hero	Frederick Feied
Rand McNally Handy Railroad Atlas	
'Renaissance on the Rails' Ft. Worth Weekly—Profile on Bo Keeley	Peter Gorman (First place for the Association of Alternative Newsweeklies Best Feature of the Year 2009)
Riding on Top: Memoirs of a Modest Master Hobo	Gordon McLean
Riding the Rails	Michael Mathers
Riding the Rails: Teenagers on the Move	Errol Uys
Rolling Nowhere	Ted Conover
Sister of the Road: The Autobiography of Boxcar Bertha	Ben Reitman
South of Heaven	Jim Thompson
Tales of an American Hobo	Charles Elmer Fox
Tales of the Iron Road	Steam Train Maury Graham
Teenage hobos: A memoir	Harry J. Bohr
The American Hobo	Nels Anderson

Work	Author
The American Tramp and Underworld Slang	Godfrey Irwin
The Hobo	Roger Quam
The Hobo Handbook: A Field Guide to Living by Your Own Rules	Joshua Mack
The Hobo: The Sociology of the Homeless Man	Nels Anderson
The Last Great American Hobo	Dale Maharidge
The Road	Jack London
Tramping with Tramps	Willard Flynt
Tramping on Life	Harry Kemp

Hobos have always been willing workers at the drop of a hat to capitalize in Kansas on the rumor of a job in Montana, to jump a freight and a few days later hop down with sleeves rolled up. Life as a hobo was romantic, difficult, and dangerous.

Hobo Symbols and Modern Nomad Codes

To help each other they developed secret hoboglyphs to direct other hobos to food, water, or work—or away from dangerous elements.

Kindhearted Lady	Kind Woman	Woman	Housewife feeds for chores	Sit Down Feed	Food for work
Food for working	Talk religion get food	Bread	Good For a Handout	Gentleman	Wealthy
I Ate	Allright (Ok)	Easy mark	Tell Pitiful Story	Work Available	Tell a Hard luck story here
Fake illness here	Anything Goes	Sleep in barn	Can sleep in barn	Good Chance to get money here	Here is the place
Help if sick	Doctor	Telephone	Poor Man	Bad tempered owner	Dishonest Man
Man with a gun	Dog	Bad Dog	Officer	Police Officer Lives Here	Judge
Nothing doing here	Doubtful	Owner Home	Owner Out	No One Home	Someone Home

264

The symbols or signs etched on a bridge, water tank or building were a silent grapevine read in singlet or sequence by all who knew the secret code.

Because hobos weren't always welcome and the majority were illiterate, these messages evolved to be simple and easy to read, while protecting a conspiracy. The innocent ones such as a cross meant a traveler could score a free meal for sitting through a sermon, a tick-tack-toe pattern signified a jail, while the more complex such as crossed circles or rectangles indicated social interactions. There were some consistencies throughout the system such as circles and arrows for direction and hash marks or crossed lines for trouble.

A chain of marks scrawled in coal or chalk on RR water tanks and fences near the yard led to neighboring doorsteps of ladies who were a soft touch for a set-down meal or had a barking dog. They told the next train tramp what to expect and saved miles of shoe wear.

Some codes are still clearly tongue-in-cheek warning modern-day hobos, and anyone else who may read them, of such perils as parking tickets, lawn sprinklers, undercover officers and biting dogs, and the welcomed locations of well-stocked bathrooms, rich dumpsters, and car washes for bathing.

However, the old hoboglyphs went the way of the stream trains in the 1950s as diesel-electric locomotives replaced steam, making them harder to chase. The water tanks were torn down destroying the hobo newspaper that he had put ads on. He scratched his moniker, an arrow in the direction of travel, and date. In this way hobos across the steel gridiron overlaying America kept track of each other.

In this appendix we wish to identify and appreciate a number of special creative people who have generously lent their art to the book.

Linda Mears

American Folk artist Linda Mears painted Hit by Train in the story 'First Hobo Ride' as part of an Adventure Art series.

Background:

After a hoboing trip in 1995, the author sequestered at Victor Niederhoffer's Connecticut home for one year to write memoirs. Mr. Niederhoffer viewed the 'First Hobo Ride' sketch and quietly commissioned Ms. Mears to paint it and seven others (shown at *bokeelytours.com/art/*) that depict the author's several international adventures—on and off the rails. Find her information and portfolio at *lindamears.com*.

Josh the Wanderer

"Travel and autonomous volunteering are the twin pillars of my existence; they have taught me more then school and given me more happiness then money. I believe we have no need for authorities and that our collective liberations are bound together. I have found fleeting moments of freedom in boxcars, mountain trails, collective squats, and riots, and I hope and strive still for the real thing."

The tunnel light photo from Josh shows on the front page of "Six Miles of Smoke" (pg. 181). Also he contributes a picture from a New Zealand run that appears in Appendix E: Glossary of Terms (across from the definition of unit-train). The Wanderer is a free spirit who maintains a blog at *saliendoestelado.blogspot.com*.

Roy Reiman

Roy Reiman is the founder of Reiman Publications which is best known for country-oriented magazines and books that often conveyed a childhood penchant for hobos. He built the country's largest, private subscription-based publishing company without selling a single ad. In 2003, one out of every eight American households subscribed to a Reiman magazine.

Rail Images _____

The clip art used as chapter heading icons comes from *ribbonwail.com*, and the author especially credits Ken Houghton for his fine sketchwork of train subjects.

Executive Tours by Dr. Bo Keeley takes professionals into remote areas of the world including the missions of Baja California, America's boxcars, and the Amazon rainforest. Dr. Keeley, a retired veterinarian, coined the term Executive Tourism two decades ago while taking corporation presidents, speculators, doctors, attorneys, talk show hosts, professors, businessmen, and musicians in boxcars across the country, deep into Mexico, and to the headwaters of the Amazon.

www.bokeelytours.com

Steven 'Bo' Keeley is a Doctor of Veterinary Medicine, former national racquetball and paddleball champion, and has traveled the world… on a wing and a shoestring.

"My life has followed the vicissitudes of Buck the Dog in Jack London's *Call of the Wild*: from comfortable back yards across America; boxcars on every major railroad; 100+ countries under a backpack; hiking the lengths of Florida, Colorado, Vermont, California, Death Valley, and Baja; to retirement in a desert burrow with Sir the Rattlesnake as a doorkeep… and a solar computer to write essays and memoirs."

In 2007, he became the first California substitute teacher—most requested by students and faculty—to be fired trying to stop a playground fight. He left to ride the rails, and then became an itinerant expatriate writing from selective global Shangri-Las including Iquitos, Peru, San Felipe, Baja, and lately, unspoiled Lake Toba, Sumatra.

Bo's Wikipedia entry reads like Indiana Jones.

---

[4] "The picture is at 14,000 ft. in the Peruvian Andes where a dog with the red-eye condition, and 10-year old girl waltzed in front of me on an empty street. They danced, she leading, he on hind legs, with a red moon hanging on the wall behind me. So I sat, traded the camera for the dog… a magic moment, and then cover material for another book of mine, *Keeley's Kures*."

www.ingramcontent.com/pod-product-compliance
Lightning Source LLC
Chambersburg PA
CBHW061339280526
45784CB00001B/64